S0-BZI-022

Incorrigible

A Memoir

W. Patrick Middleton, Ph.D.

Copyright © 2008 by W. Patrick Middleton

All rights reserved. No part of this book shall be reproduced or transmitted in any form or by any means, electronic, mechanical, magnetic, photographic including photocopying, recording or by any information storage and retrieval system, without prior written permission of the publisher. No patent liability is assumed with respect to the use of the information contained herein. Although every precaution has been taken in the preparation of this book, the publisher and author assume no responsibility for errors or omissions. Neither is any liability assumed for damages resulting from the use of the information contained herein.

ISBN 0-7414-4741-X

Published by:

INFINITY
PUBLISHING.COM

1094 New DeHaven Street, Suite 100
West Conshohocken, PA 19428-2713
Info@buybooksontheweb.com
www.buybooksontheweb.com
Toll-free (877) BUY BOOK
Local Phone (610) 941-9999
Fax (610) 941-9959

Printed in the United States of America

Printed on Recycled Paper

Published July 2008

Acknowledgments

I want to thank the lovely Irish lady from New Jersey, Ms. Christina McLean, for her early reading and very competent editing.

Melanie Rigney, the former editor at *Writer's Digest*, and current Editor for You, came along and tweaked the final draft; she made the book a better read and taught me much about the finer aspects of editing.

Finally, Jaclyn Fleming, the Bryn Mawr scholar, crawled over every line of text, finding those subtle misspellings and little errors the rest of us missed.

My aunts and siblings, Suzie and Huck, encouraged me to the final page.

All of my family, and the friends and enemies I've made throughout my life, have given me experiences that I hope have made me a better human being.

I am grateful and rich among prisoners.

This book is dedicated to my best friend, mentor, and sage inspirer, Judith Trustone.

"To bring to light the buried skeletons of our early tragedies, to understand that the evildoers who almost killed us were the victims of other evildoers, and that those again did not know how to love, because they were betrayed by their own parents—that means to acknowledge the wickedness of mankind and to forgive fullheartedly because we ourselves are badly in need of forgiveness for the ugly things we have done."

(from *Selected Writings* of Fritz Kunkel, psychiatrist)

"Come, lets' away to prison.
We two alone will sing like birds i' th' cage.
When though dost ask me blessing, I'll kneel down.
And ask of thee forgiveness. So we'll live,
And pray, and sing, and tell old tales, and laugh
At gilded butterflies, and hear poor rogues
Talk of court news; and we'll talk with them too:
Who loses and who wins, who's in, who's out;
And take upon the myster of things,
As if we were God's spies; and we'll wear out,
In a wall'd prison, packs and sects of great ones
That ebb and flow by th' moon."

King Lear

Chapter 1

I'm standing beside 301 Highway with my brother, Michael. He's five, I'm four. We wave good-bye to our father as he drives away in his new red Ford.

See you boys soon. Those are Dad's last words to us. Every day for the next three weeks I look out the front window of our apartment, hoping to see my father's car pull into the driveway. Each time I see a red Ford coming up the highway, I think it's him. I'm wrong every time.

Four, five, six weeks go by and my father still doesn't return. Moma won't talk about him. When the divorce papers arrive in the mail, Moma celebrates with a drink. I can tell she's in pain when I ask about him.

She says, He's gone, Pat, and he's not coming back. Try to forget about him.

I say, How come and where did he go, Moma?

I don't know and I don't care. Just forget about him.

Our apartment building is on the corner of 301 Highway and Hawthorne Drive. At night, the tractor-trailers scream through the intersection when the light is green and screech to a halt when it's red. Sometimes they don't. It's the spring of '57 and already this year Michael and I have witnessed seven accidents at the intersection. Seven accidents, and in every one of them a casualty. I ask Michael if he thinks God uses the traffic light to call people to heaven or send them to hell.

Michael says he doesn't know.

Every evening before we go to bed, Michael and I kneel at the windowsill and watch the traffic go by. One

1

night we see a sixteen-wheeler slice a red Ford in half in the middle of the intersection. Michael and I put on our sneakers and run to the scene in our pajamas. Michael stops at the edge of the highway. Not me. I dart around the debris and men who have come from Mr. Mack's Shell Station to help.

I can tell that the driver of the car is as dead as a stump. His right leg is hanging from the driver's seat and there are bloody cords hanging from it. I've never seen so much blood. I call for Michael to come and see, but he won't.

The dead man is lying in front of the car. A burgundy wing-tipped shoe is beside him. They're the same kind of shoes our father was wearing when we last saw him. Carroll Simpson, who is the captain of the Charles County Rescue Squad, is working frantically on the man.

I maneuver close enough to see that he is a white man. His eyes are wide open and they're as blue as our father's eyes. His hair is parted on the left side just the way our father parted his, and there's a diamond ring on his left pinkie. What if this is him? What if God worked that traffic light to send my father to hell for playing such a bad joke on us?

I start to cry. I yell for Michael.

That ain't him, Pat.

But the car's red and he's wearing the same shoes and diamond ring and—

That ain't him. Now come on.

We walk back across the highway. Michael sits in the fork of the oak tree, which also serves as the crow's nest of a pirate's ship we have captured over and over. I want to go back and look at the man one more time. Michael says no. Tears are streaming down my face as I watch Carroll Simpson pull a stiff white sheet over the man's face.

It's *him*. I know it's him.

It is not.

But this is one time I refuse to believe my brother. I'm glad my father is gone, and I don't have to wonder about him anymore.

Moma says if it weren't for our grandfather, Mr. Ernest A. Middleton Sr., we'd be in the poorhouse. Even though she works full time for the Charles County Treasurer's Office, Moma doesn't make enough money to pay all the bills. On Sundays our grandfather, whom we call DaDa, brings us fresh fruit and eggs and long links of smoked sausages and slabs of bacon that he cured with his own hands on his tobacco farm called Maple Knoll. I have also seen him give Moma wads of fresh new money on Sundays when he comes to pick us up after Mass.

Moma says that DaDa is our guardian angel. She says that we are to attend Archbishop Neale School and DaDa will pay our tuition. Susie, my sister, has just finished the first grade. Michael will start in the fall and I will start next year.

I am five now and old enough to be the mascot for the Ladies Auxiliary of the American Legion Post 82. The annual Memorial Day parade is in two weeks. Moma says the ladies are gonna turn me into a handsome soldier. We walk to the American Legion parking lot, which is right beside our apartment building. April Pace makes a fuss. She says, Pat, don't you look cute with your front tooth knocked out.

I smile and Moma says, Tell April how you lost your tooth.

I was running down the sidewalk with an orange Nehi in my mouth and fell.

The women laugh. Isn't he such a darling?

April hands me a white toy rifle and Mary Jo Hancock shows me how to rest it on my shoulder. She tells me to stand up straight and proud as she pats me on the head.

The women file into formation. April and Moma are in front of the others carrying the banner. I am in front of them, the littlest honor guard. For thirty minutes, we march around the parking lot, my legs moving like pistons, left-right, left-right, left-right.

When practice is over, Mary Jo reminds everyone that the parade will begin on Charles Street in front of the theater at exactly eleven a.m., a week from this Saturday. We will march all the way down Charles Street, past the courthouse where Moma works, and down the La Plata High School hill. At the bottom of the hill, we'll turn right and march all the way up 301 Highway to the American Legion Post.

Mary Jo says, You girls be on time, and let's look pretty.

I follow Moma and the other ladies inside the American Legion. The Legion is second home to Moma and her girlfriends. For the married ladies, it's a place where they can drink and socialize while they keep an eye on their husbands. For Moma and other ladies whose husbands have abandoned them, the Legion is a perfect place to find a new one.

The men of the American Legion are veterans of World War II and the Korean War. They drink beer and liquor and tell old war stories, and play cards and make secret deals in the smoke-filled back rooms.

Charles County is the only county in the whole state of Maryland that has legal gambling. Along one entire wall of the Legion are nickel, dime, and quarter slot machines; three horse-racing machines; and two pinball machines. When you win, these machines pay off in coins. Once, Moma hit the quarter slots for seventy-five dollars.

In a side room there are shuffleboard tables, a bowling machine, and a pool table for us children. In the very back is a huge ballroom for dances and proms and wedding receptions. Sometimes when this room is empty, I go up on the stage and pretend I'm Elvis Presley.

I'm behind my mother as we walk through the side door of the Legion. Three men who are sitting at the bar turn their heads to stare at Moma and the other women as they pass by. Moma is strikingly beautiful. Carroll Simpson says, ToTo, you get more beautiful every time I see you. Toto is Moma's nickname.

Moma says, Why, thank you, Carroll.

Moma is the prettiest woman in the room. She has large brown eyes that sparkle when men talk to her. She wears red lipstick and stands at the mirror for what seems like hours plucking little hairs from her eyebrows. Every Saturday she goes to Mrs. Murphy's house to have her long black hair done in a French twist. When she's ready to go out for the evening, I swear she looks like one of my sister Susie's dolls.

We sit at the corner table and Moma orders a beer and a Hire's root beer for me. April and Mary Jo order drafts. Moma drinks her beer and then walks to the jukebox, drops in a quarter, and plays her favorite songs: Quarter to Three, by Gary U.S. Bonds; Teddy Bear, by Elvis; and At the Hop, by Danny and the Juniors. She grabs my hand and leads us to the dance floor.

Moma has been teaching me how to jitterbug when we watch *American Bandstand.* She can dance as good as any of the girls on Dick Clark's show. She says I'm a natural-born dancer, too. We two-step, balance, and twirl in perfect timing. In the middle of At the Hop, Mary Jo cuts in and we don't miss a step. Carroll Simpson grabs Moma's hand and they dance up a storm right alongside Mary Jo and me. Moma has the sparkle in her eyes.

When the song ends, Carroll says, You're too much, ToTo.

Moma says, You ain't bad yourself, boy.

I'm sitting in April's lap drinking my Hire's root beer. April tells Moma what she's heard about Carroll. Moma goes, Oh, my God. April gives me a sip of her beer and hugs me close. I press my head against her breast. I keep my head still because I don't want the warm feeling that runs through me to end. It does when April's son, Freddie, my best friend, bursts through the side door and races up to the table.

Freddie is panting. His red hair is matted to his forehead and sweat is dripping down his face. Hey, Pat. Wanna come and play army with us?

OK, I say. I slide off April's lap.

April pulls her navy blue skirt down and says, Freddie Pace! Don't we get a hello?

Hi, Mom. Hi Toto, he says.

Moma says Freddie, you look more like your father every day.

Freddie and I run across the front lawn of the Legion. Jimmy Thompson and Travis Tucker are sitting on top the World War II cannons that are mounted on slabs of concrete. Both of their fathers are big shots in the Legion.

I'm on the USS *Missouri*, Jimmy says. I'm a gunner's mate just like my old man.

Travis says, The navy's for queers. My father was an army man. First Infantry. He killed Japs in Okinawa. He wasn't on no fricking ship.

Jimmy says, What about your old man, Freddie?

My dad was a sergeant in the Marines, Freddie says. He got his hip blown off by a stinking kraut.

Freddie and his father, Fred Senior, are the closest I've ever seen a father and son. Sometimes it makes me sick to see how close they are. Fred Senior drives a Texaco oil truck and is out on the road for weeks at a time. I always know when he's home because little Freddie's never around. When he's home, Fred Senior takes Freddie everywhere he goes in an old beat up Chevy truck.

Travis turns to me. What was your old man in, Patty boy?

The Navy, I say. My father directed traffic on an aircraft carrier.

Travis starts laughing like an idiot. Yeah, I'll bet! I heard he was in the fricking brig for the entire war.

Travis is a smart aleck. He's three years older than me and much bigger. Jimmy Thompson thinks Travis is funny. He laughs too.

I say, If he was, Travis, it was for screwing your mother in public.

And then I knock Jimmy Thompson right off the top of the cannon with a stiff-arm. I jump on top of him and punch him in the face over and over. I say, Is it still funny? Is it still funny?

The more I punch him, the madder I get until I start crying and screaming. There's a pile of dog shit in the grass close to Jimmy Thompson's head. I grab it and rub it in his face. Some of the shit gets in his mouth and he starts to vomit. I don't care one bit.

Freddie grabs my shoulder and tells me to let him up. Eventually, I do.

Travis says, Why'd you have to pick on him? You're in big trouble now, kid.

Yeah? Who cares? I say.

Travis follows Jimmy down the sidewalk. I stop crying long enough to tell Freddie I'm going home.

He says, See ya, Pat. Let's go bike riding tomorrow.

Fifteen minutes later, I'm in my bedroom watching the shadow of my Mr. Magoo puppet rise like a giant ghost on the wall. As I watch it dance and shimmy, I can hear the Three Stooges on the television in the living room and Michael and Susie laughing along. Then I hear Moma's high heels clicking across the linoleum floor and moving down the hall.

Moma says, Where's your brother? But before Michael or Susie can answer, my bedroom door swings open.

Get out in the living room now! Moma says. She stands to the side and waits until I pass in front of her, and then she shoves me down the hall.

Jimmy Thompson and his father are standing in the foyer. Jimmy's eyes are swollen from crying so much and from the punches I landed. Other than that he doesn't look any worse for the wear.

Moma goes first. What did you do to this boy, Pat? Look at his eye! Look at his shirt and pants. You made him throw up all over himself!

Jimmy says, He made me eat crap, Toto. No sooner does he say *eat crap* then he breaks out crying again.

He did what! Pat, what in the hell's wrong with you? Why would you do such a foul thing?

When I won't answer, Moma says, I don't know what to do with him, Ed. Ever since his no-count father left, he's been more than I can handle at times.

Moma is crying.

Mr. Thompson says, I understand, Toots. It's all right. Mr. Thompson puts his arm around Moma's shoulders. He says, Pat, you boys have to play nice and not be mean to each other. You could have made Jimmy real sick by what you did, son. Do you know that?

I can't bring myself to look at any of them or say a single word. I keep wringing my hands and staring down at the roses on the floor.

Moma says, Answer Mr. Thompson right now!

I still refuse to say a word.

Moma says, The least you can do is apologize for what you've done. And if you won't do that, you're not marching in that parade next Saturday.

Moma walks over and stands in front of me. She shakes her finger in my face.

This is your last chance, she says. And you're making a big mistake if you think I don't mean what I say.

I'm not about to miss the parade.

I'm sorry, Moma.

Moma says, Don't tell me, for God's sake. Her eyes are filled with tears. Tell little Jimmy.

Jimmy is clinging to his father's leg like a little girl. I swallow hard and say, I'm sorry. I'm really sorry.

But I'm not sorry one goddamn bit.

For hours I march up and down the hallway of our apartment building until the neighbor, Mrs. Clemmons, knocks on our door and says, Mary, this boy is driving me crazy marching back and forth and up and down the stairs. I'm seventy-two. I can't take it. Please make him stop.

Moma puts my rifle and shiny white helmet away in the top of the hall closet. Then she hides my new navy blue pants with the gold stripe she sewed down the sides and the new white shirt and gloves she bought me from Bowling's department store. I keep trying them on and wrinkling everything.

Moma reminds me to look straight ahead when I'm marching. She says that old Ben Porter will snap my picture when we pass the front steps of the courthouse and I'll be on the front page of the *Maryland Independent* come Monday morning.

At night in bed, all I think about are the high school bands that will come from all over the county to march and play their best patriotic songs, and the pretty baton-twirling majorettes kicking their legs high and doing cartwheels in the street. The fire departments and rescue squads will arrive in their shiny red Cadillac ambulances and trucks, and everyone will be dressed in sharp-looking uniforms. The Charles County rescue squad will show off its new cherry red ambulance, and after the parade Carroll Simpson will let me sit behind the wheel and turn on the siren.

The parade lasts for a little over an hour. I look straight ahead the entire time we're marching except once when Ike Wills, a colored boy I know, starts hollering my name out when we pass by the Foodland store. I turn my head slightly to the left and stare him down until he shuts up. He is trying to make me laugh and lose my step, which I never do.

When we march into the parking lot of the American Legion, Mary Jo shouts, *Parade rest!* The ladies fall out of line and every single one of them hugs me and tells me what a fine job I've done and what a handsome soldier I am.

Two hours later, I'm playing hide-and-seek with Freddie and some other boys. I run behind the Legion and stoop down in a briar patch to hide. After a while, no one comes and I start to leave.

That's when I see my mother standing against the back of the building with her arms around Carroll Simpson's neck.

I stand up and move toward them and the rustling leaves and cracking twigs give me away.

I say, What's wrong, Moma. She opens her eyes and looks at me. Her face is red and she's breathing heavy.

What are you doing back here?

I'm hiding from Freddie and the other boys, Moma.

You can't play back here. How many times have I told you I don't want you playing behind this building? Now go back out front and play.

Yes, ma'am.

But I don't. I turn and run into the woods as fast as my skinny legs will move. I don't stop until I reach the tree fort Michael and I built from pieces of plywood and two-by-fours we found around the neighborhood. I climb up the ladder and rest my head against the tree. I start to cry. I see my mother kissing Carroll Simpson and the look of agony on her face and I wonder why she never held me that close. I'm crying so hard I can't see. I get so angry that I think about running as fast as I can through the woods and right into a tree.

Then I start thinking about my father and the last weekend Michael and I spent with him. He had taken us to Baltimore to see an Orioles game. Later we had lobster and crabs in a dark restaurant in the harbor where we met Daddy's girlfriend. She was beautiful. I remember sitting on the toilet seat in our hotel room watching my father shave. He was as big as a lumberjack, his shoulders as wide as an old Plymouth. His voice was deep and strong and he had a funny way of laughing that made me laugh. He'd say, This town's not big enough for the two of us, and he'd say it the way John Wayne would say it. And then he would break out laughing, and so would I.

Now it's getting dark and the crickets are raising a racket. My heart is banging away in my chest and I don't know what to do because I'm raging inside and all I can think of is, I wish I could find my father so I could tell him what an awful goddamn liar he is and how God hates liars.

Chapter 2

The next spring Moma marries Jack Bair, who everyone calls Maxie. He's a big hairy man with tattoos on his forearms that he got when he was in the navy; he snores like a sailor too. Max is a veteran of World War II and a member of the American Legion.

At first, it isn't so bad having Max around. Every day when he comes home from his job at the Naval Ordinance Station, he gives Michael and me rides on his back. We play army and he makes a fine paper airplane that has more hang time than the wooden planes we buy in the five-and-dime store. Sometimes he takes me to the American Legion with him. I sit at the bar right beside him and order a Hire's root beer and a five-cent bag of Lance's peanuts. I listen to him and Fred Senior and Squeeky Hanson talk about the war and how bad it was.

After five or six beers, he turns to me and says, Boy, you don't have a clue what war's like. I want to say, How in the hell can I when I'm only six years old?

In the middle of the summer, we move to a house on Hawthorne Drive. All of the houses in the neighborhood have nice lawns and shrubs and hedges and bright colored flowers. Behind our house are thick woods to play in, and there's a small stream right _bedside_ the house. Just up the street is the Charles County Little League baseball diamond.

The day after we move in, Michael and I get on our bikes and explore the neighborhood. Michael is bigger and stronger than I am and pedals twice as fast. I have trouble keeping up. Slow down, goddammit, Michael.

When I catch up to him, he says, Pat, you gotta keep up.

We ride up and down each side street until Michael sees a boy in his class named Skippy Simpson. Michael stops to talk to Skippy, and I take off to explore the dirt road at the end of the street.

The road leads into the woods. I stand and pedal as fast as I can. Every five or six feet I have to dodge deep holes in the road. The farther I go into the woods, the narrower the road gets.

I maneuver a bend in the road, and then I see small shacks and bungalows on both sides of the road. Two colored boys are playing catch with a baseball. A fat boy who is darker than the other two boys is working on a raggedy bicycle. I stop my bike beside him and say, What's wrong with it?

He says, It's the chain. The master link broke.

I say, I'm Pat. My brother, Michael, can fix it if you want.

He says, I'm Rooney Smoot. Where's your brother?

We just moved on Hawthorne Drive. My brother's riding his bike around the neighborhood somewhere. You want me to go get him?

Rooney stands up. We are the same height. He says, No, thanks. I can fix it. I can fix anything on a bike. The other two boys walk over. Rooney says, This is Pat. These are my little brothers, Cookie and Lee.

I say, Hi, and then the blackest woman I've ever seen steps off the front porch and says, You boys get in here and eat your lunch. Who's that?

Rooney says, Moma, this is Pat. He just moved up on Hawthorne Drive.

Well, Pat, it's nice to meet you. You can come back some other time and play.

Yes, ma'am, I will. Where does this road lead to?

The boys' moma says, The dump's about a half mile down. Good-bye.

I say, Thank you, ma'am. See ya.

Down the road I meet up with two more boys and a little girl. I look in the opposite direction after I get a good look at them because Moma says it's not polite to stare at people who are different. What is different about these kids is that their skin is whiter than mine and they have nappy yellow hair. I get closer and see the irises of their eyes. They're an awful reddish-pink. As I pass by, I say, Hi.

They don't reply.

Later that night, I ask Moma about them.

She says, Those kids are albinos.

What's an albino, Moma?

They're white niggers, Max says.

Don't tell him that! Pat, albinos are the same as coloreds. They just don't have color in their skin.

I say, Is it OK to play with them? Moma tells me they stay with their own kind, but they're nice people.

How do you know they're nice, Moma?

She says, They're the Proctor children. Their mother does ironing for your grandmother.

Boy, don't you play with those kids, Max says.

How come?

They have cooties and they smell like a wet dog, he says.

Moma says, Would you for Christ's sake stop, Maxie! You know how he repeats everything he hears.

And I do. On Sunday, I ask my grandfather, DaDa, What's cooties? He is sitting in the parlor reading a *National Geographic* and listening to the Senator's game on his little portable radio. He is dressed in a neatly pressed red plaid lumberjack shirt buttoned all the way to the collar and a pair of gray Sears work pants. He pats my head and says, Son, a cootie is a bug.

I say, Max says that the albino children have cooties.

DaDa chuckles and says, Son, Max was just kidding you. Children don't have cooties. That's a term kids use to tease other kids. It's really not a nice word to use.

I say, Aunt Vera said Old Ham has the cooties and that I should stay out of his shack.

Now, now, he says. Vera doesn't really mean that, son. What she means is that Ham's place isn't very clean and she doesn't want you to get your clothes dirty.

Yes, sir, I say. Can I go play now?

Run along but don't wander off too far. I'm going to take you and Michael to the store with me a little later, he says.

It's Sunday, my favorite day of the week. Ever since I've been old enough to remember, our grandfather has picked us up after Sunday Mass and brought us to his farm. Maple Knoll is my favorite place in the world.

On Sundays, Michael and I get to jump over brooks and streams. We run through tobacco fields and cornfields that are thick with blackbirds and doves and caterpillars and scarecrows, and across meadows sprinkled with dandelions, sweet honeysuckle and cow pies. There are apples and juicy blackberries to pick, lots of animals—hogs and chickens, cows, horses and ponies—and a variety of spiders and snakes crawling deep in the green grass. There are front pastures and back pastures, haylofts and tobacco barns, and dirt trails and roads that zig and zag all around the farm. All of these joys and a loving bunch of relatives welcome Suzie, Michael and me every Sunday.

Aunt Vera, our father's oldest sister, is in the kitchen in her church dress preparing a big dinner. Her sisters, Aunt Alice and Aunt Winn, are helping her. Sitting at the table are our cousin Lucy, my sister, and my three uncles, Leo, Percy, and Sanford.

Michael and I race out of the house to go and play. First, we run through the chicken coop and stir the chickens up in a frenzy. Then we run through the pigpen and Michael gets the biggest hogs a-squealin'-and-a-oinkin'. Later, we enter the corncrib, climb to the top, and slide down the mountain of yellow-orange corn. Thump! Thump! Thump!

Michael shouts, There's a mouse in the house and I saw him first! Last one out's a rotten egg!

We run from one barn to the next looking for Old Ham. When we don't find him, we search both tobacco-stripping sheds. Ham is nowhere to be found.

Ham doesn't have any living relatives of his own. He has lived on our grandfather's farm for as long as we've been coming. His house is a one-room shack beside one of the biggest tobacco barns. Michael and I peek through the dust-covered windowpane. Ham is not home.

DaDa says that Ham is probably off drunk somewhere.

On our return trip from the general store, we are on the private dirt road that leads to Maple Knoll when Michael shouts, Look! It's Old Ham!

I say, I saw him first!

No, you didn't, Michael says.

Old Ham is lying across the dirt road.

DaDa slows the car down. I say, Is he dead, DaDa?

DaDa says, No, son. He's drunk.

DaDa stops right in front of Old Ham, gets out of the car, and opens up the trunk. He walks around to the front of the car, snatches up Old Ham and throws him over his shoulders like a sack of potatoes. Michael and I get out of the car to watch. DaDa lays Old Ham down in the trunk and leaves the truck lid open. Ham is snoring. His blue jeans and shirt are stained with black grease and dirt, and he smells like he's never had a bath.

When we arrive at the farmhouse, DaDa picks up Ham and lays him under the rusty water pump beside the house. Ham is the skinniest colored man I've ever seen. Michael and I jump up and down with excitement as DaDa baptizes Old Ham with the ice-cold water. On the third gush, Ham rises like a string puppet from his sleep, and then falls back down to the ground. He gets up and falls down again.

Get up, Ham! DaDa roars. Ham gets to his feet, stumbles this way and that way, and then takes off like a crooked man up the dirt road. We stand in the middle of the road beside our grandfather as he waits for Ham to disappear inside his little shack.

DaDa says, I don't like for you boys to see Ham like this. I can tell by the gentle tone of his voice and the kind expression on his face that DaDa really loves Old Ham.

DaDa sits at the head of the table and waits until everyone is seated before he says grace: Bless us, Oh Lord, and these gifts which we are about to receive through thy bounty and through Christ, our Lord, Amen.

Over in the corner is a little wooden table where Old Ham usually sits like a leper and eats alone. But not today. Ham is drunk and asleep in his little shack. DaDa asks Aunt Vera to make a plate for him for later.

Aunt Vera says, Like hell I will, Daddy.

DaDa says, Vera, please.

And that's the end of the conversation.

During dinner there's lots of laughter and conversation. Uncle Leo, who works for the Army Corps of Engineers, tells Uncle Percy about some mechanical project he's working on. My aunts are sharing the latest gossip about the health status of a distant relative. Aunt Vera says that the relative has one foot in the grave and it won't be long now. DaDa says that's not nice to say.

Uncle Sanford asks me if I've been good, and I lie.

Oh, yes, sir, I say.

Good, then I'll do my magic trick for you after dinner.

Uncle Sanford tells me to run to the end of the hall and back as fast as I can. I do and when I run into his waiting arms, he shows me that there's nothing in either of his hands. Then he takes his hands and rubs my ears. When he lets go of my ears, *Presto!*, in the palm of each hand is a shiny new quarter. When it's Michael's turn, I watch carefully to see how Sanford does the trick, but his hands are too quick.

Show me how you do that, Sanford, I say.

He says, I can't, son. It's magic.

Michael and I are both amazed and fifty cents richer.

After dinner Aunt Winn and all of us children hike through the woods to the estate of Dr. Samuel Mudd. Aunt Winn tells us that Dr. Mudd set the broken leg of John

Wilkes Booth, the man who shot President Abraham Lincoln while he was watching a play at Ford's Theatre in Washington, D.C. She says Dr. Mudd went to prison for it and that it wasn't right because he had taken an oath to treat people who are sick. Suzie says that she can't wait for school to start back so she can tell her class how the doctor who treated President Lincoln's assassin lived on the farm right beside our grandfather's.

In the evening we gather in the parlor around our grandfather for ice cream and storytelling. Everyone is happy and having a good time until I go and spoil everything. I haven't thought of my father all day, but suddenly I get the urge to ask about him. How is a six-year-old boy supposed to know that inquiring about his father would turn a room full of adult faces upside down?

No one wants to talk about him. I am hurt and angry and I want to go home.

When it's time to leave, Suzie, Michael, and I gather up our new clothes and toys. Everyone hugs and kisses us and says, We'll see you children next Sunday. Then we pile into the backseat of Uncle Leo's new Thunderbird for the fifteen-minute ride home.

On the way I entertain myself by counting the cars that go by in the opposite direction. I stop when the eighteenth car passes. That's how many days are left before I start the first grade.

Chapter 3

On my first day of school, Moma walks me into the classroom and delivers me to Sister Priscilla. She is young and pretty and has blue eyes. She was my brother's first-grade teacher, and Michael says she is the nicest Sister in the whole school. These are the Sisters of the Immaculate Heart of Mary. They wear long navy blue robes that fall below their ankles. Their heads are covered with a long black veil draped over a white bonnet that wraps around their head like a giant bandage. A round white cloth covers their chests. The cloth looks stiff like a corpse. Hanging from their necks and falling just below the white cloth is a heavy crucifix.

Moma says, Good morning, Sister Priscilla. This is my youngest child, Pat.

Sister Priscilla says, Good morning to both of you. How are you, Patrick?

Fine, Sister.

She shows me to my seat. Second row, second chair. Moma tells me to be good and then says good-bye. When she leaves, I look around the room and see my first cousin, Andy Mills; my second cousin, Sally Middleton; and several other boys and girls I know from my parish: B. B. Kemp, Danny Miller, Sally Cruikshank, Marianne Gardner.

The seats are almost all taken. The room has more windows than I can count. There's a crucifix on the wall high above the blackboard. Below the crucifix is an American flag, and below that there's the alphabet in large and small letters. On the wall beside the blackboard is a large bulletin board covered with bright colored paper.

When the last seat in the room is filled, Sister Priscilla tells us to stand. She shows us the proper way to place our hands together for prayer. Then she tells us to bow our heads. She leads us in prayer—one Our Father, one Hail Mary, one Glory Be to the Father. We will have to memorize these prayers by heart if we don't already know them, she says.

I already know them, Sister, I say.

That's fine, Patrick. Now you must learn that we don't speak out in class unless we raise our hands and are called on.

Yes, Sister.

Now, class, remain standing and place your right hand on your heart like this. We're going to learn the Pledge of Allegiance now. Please repeat after me: I pledge allegiance (I pledge allegiance), to the flag (to the flag), of the United States of America (of the United States of America), and to the republic (and to the republic), for which it stands (for which it stands), one nation (one nation), under God (under God), indivisible (indivisible), with liberty and justice for all (with liberty and justice for all).

That night I tell Moma and Max how much I like school and Sister Priscilla. Max says, Well, just wait until you start getting all that homework. Then we'll see how much you like school.

Moma says, You're a smart boy, Pat. You'll do fine. She says it's good that I like my teacher and to behave and not cut up in class with my cousin Andy.

In my second week, I run through the door of the classroom. I am late and my tie is crooked. My navy blue trousers and white shirt are covered with dirt and grass stains. Sister Priscilla looks at me and throws her hands toward heaven. She says, Patrick, you're a mess! Come with me, sir!

She takes my hand and leads me to the boys' lavatory. We walk inside and she says, How did you get so dirty so early in the morning, young man?

Sister, I was fighting.

Who were you fighting with? she says.

My cousin Andy.

You were? Well, why doesn't Andrew look like he's been fighting?

He was on top of me, Sister, and I couldn't get him off.

I see.

Sister puts her hand inside her robe and produces a clean white handkerchief. She places it under the faucet and then gently wipes the dirt from my face and hands. When she finishes, she sprinkles water on my head and pats my hair in place.

She says, Patrick, you must never come to school looking like this again. She is smiling at me as she flicks water in my face.

I say, Yes, Sister, smiling back at her.

Sister tells us how Adam and Eve brought original sin into the world. As a result of their downfall, all of mankind is doomed by original sin. I want to raise my hand and tell her I don't understand original sin, but my second cousin, Sally Middleton, beats me to it.

Sister says, You're all too young to understand right now. You just have to have faith and believe that it's the truth.

We learn about Adam and Eve's oldest son, Cain, and how he killed his brother Abel and about Moses and the burning bush and how he parted the Red Sea. We recite the Ten Commandments over and over until we know them by heart.

Sister shows us the proper way to genuflect, make the sign of the cross, and bow our heads whenever Jesus's name is said out loud.

One day, Sister brings Jesus down off the cross and into our lives in the form of the Holy Ghost, the third person of the Blessed Trinity. There's the Father, whose shape and form we do not know. There's the Son, Jesus Christ, who came in the form of man. And there's the Holy Ghost. Sister Priscilla confesses that she herself does not understand this great mystery, that it's beyond our ability to understand it. It's good enough, she says, just to know that God exists in three persons, and to BELIEVE.

In our Baltimore Catechism books, we learn how Jesus went about his life performing miracles—healing the sick, raising the dead, restoring sight to the blind. Sister says that Jesus died on the cross to save us all.

These instructions fall from Sister Priscilla's lips with such conviction and authority that I can't help but BELIEVE everything she says.

When I get my first report card, I earn S's, for Satisfactory, in every subject. Moma drives me downtown and we have an ice cream soda at the counter of the County Drug Store. Afterward, I commit my first crime while Moma is shopping in the aisles. I see a patent leather purse in the toy section and fill it with penny candy and bubble gum. When no one is looking, I stuff the purse underneath my Washington Senators baseball jacket. The purse is going to be a present for Suzie's tenth birthday. The bubble gum and candy are for my friends at school and me.

When we get home, I stash the purse behind Moma's rhododendron bush in the front yard. Max is standing behind me when I turn around. He has a beer in his hand and a scowl on his face.

What in the hell are you doing, boy! He says. What do you have there?

He picks up the purse and opens it. He says, what are you doing with a purse? You're not a little girl, are you? Where'd you get this?

I say, I got it from the drug store. It's for Suzanne.

Max tells me to get inside the house.

Moma says she didn't see me buy the purse or the candy.

Get your ass out in the car! Max says. He drives me back to the store and makes me confess to the store manager. The man is nice. He says he'll have to watch me from now on when I come in the store. I start crying because everybody in the store is staring at me as Max scolds me.

On the way home, Max tells me how stealing is a crime. He says how they can put me in reform school for stealing. All the while he is talking, I'm staring out the window and counting the houses we pass. I don't want to listen to what Max has to say. I already know that stealing is wrong. It's a *mortal* sin to steal. I have broken God's seventh commandment: *Thou shalt not steal.* That doesn't bother me. What bothers me is that I got caught and now I'm going to get a whipping.

From 301 Highway, there are exactly fifteen houses on the left side of Hawthorne Drive before we reach our house.

I'm in the top bunk bed pretending to be asleep when Max walks in. Without saying a word, he yanks his belt off, pulls the covers back, and let's loose. I try to curl up in a ball and ease the blows with my hands, but every snap of the belt gets harder and faster.

Now he's yelling at me, I won't have any criminals living in my house, you hear me! You'd better *never* pull that kind of stunt again!

Just when I'm ready to leap off the bed and make a run for it, Moma comes into the room. She says, That's enough, Maxie!

The next week, I get another beating. I'm hiding in the coat closet near the front door of our house. I have the door slightly cracked because I'm afraid of the dark. Michael and Suzie are running all over the house looking for me. Max sees me peeking from the crack in the door. He walks right up to the door and slams it shut. He makes noises like a monster. *G-r-o-w-l-l! Boo-hoo-hoo. Aggghhh! Fe-fi-fo-fum!* I'm crying and screaming and kicking at the door. Let me out! Let me out!

When he does, I shoot out like a cannon. While everyone is bent over in laughter, I run to Moma's knickknack table, scoop up a ceramic geegaw of a little shepherd boy, and fire it across the room. It hits the closet door and shatters into tiny pieces.

The explosion knocks the laughter right out of Max and turns his smile into a scowl. He charges after me. I try to hide behind Moma, but Max manages to slap me twice as Moma tries to keep him in front of her. I run to my bedroom and slam the door. Moma says, That's enough, Maxie! You made him do it! You know he's afraid of the dark!

The door opens with a *whoosh!* and Max picks me up in a waist lock. He spanks me with his belt until the left side of my ass is numb. I kick and flail and scream until he stops. He puts me down and says, That'll teach you to break things in my house.

I wipe the tears from my face. No, it won't! I say. You're not my father!

Do you want more, smart mouth?

Moma tells him to leave me alone.

Later, I hear them arguing over what's the best way to discipline a child. Moma says it's enough to ground me to my room or put me on yard restriction. Max says that's bullshit! He says, ToTo, haven't you ever heard, Spare the rod and spoil the child? An old-fashioned ass whipping is the only way that boy'll ever learn.

We have a parakeet named Peetie and a big beautiful collie named Laddie. Peetie is almost human. He flies around the house and lands on our shoulders. Once he landed on the side of Michael's cereal bowl and ate a cornflake. We have to keep Peetie in his cage when the windows are up because he'll fly away, Moma says.

Laddie stays outside most of the time. He has his own little house and when he sees me, he is up and ready to play. When Moma's at work, I bring Laddie into my bedroom. Elizabeth tells me not to let the dog get on the bed because he sheds. Elizabeth is our maid. She wears a white uniform and cleans and irons and opens the front door for us every day when we come home from school. Elizabeth is half Chinese and half colored. We all love her very much.

One afternoon, Elizabeth takes a drink from the vodka bottle Moma keeps hidden under the bathroom sink. When she puts the bottle back and turns to leave, I am standing in the doorway waiting to pee.

She pulls me into her arms and says, I know how much you children love Miss Elizabeth. If you tell anybody about this, Miss Elizabeth will be in big trouble. She's holding me close and combing my hair with her fingers. I love the way she smells. I promise her I won't tell a soul. She smiles. She knows I won't tell.

The next day Elizabeth doesn't come to work and I'm crying. Moma, where's Elizabeth? Did she get fired?

Moma says, Did you fall out of bed and hit your head? Why would I fire her? It's the Fourth of July. Don't you know where we're going today?

Oh, yeah, I say. We're going on a picnic. We're going to Chapel Point.

Moma tells me to put on my bathing suit.

When we get to Chapel Point, Moma and Max pull two picnic tables together. Moma covers the tables with old sheets and lays out paper plates that blow off the table. Michael and I laugh and then we run and pick them up. Max sets the coolers down beside the tables. One cooler is filled with beer and sodas. The other is filled with large Tupperware bowls of potato salad, coleslaw, fried chicken, butter and rolls, and chocolate chip cookies that Moma made especially for me.

Michael and Suzie want to go swimming. I want to roller skate. Max walks Mike and Suzie down to the water. Moma takes me to rent skates. Mrs. Murphy and her son, Johnny, are ahead of us in line.

Moma says, Hi, Sara. I'll see you Saturday, won't I? Mrs. Murphy tells Moma that her hair looks great. Moma says that's because Mrs. Murphy is the best beautician in Charles County.

I skate around the rink so fast that the manager comes from behind the counter and tells me to slow down; I'm scaring the little ones. I want to tell him that I'm only eight myself, and how little is that? I slow down each time I pass the manager's desk, and then speed up again after I go by. I'm having the time of my life until Travis Tucker skates by and almost knocks me over the rail. Get out of the way, shrimp, he says. After that, all I can think about every time Travis passes is tripping him and laughing in his face.

As it gets dark, the fireworks light up the sky. I'm sitting in Moma's lap drinking the last orange Nehi in the cooler. Every time the sky explodes, I hold my ears and watch the colors shoot down. Moma and I both burst out laughing when Max falls out of his chair as he tries to reach into the cooler for a beer. He falls right on the cooler and his ass is soaking wet. The Styrofoam cooler breaks in two and the icy water makes a stream under our picnic table. Moma cracks me up. She says, That probably means you've had one too many, Maxie.

Max is on all fours searching for a beer in the dark. Don't worry about me, woman, he says. I'm doing just fine.

They are both good and crocked.

On the way home, I huddle in the backseat with Michael and Suzie. Moma and Max are arguing over something stupid. Moma is yelling at Max until he tells her to shut her mouth. Eventually, she does, and there is silence for the rest of the way home. I count the cars that pass by, one by one. Suzie and Michael are asleep.

A red Ford is about to pass us and there's a man driving. I think to myself, Maybe it's my father. I press my nose against the windowpane. It's not him.

Chapter 4

Max says it's almost time for Moma to go into the hospital to have a new baby, and I have to stay with the Paces for a while.

I'm confused about why I have to go and Michael and Suzie get to stay at home. Max says it's because it will make things easier on everyone until Moma comes home with our new brother or sister. But I know there's more to it because I overhear Moma say she feels like she's going to have a nervous breakdown.

April and Freddie and his little brother, Jack, and sister, Dee Dee, make me feel welcome. Jack gives me his bed so Freddie and I can stay up late and play Monopoly and tell stories of heroes and bogeymen. Freddie insists that I ride his new three-speed Schwinn while he rides my Ross that wobbles in front because I ran into a tree and bent the fork. I have a grand time staying with the Paces.

On October 6, 1960, Moma brings Johnny Bair into our world. Moma is home from the hospital a week later, and I'm there to greet them. Michael, Suzie, and I take turns holding and feeding our new brother. Suzie makes a big fuss about the proper way to hold him so I don't break his little neck. She shows me over and over until she's satisfied.

When he's nine months, Suzie has him on her lap shaking him up and down until he shits himself. She is tickling him as she changes his diaper for the third time that morning. She says to him, Are you Huckleberry Hound or Huckleberry Finn? Johnny's brown eyes sparkle and he giggles. He breaks out laughing like a hyena, and from that day on, we call him Huck.

Moma cries off and on for days. She won't even talk to us or look at us, and I begin to think she doesn't love us anymore. I try to hug her, but she tells me to go and play. I get anxious and nervous because she's my mother and I don't know what to do.

When she gets like this, I put on a stack of her 45 records and play them. I press my ear against the speaker and listen to the Coasters, the Drifters, the Platters, and the Five Satins. I learn all the words to my favorite songs. Moma sips on a beer while she waters her African violets. One of my favorite songs is playing. It's Poison Ivy, by the Coasters.

Come on, Moma, let's dance, I say.

Mom says, Not now, Pat, maybe later.

Max has bought a bar and grill and spends most of his time tending to the place. He still works full time at the Naval Ordinance Station, so he's away from home most of the time. He comes home late and Moma accuses him of having an affair with one of his barmaids. They argue and shout and it makes me nervous.

Michael and Suzie don't listen to their arguing. I keep the door to my room cracked and listen to everything they say. What bothers me the most is seeing Moma so sad and quiet. She drinks more and more and talks less and less to us, and I get more nervous and angry and think, we should all be quiet. We should be a house of deaf-mutes.

Suzie has learned the trick. She clams up one day and is never the same again. Sometimes I'm mean to her. I pull her hair and spike her tea with table salt. She stays in her shell. Michael is quiet too, but in a good-natured way. He is never mean to me and always lets me play with him and his friends. Huck is like a well of love that we all draw from. He never gets tired of being hugged and loved and pulled at like a Raggedy Ann doll.

During the worst of times, Max is like Brutus in the Popeye cartoon. He gives Huck all of his attention, ignores me altogether. He acts like everything's hunky-dory. It doesn't bother me though. As a family, we are a sorry bunch.

Sister Thomas Mary, my third-grade teacher, tells Moma at the spring PTA meeting that I am one of the best readers to ever come through her class. Sister Thomas Mary is young and pretty and full of energy.

The day before school lets out for the summer, she takes us hiking behind Brent Hall. She points out bamboo grass growing on the side of a steep hill. She says that it's the strangest thing because bamboo usually grows in tropical regions. Francis Flynn says maybe it's not bamboo, maybe it's something else.

Sister says she knows bamboo when she sees it, and we should trust her. Francis says, My father says not to trust anybody, Sister, especially used car salesmen. Sister says, Francis Flynn, do I look like a used car salesman? I'm your third-grade teacher, and if you don't trust me, sir, I'll box your ears.

Francis says, Sister, what's black and white, black and white, and black and white? Sister tells him it better be good. Francis says, A nun standing in front of venetian blinds. Sister laughs along with the rest of us. Then she balls her fists up and sticks them out in front like a boxer.

OK, Sister, OK, Francis says, I trust you. We all laugh some more.

When we get back to the schoolyard, Sister splits the class into two groups and we play Red Rover. Sister is on the same team with Francis and me. Our opponents go first. Red rover, red rover, I dare Sister Thomas Mary to come over. Sister rolls up her sleeves and takes off running. She runs smooth like a boy. She breaks through the line and brings Hilda Brown back. Hilda is a pretty colored girl.

Later, when we're in the cafeteria eating lunch, Sister Thomas Mary moves from table to table to see what each of us has brought for lunch. Francis peels the bread back on his sandwich to show off his slice of bologna and cheese and brown lettuce. I have peanut butter and jelly.

What are you having for lunch, Sister? Marianne Gardner asks. Sister says she's having an apple and a glass of milk.

The next day, we say good-bye to Sister Thomas Mary and the classmates we won't see over the summer. Then we go outside to play until the buses come to take us home.

On the first day of summer vacation I ride my bike all the way into the city of La Plata. I march into every store in town. I walk up and down the aisles of the County Drug Store, Farrell's and Bowling's department stores, and the Western Auto. I sit at the bar of the Stumble Inn pool hall and order a large cherry soda and a bag of Lance's peanuts. This is my first time in town without a grownup and it feels good to be on my own.

I visit Mr. Spaulding, the only barber who's ever cut my hair. He gives me a Tootsie Roll sucker and tells me a corny joke.

Later, I ride my bike alongside the county jail and yell obscenities at the prisoners whose shadows I can see behind the dark screens.

The next day I meet up with Billy White in front of my Uncle Bernard Reese's lumber and supply store. We ride all over town collecting soda bottles in ditches and alleyways. When we have more bottles than we can carry in our baskets, we turn them in at Foodland for two cents apiece. Billy has three large bottles that he gets five cents apiece for.

Three weeks later, Billy and I see old man Willie Bowman, the town drunk, coming through the woods behind the Foodland. Billy says maybe he's got something stashed back there and we'd better check it out. We set our bikes against the side of the building and head in the direction where we think we saw Willie Bowman coming out of the woods. The only thing we find is a well-worn path. It leads all the way down the hill and stops ten feet behind the A&P store. Billy says, This is a hell of a nice shortcut, ain't it?

Heck, yeah, I say.

When we come out of the woods at the top of the hill, Billy says, Holy, shit, Mother of God! Look at that gold mine, Pat!

And pray for us sinners! I say. We're fricking rich!

Against the back wall of the Foodland, stacked six feet high, are wooden crates filled with empty soda bottles. We load our bike baskets till the bottles start tumbling out and then we each balance a crate on our handle bars and head back down the path to the A&P. We cut across the parking lot, around to the front of the store.

Billy is whistling "Dixie" as we enter the front door. We walk to the first checkout clerk. It's Mrs. Dobry. She's chewing gum like it's her last supper. Put them over there with the others, she says after she counts them.

We ain't done, lady, Billy says. We got more out on our bikes. Mrs. Dobry says, Well, hurry up and go get 'em. It's time for my lunch break.

After we bring in the rest of the bottles and Mrs. Dobry counts them, she lays a pile of quarters, dimes, nickels, and pennies in my hand. Thank you, Mrs. Dobry, I say.

Back outside, we split up our coins and laugh like drunken pirates as our pockets jingle all the way up the hill. Billy and I make a pact between us. For the rest of the summer, we only steal from our gold mine when we're together. And we don't tell any other boys about our stash.

Mrs. Margaret McGinnis is my fourth-grade teacher. She's the only teacher at Archbishop Neale School who is not a Sister of the Immaculate Heart of Mary. She has white hair that's tinted blue and thin like a baby's. Every day she wears a look of agony on her wrinkled old face. She has a sorry method of teaching, too. We have to memorize everything.

Mrs. McGinnis keeps a daily record of my behavior. After two months, she tells me I have accumulated fourteen demerits for speaking out in class, chewing gum, and throwing paper. But you already punished me for those things, Mrs. McGinnis. What's the demerits for?

There are merits and demerits, young man, she says. You have no merits. You are one of the worst boys ever to come through my room. You and Francis Flynn. You will repeat the fourth grade at the rate you're going. You are not here to gaze out the window all day. You are not here to pull Sally Cruikshank's pigtails, or to throw paper objects across the room, or to erase the blackboard without being asked.

But you punished me for those things already, I say. I turn my homework in every day, Mrs. McGinnis. She says that it's not my homework, it's my deportment. Look at Mr. Miller. Do you ever see him misbehaving in class? You should act more like him.

Danny Miller is the smartest and nicest boy in our class. He always picks me on his team at recess because I can run faster than any other boy. Every day we sit together in the cafeteria and he tells us the funniest jokes:

The Mother Superior calls all the nuns together and says to them, I must tell you something. We have a case of crabs in the convent. Thank God, says an elderly nun sitting in the back. I am so tired of eating sardines.

We all fall out laughing. You'd better not let Mrs. McGinnis hear you telling that joke, Danny, I say. She thinks you're a fricking angel.

Danny says, I am. Didn't you know?

Yeah? Where's your wings?

The next week I learn what it means to reach twenty demerits. All I do is pass a note from Sally Cruikshank to Sally Middleton, but old Ginny sees me.

She calls me to the front of the room and takes out a long wooden ruler from her desk. Stick your knuckles out, she says. I'm laughing inside because I'm thinking, how hard can it hurt?

She smacks my knuckles four or five times before I can't hold back laughing like an idiot. After that, she turns three shades of red and let's loose. The blows sting and my knuckles turn blood red. I think of Jesus in the garden of Gethsemane and my facial expression immediately turns sorrowful. She stops and tells me to return to my seat.

The day before our Thanksgiving holiday, she's at the blackboard writing out the Southern states and their capitals. Francis sneaks to the front of the room and sets a rubber vomit pad on the edge of Mrs. McGinnis's desk. It slides off and lands on the floor. Francis is back in his seat, and who else is going to pick it up. I've got it in my hand when she whirls around.

Do you think because I'm old I didn't see you the first time, Mister? She says. She is smiling like a goddamn crazy person. Hand that to me and go to the back of the room.

We're in the cloakroom and Mrs. McGinnis tells me what a bad and hopeless boy I am. There's wrath in her voice and she's spitting the words at me. Now I'm angry as hell. I wipe her spit from my cheek and shove away the finger she's wagging in my face. She rears her hand back and is about to slap my face. I duck. Her hand lands with a *thump!* against the heavy iron pole that holds our coats.

She grabs me by the shoulder and shakes me. You are a hopeless, hopeless boy. Do you understand? You had better learn to behave, Mister!

On Monday, Mrs. McGinnis is wearing a cast on her hand. Francis tosses a note on my desk before we start going over our arithmetic homework. The note says, *Serves her rite. The wich of a bich.* We both muffle our laugh.

Spring comes and then summer and I am, thank the Holy Mother of God, finished with the fourth grade and Mrs. Margaret McGinnis. Max says it's fine if I use our lawn mower to start my own lawn mowing service. I ask Michael if he wants to go in halves, and he says he'd rather play baseball. Michael is an all-star third baseman for the La Plata Giants. This is his second year in Little League and my first. Mr. Joe Tucker, who is our coach, says I'll make the team but don't expect to play much my first year. That doesn't bother me. It's enough that I've made the team and I get to be around Michael who is a big star and we're all proud of him.

At the upper end of Hawthorne Drive where it intersects Washington Avenue, there are several houses with high grass in their front yards. The first door I knock on, Mrs. McGinnis answers. She stands there hunched over like a broken weed and her damp gray eyes are locked on me.

Cut your grass for two-fifty, I say.

She hires me on the spot.

After her lawn is cut nicely, I rake up the dead grass and throw it over the hill behind her house. Then I start pulling weeds in her flower bed until she tells me to come inside. I don't want to go inside. *God, please don't make me go inside!* She stands there holding the door and I'm still on my knees with a handful of ragweed.

Well, come on, she says. I've got things to do, too.

Butterflies are churning and fluttering in my stomach as I walk through her living room. The drapes are shut and it's dark and all I want to do is collect my two dollars and fifty cents and go home.

I follow her into the kitchen where she directs me to sit down in front of a tall glass of milk and a plate of chocolate chip cookies. It's too hot to drink milk, but I'm afraid to tell her because I know if I open my mouth, a hundred butterflies will fly out. The cookies are soft and chewy, and the milk is cold. I down it all in a hurry because I'm nervous and don't know what to say.

Mrs. McGinnis tells me how she and her late husband, George, never had any children. She loves children and that's why she's been a teacher for forty years, she says. As she goes on, she sounds like a little girl, and what she tells me almost makes me choke. She says I am a good boy and I did good work in her class and I am destined to be a scholar some day.

Moma's aunt, my Great-Aunt Fanny, used to say things sometimes that didn't make sense to anyone, and Moma said it was because Aunt Fanny was old and her mind was going. I look up into Mrs. McGinnis's wet gray eyes and I know that her mind is going too or she's playing a joke on me. I wait for the punch line, but there is none.

She hands me a crisp new five-dollar bill.

Mrs. McGinnis, I only charge two-fifty.

Yes, I know, she says. You did a fine job and I want you to have it. And I want you to come back every three weeks for the rest of the summer, you hear?

Oh, yes, ma'am, I say. Thank you, Mrs. McGinnis.

On my way home, I get off my bike at the intersection of 301 Highway and Hawthorne Drive and wait for the light to turn green. As I'm standing there, I feel sad for Mrs. McGinnis and I'm sorry that I misbehaved in her class. When the light changes, I walk my bike quickly across the highway because Moma told me I'm not allowed to ride through the intersection. On the other side of Hawthorne, I jump on my bike and pedal home as fast as I can. On the way I make a solemn promise to be a better boy in school next year.

There are signs all over the town of La Plata that say WHITE ONLY, COLORED SERVED IN BACK, and COLORED ENTRANCE. In the alley behind Vic's bar, the colored men lean against the building or sit on the side of the curb and drink from bottles hidden in paper bags.

When I ask Moma why they don't go inside, she says because Vic's has only takeout orders for coloreds. I discover that's the way it is at Tony Vacchiano's restaurant and at the Stumble Inn pool hall, too. I ask Moma why, and she says it's always been that way.

One Sunday I ask my grandfather why, and he says it's because of Jim Crow. I say, Who's Jim Crow? and DaDa says Jim Crow's not a person. Jim Crow's the law that has to do with segregation. What's segregation? I ask. Segregation keeps coloreds separate from white people, he says. So that's why the colored families sit in the balcony at church and at the Charles Theater? Yes, son, that's why, DaDa says.

Twice that summer I meet Jim Crow face to face. The first time, I'm with Billy White and Leroy Proctor. We are racing our bikes up and down Charles Street. It's hot as hell and we all know where the coldest sodas in town are sold. The three of us lay our bikes against the side of Tony Vacchiano's restaurant and burst through the front door. We slam our coins down on the counter the way we've seen John Wayne do it a hundred times in the movies and then we stare up into the eyes of Fat Tony.

Tony stares down at Leroy and says, Now, son, you know you got to go 'round to the side door.

Leroy is an albino. He shrugs his shoulders and picks up his dime; Billy and I do the same. We race out the front door and around to the side door with the big sign over it that reads COLORED. We walk inside and Fat Tony looks down at the three of us. He is muttering strange words we've never heard before.

We order three grape Nehis. When Tony turns his back and leans over to get them out of the icy water, I imitate his clumsy waddle while Billy and Leroy make funny faces. In one motion Fat Tony sets the sodas down and scoops up our coins. We snatch the sodas off the counter and bolt out the door. All three of us are singing, *Fatty-fatty, two-by-four, can't get through the bathroom door.*

A couple of weeks later, Jim Crow is at the town playground. This time I'm playing follow-the-leader with Rooney Smoot and his brother, Cookie. We're on our bikes and Rooney is leading Cookie and me between tightly parked cars, across busy intersections, through narrow alleyways and side streets, and down the crowded sidewalks. We ride all the way around the town playground and then through it.

We stop for a drink at the two water fountains near the pavilion. Above each fountain is an old wooden sign. One says COLORED and the other says WHITE ONLY. There are four or five children waiting at the WHITE ONLY fountain. Rooney and Cookie drink from the COLORED fountain and when they're through, I do the same. The spout is rusty, but the water is cold and it tastes as good as any water I've ever had.

Chapter 5

On the first day of fifth grade, we all shout *hooray!* when Sister Thomas Mary walks in and announces she's going to be our teacher for the year. She says we're going to have a spelling bee every Friday afternoon and the best two spellers will get to compete with students from other schools in the spring.

On Fridays, the boys line up on one side of the room and the girls line up on the other side. Every week, I'm the last boy standing, and Julie Posey is usually the last girl. I can never beat her.

Sister Thomas Mary gives me advanced word lists to study. Moma and Suzie quiz me on the words and I learn them easily. Sister Thomas Mary says I'm a natural and I'll do well representing our class in the diocese's spring spelling bee along with Julie. I'm thrilled out of my head. My classmate Danny Miller is the first to congratulate me. He tells me I'll do great. Francis ribs me and says that spelling is for girls and why would anyone want to memorize all those words anyway.

When my Aunt Vera finds out that I'm a top speller, she and Uncle Leo take me to the Woodward and Lothrop store on a Saturday afternoon and buy me a new navy blue blazer and trousers. Afterward, we ride the escalator down to the basement and eat lunch in the store cafeteria.

The day before the spelling bee, Moma buys me a new dress shirt and a model Corvette and tells me she's never been prouder of me.

The word that does me in is *innocuous*. There are three of us standing, a girl from Our Lady Star of the Sea, a boy from St. Michael's, and me. When it's my turn, Mrs. Rudy, the librarian, pronounces my word, and I know in a flash I'm done for. I say, *Innocuous, I-n, Innocuous, I-n-o-c-u-o-u-s*. I'm sorry, she says, It's *I-n-n-o-c-u-o-u-s*. I forgot the second *n*.

The next day at school, every Sister I see in the hallway and all my fellow classmates congratulate me for doing a fine job. Everyone is proud of me and I feel like a king.

Two weeks later, I ruin everything.

I'm riding my bike on a long and winding trail through the woods. As I'm racing down the steepest hill and about to make the turn, Timmy Garner, the son of Sheriff Buddy Garner, runs me off the trail. I crash head-on into a tree. I'm sitting on the ground crying and my nose is bleeding like a faucet. Accident or not, I'm going to pay Timmy back.

I get up and hide behind a tree. When I see him coming, I reach out and clothesline him, knocking him right off his bike. I attack him like a shark. I punch him in the face over and over. When he tries to fight back, I bite him across his shoulder.

After a few minutes, I get off him. His nose and lips are bleeding. I pick his bike up and throw it down the hill. My bike is bent and twisted and I leave it lying right there in the bushes.

Later that night, Sheriff Garner pulls into our driveway. I bolt out the back door of the house and run into the woods to hide. My collie, Laddie, follows me. I think about running away with him, but I don't know where to run to. We are sitting below my tree fort when I hear Max's voice. Boy, I know you hear me! You'd better get back in that house before I have to come in these woods and drag you out!

The beating is worse than ever. Max uses a belt he's never used before. He grabs me by the scruff of my neck and bends me over. He strikes me several times across my ass and legs. He's wearing a scowl on his face like I've never seen before.

I cry and scream. The first time I attempt to break free, his hand grips my neck and I can't move a muscle. I hear Moma come into my room and tell him to stop, but he doesn't listen. Moma is yelling, Leave him alone, leave him alone! He only stops when he's done.

That boy needs help! he tells Moma. And I'd better not catch you leaving this yard for a month! Do you hear me, goddammit! I don't answer him. I am crying and he can go fuck himself or beat me some more because I'm beyond feeling pain now.

You didn't have to beat him like that, Moma says.

That boy needs help. How's he going to learn if he's not disciplined? And how in the hell can I discipline him when you're always taking up for him? He's your son. You deal with him. I'm through with him.

Later, Michael comes into the room for bed and tells me I can sleep with him if I want. Our bunk beds are against the wall and there is just enough room for me to slide down into Michael's bed. When I do, he tells me I have to stop crying and go to sleep. Michael might have cried when he was a baby, but I've never seen him cry once. He doesn't know what it's like to lose your temper because he doesn't have one.

I stop sniveling but I can't sleep because there's a volcano erupting inside my head. I feel helpless and alone. I think about Timmy and what I did to him and how I wouldn't have done it if he hadn't run me off the trail. I'm not sorry one bit. He deserved what he got, and Max can go fuck himself.

After two days, Moma lets me leave the yard to play.

She says, You'd better be in this house before Max gets home from work.

I have fifty cents and I want a pet rabbit. I have to ride my bike across the highway to the other side of Hawthorne Drive to buy one. Travis Tucker and his little brother, Wayne, raise rabbits in a little barn behind their house. A sign over the door reads: Rabbits for Sale—$2.00.

Hey, Wayne. Hey, Travis, I say. I wanna buy a rabbit.

Travis says, OK, sure. He picks up a little brown and white rabbit. You got two dollars?

I only got fifty cents, but I can pay you the rest later.

No, you can't. You gotta have two dollars. Come back when you got it all.

Wayne removes a big black rabbit with red eyes from its cage and holds it out to me. You can hold her if you want, he says. I hold the giant rabbit while Wayne cleans out the cage. It's fat and warm and very soft. I can hear it breathing. I can feel its heart beating.

If you really wanna buy one that bad, Travis says, I'll sell you this one for fifty cents.

I hand the big rabbit back to Wayne and run over to where Travis is standing. Be careful, he says. He gently lays a little gray and white baby rabbit in my outstretched hands. It's asleep.

The rabbit doesn't move. It just lays there in my hand, warm and limp as a cooked noodle. I place it in my coat pocket and hand Travis the fifty cents.

All the way home I keep my hand in my pocket, petting and stroking the rabbit's soft fur. When I get home, I show my sister Suzie. She laughs and tells me I'm stupid for playing with a dead rabbit. She must have told because Moma finds me sitting on the back steps and tells me I have to get rid of it. I start to cry. I put the rabbit back in my pocket and run into the woods. After a while, I bury it near a stream.

The next day, Max comes home and his white shirt is covered with blood. There's a cut over his eyebrow. He tells Suzie to put some ice cubes in a towel and bring it to him.

Moma walks out of the bathroom and looks at Max. She has her makeup on and she looks beautiful, even though she's angry.

Jesus Christ, Maxie, look at you! she says. You haven't taken me out in six months and you come home all beat up and covered with blood. Why didn't you call to tell me you were going to be late? I would have gone out by myself.

I'm sitting on the couch beside Sheri Murphy, who lives across the street and is here to babysit Huck. Max looks funny with a swollen eye and blood caked to his eyebrow. I start to giggle and Sheri nudges me with her elbow. It's not funny, she says. She's laughing too.

Max says, I know I didn't see your little ass on the other side of the highway today, did I, boy?

No, Max. I never left the yard.

I had to kick two drunks out of the bar, ToTo, and I did it by myself. Do you want to go dancing or not? Get me a clean shirt.

Like hell I will, Moma says. Get it yourself!

Max says for everyone to be quiet, he's trying to hear the news on television. An important leader of the National Association for the Advancement of Colored People was shot and killed in his driveway in Jackson, Mississippi. His name is Medgar Evers and he was only thirty-seven years old. The police suspect the Ku Klux Klan killed him.

I ask Max, Why'd they kill him? He says they killed him because he stepped out of line.

When the story ends, Max says, They're never satisfied. He was probably one of those damn freedom riders. They got all the freedom they're ever going to need, and they're still not satisfied. They keep at it and they're going to start a goddamn race riot in this country. Then all those niggers will be dead.

Moma comes back out of the bathroom. You've got the commonest mouth I've ever heard, Maxie. Do you have to talk like that in front of those kids? Sheri, I'm sorry. Don't listen to him.

Max asks Sheri what her father thinks about the freedom riders and all this civil rights crap.

Daddy says they're treated awful down South, and they should have the same rights white people have, Sheri says.

Max says, He does? Well, I don't know if I agree with your father. That's going a little too far for me. He buttons his clean white shirt and then kisses Moma on the neck until she tells him to get away from her. Then she tells Sheri that she and Max won't be out too late.

Sheri has freckles on her nose and the bluest eyes I've ever seen. She's in the ninth grade at Archbishop Neale School, and she's no taller than me. After Moma and Max leave, we listen to records and dance. She's a good dancer and we make up our own steps. It's almost midnight when she tells me it's way past my bedtime. I promise her I'll go if we can dance to one more record. Three records later, I'm still not ready to leave her.

Finally, I say, I'll go to bed if you'll kiss me on the lips for five seconds.

She says, How old are you?

I lie. Twelve.

All right, she says, but then you've got to go to bed.

I tell her to sit down in the chair and when she does, I sit on her lap, close my eyes, and press my lips against hers. My arms are locked around her shoulders and I know I will not let go in five seconds. She's the first girl I've ever kissed on the mouth, and it's the most wonderful thing I've ever done. I know I must be doing it right, too, because when I open my eyes hers are closed. *Holy Mother of Christ! I've never felt this excited before!*

We are both breathing fast and I have a hard-on. I go to touch her and she grabs a handful of my hair and pulls my head away from her mouth.

Now go to bed! she says. Her face is as red as Moma's lipstick.

After that night, all I want to do is kiss girls. After I kiss Peggy Steltzer in the woods while we're playing army, I kiss Carol-Ann Simpson on her back steps after she makes me swear I won't tell anyone. Each time I kiss another girl, I get more excited and want more. At night I touch myself and twist the hairs growing around my groin.

When Debbie Garner visits one day with her Aunt June, we're playing in my room and I push her down on my bed. I fall on her and kiss her until we're both breathing hard. Then I start to move up and down on top of her because it feels even better that way and she says, No! Now let me up! I get off her and I feel like Superman. Kissing girls is the most wonderful thing in the world.

The first day in sixth grade, I drop a note in Marianne Gardner's lap asking her to go steady with me. She is the prettiest girl in our class. She has brown hair that falls and flips over her shoulders and deep brown eyes that are as bright as stars. Over the summer, she grew taller and now her blouse sticks out. I want to kiss her so bad I don't know what to do.

After lunch she walks by my desk and slides a note under my geography book. I open it and my heart pounds like a bass drum. There's a big heart on the page and the word YES! is written in the center.

Every day after school, we talk on the phone. Suzie tells me to get off the phone because she's expecting a call. I cover the mouthpiece so Marianne doesn't hear me tell Suzie to go to hell and don't come back.

On Friday nights, Marianne and I meet in the lobby of the Charles Theater. We take the corner seats where it's very dark and make out until Jack Palmer, who's in the eighth grade and whose father owns the theater, shines a flashlight on us and says he's going to tell my mother. I say, Go ahead and tell, you moron.

He doesn't tell Moma, but I do. I tell her how wonderful it is being in love with Marianne and how I've never felt this way before. She says whatever it is, she hopes I keep it because I've turned over a new leaf and she likes it.

The Saturday before Thanksgiving, Marianne invites me to her house to go horseback riding. She lives in the country in a big white house on a hill surrounded by pastures and corrals and flower gardens. I'm getting out of the car and Moma reminds me to please behave myself. But I don't need reminding. I'm in love and nothing could be more wonderful than being in love.

Yes, ma'am, I say.

Marianne and I ride on trails through the woods, around the main corral, and across a field that is set up with several equestrian hurdles. Marianne gracefully guides her horse over every jump while I watch. I want to try too, but she says it's not a good idea because the horse I'm riding has a mind of its own.

When it's time for lunch, I meet her father, who's sitting at the dining room table finishing his lunch and reading the newspaper. Marianne bends down and kisses him on the cheek, and he takes her hand in his. Mr. Gardner is a very nice man. He is warm and soft spoken. I remember Moma telling me that Mrs. Gardner died of cancer when Marianne was just a little girl, and Mr. Gardner raised her all by himself. He's the perfect father.

During lunch, the maid, a middle-aged woman who speaks with a foreign accent, asks us what we are learning in school. Marianne tells her matter of factly that I am one of the smartest boys in our sixth-grade class. At that very moment I feel so proud that I want to cry.

There are fresh-cut flowers and antiques in every room of their house. Moma says their house is as old as the Civil War. It has high ceilings and shiny wooden floors and lots of windows draped with long transparent lace curtains.

In Marianne's bedroom, there are trophies and blue ribbons on the dressers and shelves. Over her bed is a large portrait of Marianne sitting on her champion horse. Her chestnut-brown hair is pulled back, and she is wearing a smile that would make any boy melt. I look up at the canopy of lace and pink satin that hangs over her bed, and I count my lucky stars because we are in love and it's the greatest feeling in the world.

On the way home, I tell Moma how sad I am because we had such a great time together and it had to come to an end. I know, Moma says. But you'll see her in school every day.

I say, It's not the same, Moma. I wonder to myself if there will ever be another day in my life like the one I just had.

Marianne and I are inseparable at school. Every day we hold hands in the cafeteria line, and after school I carry her books while I walk her to her bus. One day I kiss her in the back of the classroom while the entire class looks on. Marianne blushes, but not me.

One day we even pray together. It's November 22, 1963, and we're sitting at our desks reading about the adventures of Marco Polo. The voice of Sister Isidora, our principal, comes over the PA system, and it is filled with sorrow. Attention, boys and girls. President John F. Kennedy has been fatally shot in Dallas, Texas, she says. We are to begin saying the rosary for the repose of his soul.

After she signs off, a cloud of silence passes over our room and lasts for several minutes. Sister Roberta is shaking and there are tears in her eyes. Several girls and a few boys are crying too. Though I'm not crying, I'm still sad and afraid. President Kennedy was a Catholic and everybody in our family voted for him. DaDa and Moma both said that President Kennedy was going to make America a better place than it already is.

One of the high school Sisters comes into our classroom to talk with us and distribute rosaries to those of us who don't have our own. I look over at Francis and he has his head bowed in reverence; he is holding his beads between his fingers. We all begin to pray. I've always hated holding the plastic rosary beads because they make the palms of my hands sweat. I hate even more saying those prayers over and over again. Today is different, though. I pray all five of the sorrowful mysteries of the rosary with Marianne, and I pray with deep sincerity.

That night we all gather around the television to find out who killed President Kennedy. A man named Lee Harvey Oswald is in custody. Max says that Castro probably had President Kennedy killed because of the Bay of Pigs disaster. What's the Bay of Pigs, Max? I ask. He says that's when Kennedy sent Special Forces into Cuba to try to overthrow Castro. Then Max says maybe the mob killed him because his brother Robert, who is the attorney general, was on their backs.

On Sunday, I ask my grandfather who killed the president. He tells me they don't know, and if they do they're not telling us. He says that President Kennedy was the fourth president to be assassinated and do I know who the other three were. I know that one of them is Lincoln, our sixteenth president, because just last summer DaDa and our aunts took us to Ford's Theatre to see where President Lincoln was sitting when John Wilkes Booth shot him.

DaDa says the other two are James Garfield, the twentieth president, and William McKinley, the twenty-fifth president.

I ask DaDa what's going to happen now. He says these are very difficult times for our country. It was only two months ago when four little colored girls were killed in their church down in Birmingham, Alabama.

Who killed them, DaDa? I ask.

DaDa looks sad. He says, The Ku Klux Klan, son. I don't know why there's so much hatred in this world. He squeezes my shoulder with his large hands and pulls me close to him.

There's no school on the day of President Kennedy's funeral. We all watch the procession on television. Mrs. Kennedy has a black veil over her face and she's holding her little son John-John's hand. It's enough to make anyone cry. And we all do when John-John salutes his father's casket as it goes by. I'll never forget how sad we all are as we watch President Kennedy's casket being carried to his gravesite in Arlington National Cemetery.

The cold weather is gone, the birds are singing again, and we're moving into a new house on the upper end of

Washington Avenue. The lower end of Washington Avenue takes you right into the town of La Plata and has the most beautiful houses in the whole county.

My Aunt Frances, Moma's oldest sister, lives in one of these houses. Beside her house is a goldfish pond where the biggest frogs I've ever seen hop around all day on giant water lilies. Up the street from Aunt Frances is Judge Diggs' mansion that's surrounded by beautiful green lawns, a maze of equestrian hurdles, and a field of roving Tennessee Walkers. Right across the street from Judge Diggs' place is our Grandmother Lorenz's old house. At least half a dozen kids from my class live along this stretch of Washington Avenue or on one of the side streets. It's a beautiful neighborhood, and I know every inch of it.

The middle section of Washington Avenue is a densely wooded area where several poor colored and white families live in tiny bungalows and shacks. There's an abandoned baseball field where Max says the old Negro teams used to play. The infield is all weeds now, and there's just a trace of the dirt paths around the bases. Beside the field is the state Roads Commission shop and a sawmill. Max's mother, Mrs. Alberta Bair, lives in a big house across the street.

Another quarter mile up the road is Kline Drive. Our house is the second to the last one on the right. It sits on a half-acre lot. There are woods in the back and on the right side of the house. The only tree on our green lawn is a big oak that stands like a giant umbrella in the front corner of the yard. Along the new blacktop road are several new houses that are ready for occupancy and several that are still under construction. A few families have already moved in the day we move.

While Moma and Max arrange the furniture, I speed up and down Kline Drive watching the moving vans unloading other families. I see lots of children moving in, and I'm excited.

The next day, I ride off Kline Drive to the end of Washington Avenue where it runs into 301 Highway.

There's another new housing development at the very end of Washington Avenue. It's called Warlinda Village. I'm riding through it when a man stops me in a yellow truck. Hey, son, he says. Do you live around here? Yes, sir, I tell him. He asks me how would I like to have a job. Doing what? I ask. He says, Delivering the *Washington Post* seven days a week. I tell him I'll have to ask my mother, and he follows me all the way home.

Moma is in the yard planting flowers. She tells the man it's OK with her, and then she tells me not to expect her to take me around when it's raining.

Then the man and I sit down at the picnic table and he shows me the forms I have to fill out each time I sign up a new customer. I'm starting with twenty-three daily customers and seven Sunday-only customers. The newspapers will be dropped off on our carport every day by two in the afternoon on weekdays and four thirty a.m. on Sundays. He says the daily papers have to be delivered by no later than five o'clock, and the Sunday paper by seven a.m. Every month I have to go to each customer on my route and collect for the service.

The man shows me how to calculate my monthly earnings, and then we get in his truck and he takes me up and down our street and all around Warlinda Village to show me the route. When he drops me off, he reminds me that the more new customers I sign up, the more money I'll make each month. Then he gives me a card with his name and phone number on it, and tells me to make sure I call him if there's ever a time when I can't deliver my papers.

For the next couple of weeks I stop at every house on our street and in Warlinda Village that doesn't get a paper. I feel like a big shot every time I ring a doorbell and say, Paper boy. Would you like a subscription? Sometimes children answer the door and I say, Hi, my name's Pat, and I'm the paper boy. What's your name? Then I ask if one of their parents is home. After a month, I have eleven new customers. I'm as proud as all get-out to be earning my own money.

Having my own paper route has another advantage. It keeps me out of the house. You would think that moving into a brand-new house would make everyone happy, but it doesn't. Moma and Max argue every day. Sometimes they scream and yell until one of them storms out the door and drives up the street. After they fight, there's silence for days. I hate the silence. I hate the way Moma and Max treat each other. And I hate the way Max talks to me when he talks to me at all. As if I was some kind of goddamn criminal.

Chapter 6

Ever since I've been old enough to observe the Mass, I've wanted to be an altar boy. Before we moved into our new church, I often sat in the balcony of the old Sacred Heart Church with the colored parishioners and watched as the Mass unfolded.

I was always impressed by the actions of the altar boys. Dressed in bright red vestments, they genuflected and knelt with style and grace and they looked like angels. Leaning over the old wooden railing around the front pews of the balcony, I watched the flames of the tall white candles dance and flicker and the sweet-smelling smoke from the burning incense rise over the altar like clouds. I dreamed of playing a part in these glorious rituals one day. I was also attracted to the idea that God was down there hiding inside the tabernacle and being an altar boy meant you got to be closer to him than other people did. Becoming an altar boy would make me a better person, I thought.

My first week in seventh grade, Father Kelly Reese comes in and tells us boys if we want to become altar boys, we need to learn our Latin. He hands out plastic cards with black and red print on them to the boys who raise their hand.

I study these prayers every day for a week, but I just can't learn them. Michael, who has been an altar boy for a year now, tries to help me; he knows the prayers in his sleep. I still can't learn them. The shorter prayers that come at the beginning of Mass are easy. But the Confiteor, the Creed, and the prayer during the Orate Fratres drain my confidence. I can't for the life of me memorize these long prayers.

Michael is patient. He says to learn them a phrase at a time. I try that but when I go to put three or four phrases together, I forget the ones in front. Michael says to keep trying.

Danny Miller and his four brothers are altar boys in our parish. I ask Danny for help and he says come to his house next Saturday. I walk a mile and half up the railroad tracks and Danny and his brothers Philip and Anthony drill me for two hours. In the end, all I can do is say the initial phrases of the longer prayers. Philip says, Kid, you're an imbecile.

I'm angry as hell. That's very goddamn funny, I say.

Hey, you don't have to get sore, I'm only joking. Keep studying. You'll learn them by the time you graduate from high school. The older boys laugh. Danny smiles and so do I.

For the next month every Saturday afternoon, I go to altar boy practice at Sacred Heart Church. We learn the movements of the Mass, where to stand, when to sit; how to hold the water and wine cruets and how to pour them so as not to spill a drop of wine on Father Danvea's precious carpet. We learn when to ring the bells and how hard to ring them. I learn everything I'm supposed to do, and I can go through the Mass in my head in two minutes. Father says, Who wants to go first?

Billy White goes first. He trips coming out of the sacristy and Father says, Look at you, son. Were you in one of my wine bottles? Billy says, Sorry, Father.

Billy says every prayer properly and makes all the right movements. I go last because I'm hoping that Father will be tired of listening and less attentive, and, besides, I have a genius of a plan.

When it's time for the Confiteor, I articulate the initial phrases clearly and dramatically. Then I ride out the rest of the prayer on a wave of Latin and gibberish: *Confiteor Deo ominipotenti, beatae Mariae semper virgini, beato Michaeli Archangelo, beato Joanni Baptistae...sanctis...Apos'...et tibi...Pat'...quia pecca'...cogitato verbo et opera.*

This is followed by a most sincere sign of contrition, which involves a thunderous and passionate striking of my heart three times while reciting: *Mea culpa, mea culpa, mea maxima culpa.* (Through my fault, through my fault, through my most grievous fault.)

It works. Only Danny knows I faked my way through it. Father tells us we all did good and we're official altar boys now. The rear of the church is filling up with old ladies who've come for Saturday confession. Father says we can go first.

I walk in the confessional, kneel, and make the sign of the cross. Bless me, Father, for I have sinned. It's been a week since my last confession. These are my sins. I lied to my grandfather when he asked me if I was behaving. I stole fifty cents from my stepfather's pants, and I've daydreamed about bashing his head in with a rock. I stole a friendship ring from Bowling's department store and two 45 records. And I flushed my lima beans down the commode at supper last night.

I pause, and after several seconds, Father says, Is that all, my son? No, Father, I'm examining my conscience, I say. Father, I watched the girl who moved next door to us get undressed and I got an erection. Father interrupts me before I can go on.

What were you doing in her bedroom? he asks. Did she invite you?

No, Father. My brother hit the baseball two hundred feet and it landed in the new neighbor's yard. I went to get it, Father, and I peeked in their window.

Father says, All right, son. Is that all?

One thing, Father. Sometimes at night I touch myself. I pause again, and then say, These are my sins.

Father says, Son, it's a mortal sin to steal. And you know it's wrong to invade other people's privacy, don't you?

Yes, Father, I know. I'll never do it again.

Then he says, And you shouldn't touch your private parts except when you're using the bathroom or bathing.

Yes, Father, I say. And then I pray: Oh, my God, I am heartily sorry for having offended Thee. And I detest all my sins because I dread the loss of heaven and the pains of hell. But most of all, because they have offended Thee, my God, who art all good and deserving of all my love. I firmly resolve with the help of Thy grace to confess my sins, to do penance, and to amend my life, Amen.

For penance, Father tells me to say ten Our Father's, ten Hail Mary's, and ten Glory Be to the Father's.

I'm in Sister Isidora's seventh-grade English class, and I have my hand raised for ten minutes before she recognizes me.

She finally says, What is it, sir? I say, Sister, may I go to the lavatory?

She says, Why is it that every day you come into my class and need to be excused? I tell her I don't know the answer. She says, Make it back fast, Mister.

Five minutes later, I'm standing at the urinal peeing and puffing on a Marlboro cigarette. Francis Flynn is standing by the window waiting for his turn at the cigarette.

Suddenly, the door opens and Sister Isidora storms in. She wraps her fat fingers around my earlobe and yanks me away from the urinal and then grabs Francis by the arm. I'm still peeing and it drips on the floor and down the front of my pants before I can cut the flow off and put it away.

Sister rushes us down the hall. She's pulling hard on my ear, and it hurts. I stop dead in my tracks.

Let go of my goddamn ear, Sister! I say. When I free myself from her grip, I accidentally knock her headpiece sideways. Sister explodes. What did you say, Mister! Get in my office and take a seat!

I can hear her in the hallway chewing Francis out.

Francis Flynn, why didn't you report to English class today? she asks.

Sister, you told me I could go to the library today and work on my report, he says.

Sister says, Since when did the boy's lavatory become the library, Mister?

I had to go, Sister, Francis says.

You'd better get in that library right now, and I'd better not see you leave there until the end of the day. Do you understand me?

Yes, Sister.

She walks into her office and starts fidgeting with papers on her desk. Then the phone rings and I can tell from her conversation that she's talking to a priest. Yes, Father, she says. We will, Father. Thank you, Father. Good-bye, Father.

She hangs the phone up and rearranges the knickknacks on her desk. She forces me to sit in silence directly in front of her just like she has the other three times I've been here. This is her second year at A.N.S., and she's our principal and English teacher. I'm certain that her only purpose for coming here is to make my school days a living hell. She moans and sighs all the time. We boys call her Our Sister of Great Agony.

She smacks her lips together, and says, Now where were we?

I've been right here, you iguana-neck-old bitch! I say to myself.

She says, Is your mother working today, sir? She is calm now.

Yes, Sister.

Do you know that smoking will stunt your growth?

Yes, Sister.

And do you know it's a sin to use the Lord's name in vain?

Yes, Sister.

She looks up my mother's work number in my school records and dials the number.

Hello, Mrs. Bair? This is Sister Isidora. I'm calling about your son Patrick. He's earned himself a suspension, Mrs. Bair. You'll have to pick him up as soon as possible. What did he do? He was smoking a cigarette in the lavatory and he used the Lord's name in vain. Thank you, Mrs. Bair. She hangs up the phone and says, Your mother's coming to get you.

I'm sorry, Sister, I say.

Well, you should be. You're going to have three days to think about it. We will not tolerate any student using the Lord's name in vain, let alone smoking cigarettes on school grounds. Does your mother know you smoke, sir?

No, Sister, I say.

Well, she does now.

When Moma arrives, Sister Isidora tells her again I was smoking a cigarette in the bathroom and I almost knocked her head off coming down the hall. And he used our Lord's name in vain, she says.

Moma looks shocked, even though she uses the Lord's name in vain twenty times a day. She says, What's gotten into you? Have you lost your mind?

Moma is silent all the way home. When we pull in the driveway, she tells me to stay in the house until she gets home from work. She says, You know I'm going to have to tell your stepfather about this.

I don't care, I say. I wasn't doing anything wrong.

You weren't doing anything wrong? You're too damn young to be smoking, Pat. And you've got some nerve cursing at one of those Sisters. You don't think that's wrong? You better hope your grandfather doesn't find out about this. Sometimes I don't know what to do with you.

I know, Moma.

Moma doesn't tell Max. Instead, she gives me the silent treatment for the next three days. I spend the time at home playing with Huck. He's five now and he loves to play in the woods.

Elizabeth makes us peanut butter sandwiches and puts them in a paper bag along with red apples. We drop our sandwiches off at our tree fort, and then we set out hiking across a deep ravine where we see a doe and her fawn drinking water from the stream. The deer see us and disappear in three flashing leaps. Huck is excited. We're standing near a maple tree and I show Huck something Aunt Winn showed me when she was teaching me how to identify trees on my grandfather's farm. I pull a cluster of samaras from the branches of a maple tree and show them to Huck. I crack one open to show him the seeds inside.

Now watch me make them fly, Huck, I say. I split two of the winged seeds apart and toss them in the air; they spin and spiral to the ground. Huck is amazed. Let me try, let me try, he says. He does and he laughs when they spin.

My Aunt Winn taught me how to distinguish one kind of tree from another by learning the shapes of the leaves and the texture of the bark. I see a beech tree with its glossy straight-veined leaves that are perfect for using as a whistle when you place them between your tongue and upper palate and blow ever so gently. I show Huck how to do it and he tries. He gives up after spitting all over the leaf and trying one more time.

On the opposite side of the ravine we come to a dark curtain of tall pine trees. I've seen pine trees many times before, but never have I seen so many together in such a dense tangle. At first I'm reluctant to go any farther because I have Huck with me and I'm responsible for him. But Huck wants to keep going, so we do.

We walk ten feet into the forest and we're forced to change directions several times. There's darkness in every direction and dead silence but for the crackle of twigs under our feet.

I look over my shoulder once and Huck is gone. I stop and call for him. I'm stuck, he yells. He's ten feet behind me caught up in a snag. We stay close together after that.

The next day, we're playing army at the edge of the woods behind our house. To make our war games more exciting for Huck, I take along a Mason jar filled with gasoline and a rag. Huck and I are crouched down behind a small hill. I tell Huck there are Germans just ahead of us. Then I light a match to the rag and throw the jar onto the hill in front of us.

The flames explode into the air and ignite several branches. I try to put the flames out with my t-shirt, but I can't. I yell to Huck, Go tell Elizabeth to call the fire department! And hurry up!

Luckily, the fire doesn't spread far before the fire trucks roll into our backyard. The fireman puts out the flames quickly and then soaks down all the trees in the area.

Moma pulls into the driveway and after talking with the firemen, she shakes her finger furiously at Huck and says, Your father's on his way home, and both of you boys are in deep shit when he gets here. Huck is crying. He says he didn't set the woods on fire.

From my bedroom I hear Max enter the house and scold Huck. Minutes later, he storms into my room with his belt in his hand and starts beating me. I am much quicker then he is now and, after two or three slaps, I get away.

Max forbids Huck to ever play with me again. Huck says, Yes, sir.

But the minute Max is out of sight, we are together again. We have too much love for one another to let Max come between us.

After three days, I'm allowed back to school and Sister Rosemaron, who teaches every seventh-grade subject except for English, says, Welcome back, Patrick. She says it in front of the whole class. She's the nicest Sister in the whole school.

At the end of the day, she asks me if I can make plans to stay after school tomorrow, and I say, Why, Sister? I didn't do nothing.

She says, Didn't do anything.

Huh, Sister?

You didn't do anything, Patrick. Didn't do nothing is a double negative.

Oh, yes, Sister. I didn't do anything.

No, you didn't, she says. I need you to help me.

All right, Sister.

The next day she has me clapping erasers on the back steps of the school. After I straighten up the chairs in our classroom in neat rows, she says to follow her. We walk side by side toward the back of the convent. When we get there, Sister rolls up her sleeves and opens the door. Well, come on, Mister, she says.

She sits me down at a wooden table in the basement of the convent. I hear washing machines and dryers tumbling in the next room and someone with a sweet voice is singing. It's Mrs. Brown, the cook. She's singing as she walks into the room carrying a tray of cookies and punch.

Sister says, I don't have to ask you if you like cookies, do I, Patrick?

No, Sister.

Then she says, Now, you need to work on your math because you're behind the rest of the class. But before we do that, I want you to tell me what's troubling you.

Nothing, Sister. I feel fine.

She says, Don't play games with me, Mister, because I know better. All year you've been restless and daydreaming in class and wanting attention.

I don't know, Sister. I promise I'll start paying attention.

She doesn't ask me what it's like at home. If she did, I would tell her that Moma and Max make my life miserable by arguing all the time and Moma's crying spells and silent treatment make me worry like crazy.

Sister tells me I'm a bright boy and I have so much potential if I would just buckle down and concentrate.

And another thing, Patrick, you should watch the company you keep.

What do you mean, Sister?

You know very well what I mean. You and Francis Flynn. You're not good influences on one another. He's a good boy, but every time the two of you are together, there's chaos, Mister.

Since the first grade, Francis has been my boon companion. Moma once told me that his family has more mouths to feed than food to go around. Francis wears thick Coke-bottle eyeglasses that are taped together, and he wears the same pair of navy blue pants to school every day and a white shirt that's two sizes too small. His hair, which is the color and texture of straw, is never combed, and his shoes are falling apart. Julie Posey tells him he's a sight for sore eyes and where did he get the high waters anyway. Yeah, Francis, where's the flood? I say. His cuffs are two inches above his ankles.

Very funny, I'm sure! Francis replies.

Sister Rosemaron says I have to stay after school at least once a week to catch up on my math.

When it's time to leave, I thank her.

What are you thanking me for? she asks.

For helping me, Sister.

That's what I'm here for, my child.

The next day I'm standing in line waiting to go to confession. Francis is in front of me. We're all supposed to be examining our consciences. Julie Posey, who's standing in front of Francis, turns around suddenly and slaps Francis across the face.

You dirty, filthy creep! she shouts.

Francis is appalled. His face is cherry red and he looks like he's ready to cry. I didn't do nothing! He says. He turns around and points to me. This jerk pushed me into you, I swear!

Francis had thrust his body up against Julie's as if he'd been pushed into her. When he did, Julie lost her balance and fell forward with Francis clinging to her. To prevent her from falling, Francis grabbed her around the chest and held on to her breasts.

No way, Julie! I say, looking angry and amazed. He's lying through his teeth. You know I wouldn't do that to you.

I know the little creep did it! she says. You're a pervert, Francis. I should tell my brother.

Later in the lavatory, Francis and I celebrate his victory. Man, she's got the softest titties, he says. We laugh until our sides ache.

No one can console me on the last day of seventh grade when Marianne Gardner tells the class she's not coming back to A.N.S. next year. My heart sinks and I'm both sad and afraid. I know that once she gets to Milton Summers Junior High, she'll fall in love with some other boy. I'm afraid, too, because I can't stand the thought of being alone again.

That night I tell Moma how terrible I feel and she says I'll probably feel this way a hundred times before I'm eighteen. She's laughing like it's real cute. I say, It's not funny, Moma. She says, I know, son. But you'll find another girl soon enough, just mark my word.

At Mass the next Sunday, I pray three Our Fathers and ask the Blessed Mother to please send me another girl to love.

After Mass, I see Father Danvea in front of the church and ask him why I haven't been called to serve. He says for me to be patient, then he asks me if I have strong arms.

I say, Yeah, Father, why do you ask? He says, Would you like to caddy for me next Saturday? What's caddy, Father? I ask. He says, Carrying my golf clubs around the course.

Sure, Father, I'll do it.

The next Saturday I carry Father Danvea's golf clubs around the eighteen holes of the Naval Ordinance Station's golf course. At every other hole, Father sips whiskey from a silver flask and knocks more balls in the pond and sand-traps than he does on any green.

Once I say, Father, your aim is off a little, and he says, Yes, I think I need to adjust my swing. He tees off and the ball slices into the woods. He curses and kicks his tee out of the ground. He stubs his toe and laughs like hell. I laugh too.

That whole summer, I caddy for Father every Saturday. Sometimes on our way back to the rectory, Father lets me drive his car on the backroads of Charles County. He tells me I'm a good driver and when I get my license I can be his chauffeur.

When we get to the rectory, he asks Mrs. Sinclair, the cook, to make me two grilled cheese sandwiches. Mrs. Sinclair asks me how I like them made, and I tell her dark brown with lots of butter. She asks me how Father did on the golf course today. I say, He hit three balls in the water and one in the woods, ma'am. But he's getting better. She laughs and turns my sandwiches over. Father comes into the kitchen and hands me a five-dollar bill. Don't spend it all in one place, he says. I'm off to hear confessions now.

Thank you, Father, I say. I'll see you next Saturday. I'm relieved when he doesn't ask me if I'm coming to confession. I don't want him to hear my confession today because my sins are multiplying and I don't want him to lose confidence in me.

I have a new girlfriend. Her name is Sandy, and she's fifteen. She lives two houses up the street in a prefab. Sandy's mother is a waitress and works nights at Shorty Michaels' restaurant. When Buck, the man who lives with Sandy and her mother, leaves the house, Sandy calls me on the phone and I tell Moma I'm going up the street to study.

Sandy opens the door and she's in her pajamas. She says, Go in my room and put on some records. I find Little Richard, Buddy Holly, and Ritchie Valence in a stack of records and put them on. Then I sit on her clothes hamper and look around the room.

I see a brassiere draped over the footboard of her bed and my heart begins to pound. I'm excited and there she is with two Royal Crown sodas in her hands. She puts them down on the dresser and there they stay.

We start kissing and pressing against each other until we fall back on her bed and her pajama top is up around her neck. I touch her pink titties and she's crying, Let's do it and I know if we don't I'm going to die.

She's still crying out when I slide my hand inside her underwear. Two minutes later, she says, Put it in me, stupid!

I pull my pants down and put it in her. We move up and down and Holy Mother of God, I'm crying and she's crying and there's nothing in the world that feels as good as when my groin explodes.

I'm pulling my pants up when she says, Was that your first time?

No, I lie.

I don't bother to ask her if it was her first time because I know it wasn't by the way she did it.

Did you like it? she asks.

Yeah.

I did too.

For weeks after that, we do it on her bed every Friday night. Sometimes we meet in the woods after school and do it on the floor of my tree fort. When I get paid from my paper route, I buy her a gold friendship ring from Bowling's department store and two new records.

She puts the ring on her finger and says, Does this mean we're going steady now?

I say, You're my girlfriend, aren't you?

Of course, she says. You're so sweet, Pat. No boy has ever given me a ring this nice before.

I'm glad you like it. It cost me fifty dollars, I say. What a liar I am!

Chapter 7

Father Danvea pulls Danny Miller and me out of class in our second week in eighth grade. He tells Sister Isidora he's taking us to a funeral. He says every time a Catholic dies in our parish we're going to get out of school a half a day to serve the Mass.

I say, Father, I'd serve a hundred Masses just to get away from Sister Isidora for one period.

Father says, Ah, she's a lovely nun, Pat. You just have to get to know her.

That's OK, Father. I don't want to know her any better.

Father says, When they get that old and crabby, they should put them out to pasture, shouldn't they, boys?

Yeah, Father. You know what we call her sometimes, Father?

I'm afraid to ask, but I know you're going to tell me.

We call her Our Sister of Great Agony, Father, on account of she always looks like she's in pain.

She is! Father says. She suffers from chronic constipation, boys. Father taps his finger against his lips telling us to keep this a secret. Then he laughs right along with us.

The next day we're marching from A.N.S. up to Sacred Heart Church with the sixth and seventh graders for a special Mass. Sister Isidora tells me that the first time I act up in school, she'll put a stop to my altar boy duties. She makes me walk beside her all the way up Charles Street and down Kent Avenue and I'm so angry I could chew nails, because she's punishing me for no reason at all.

When Mass is over, we're sitting in our pews meditating. I'm praying to the Blessed Mother, *Hail Mary, full of grace, the Lord is with thee*, when Margaret Kemp, who's sitting in the pew beside me, finds a foreign object stuck under her seat.

Sister! Sister! Look! she says. Margaret takes the object to Sister Isidora who's sitting in the front pew. Sister stampedes to the front of the altar and from the top of her lungs demands to know what sinful creature among us has committed this sacrilege of all sacrileges. She places the object in her handkerchief and holds it over her head. It looks like a piece of chewing gum. Someone says, What is it, Sister?

What is it! She explodes. It's a sacred host! That's what it is!

An intense silence brought on by the magnitude of this evil act overcomes us all, and not one of us moves a muscle. Sister paces back and forth on the altar, her face is beet red, and her fists are clenched so tight that her fat knuckles turn bone white. She's waiting for the sinner to come forward.

It had to be a boy! she says. No girl would ever conceive of such an act.

I wonder if she's thought of the possibility that someone other than one of us could have abandoned the host. But I don't dare say a word.

With her hands locked behind her back, she paces up and down the aisles and scans the face of every boy, looking for a sign. Suddenly, she stops beside my pew and shouts, Mr. Middleton! This is something you would do! She stares at me in disgust, her eyes like two black stones.

I'm filled with rage and I want to stand and rip her bonnet off her head and expose her ugliness. I want to rip her precious crucifix from her neck and throw it through the stained-glass window above the altar and humiliate her the way she has just humiliated me.

I also want to hang my head and cry because I didn't commit this horrible act. But I don't. I just sit there staring holes through her and wishing she would drop dead.

Sister says to Francis, Why don't you act your age and sit up straight? Francis squirms in his seat and then sits up straight. He says, Yes, Sister, and blushes.

She says, One of these days you're going to cross your eyes and twist your face up the way you just did and they're going to stay that way forever.

Francis says, Yes, Sister.

Sister says, Go and stand in the hall. Place your nose against the wall and keep it there, Mister!

Francis sneers at Julie Posey. When he passes her desk he whispers, You're wearing pink underwear. Julie gasps and sneers back at him.

After recess we're standing outside the boy's lavatory and Francis says, I told you I'd show you a new trick today, didn't I! I say, Yeah, What's the trick, Francis? He tells me to look down at his shoes. There are pieces of a broken mirror glued to the inside heels of his shoes.

Francis says, Now just watch. We stand at the water fountain, and Francis tells each girl who stops for water to go in front of him. He sticks his foot out and turns his shoe at just the right angle and then whispers, White with red hearts. Next girl, it's pink. The girl after that, it's baby blue.

When Teresa Fowler bends over, Francis looks back at me and his eyes are bulging like a frog's. He's giggling and I'm giggling and there's spit hanging from his buckteeth. Oh, Mother of Christ! He says. She ain't wearing none! We both fall out of line laughing like two idiots.

A few days later Francis and I walk into Bowling's department store after school and fill our gym bags with mod shirts, jeans, socks, and forty-five R&B records. Then we go to Barry's and Francis steals a pair of sharkskin pants, the same kind the older sharp-dressing black boys wear. Barry is a Jewish man and his store sells mostly continental clothes for black men. They are expensive and sharp-looking clothes. In the alley behind the Chesapeake and Potomac Telephone Company we split up our booty and go our separate ways.

The next day Francis comes to school wearing the sharkskin pants with, of all things, a pair of white socks and black penny loafers. The sharkskin pants stand out like a neon sign. All of us boys tease him until he wants to punch us in the face. Teresa Fowler tells him white socks don't go with penny loafers and penny loafers don't go with those pants. Francis says, Yeah, and you're the goddamn queen of the hop.

When we're alone in the lavatory, Francis asks why I didn't wear my new shirt with the paisley collar. I'm saving it to wear at the Friday night firehouse dance, I say.

He says, Yeah, I guess I'll come and hang out with you.

No way, Francis, I say. I'm going to be with my girlfriend the whole night, and I don't want you screwing around and pissing her off.

He says, I wonder if Margaret Simpson is going. She's easy to feel up.

I don't know. Why don't you ask her?

After supper that night I race up the street to tell Sandy about the dance even though her mother has warned me three times not to come over on weeknights. I can hear her records playing and when she doesn't answer the third time I knock, I go around to her bedroom window and look through the venetian blinds. There she is, lying on the goddamn bed with Earl Brown, a boy who just moved into Warlinda Village. I slap the windowpane and Sandy jumps up like a jack in the box.

I yell, You slut, Sandy! I want my fucking ring back! Give it to me now or you'll be sorry!

She lifts the window and my ring rolls across the ledge and falls to the ground.

Here, you peeping tom! Now get away from my window or I'll call the cops.

Screw the cops and screw you too, you little bitch! I say.

I pedal my bike up the street so fast that the wind holds back my tears. When I turn on to Washington Avenue, I speed down the hill all the way to the Esso station. I slam on the brakes and gravel splashes all over the Coca-Cola machine. Then I throw my bike down, buy a Dr Pepper and sit on the curb.

Goddamn, I say. What a two-timing liar. Tears are streaming down my face, and I feel that awful emptiness inside me again. It's the worst feeling in the world.

Michael says they need another bellhop at the Martha Washington Hotel where he works. I ask him what a bellhop does and he says they escort guests to their rooms and help them with their luggage and bring them ice and the newspaper.

I say, How much does it pay?

He says, A lot more than your paper route.

Yeah, but how much?

Seventy-five cents an hour plus tips.

Holy shit! I'm going to be a bellhop, Moma.

That's nice—and watch your mouth, she says.

That night, Michael comes home from work and tells me I got the job. He says, Don't go screwing it up, Pat.

I won't, I say. I've already found somebody to take over my paper route, so when can I start?

Tomorrow. And you have to wear a white shirt and tie.

What about a blue shirt and tie, Mike?

Aw, for Christ's sake, Pat, you're going to screw it up already.

But most of my goddamn dress shirts are blue.

You've got to wear white, Pat. Not blue or gray or paisley.

I ask the owners on my first day if light blue is OK and they say it's fine. They're an older couple and they know our grandfather. They tell Michael and me to set up our own work schedules. Michael pulls rank and says I have to work on Friday nights because he has basketball games to go to. He takes Monday, Tuesday, and Thursday nights and gives me Wednesday and Friday. We both work on Saturdays.

After my first week, I tell Moma I should be paying the owners to let me work there. It's the best damn job any boy could ask for. Each time I lead a lady or a family to their room and unlock the door for them, I get a new thrill. I learn to bring them a bucket of ice whether they ask for it or not because it usually results in a tip, and I always tell them to pick up the phone and call the desk if they ever need anything.

Just about every night we have to hitchhike home. The only time it's a pain in the ass is when it's pouring down raining or when a sixteen-wheeler goes by. When I see one coming, I put my thumb down and turn my back to it. Ever since Michael and I saw the story on the news about a boy who got picked up by a trucker and was molested and killed, neither of us will ride in a sixteen-wheeler. We'd rather walk the seven miles home than take a chance on getting carried off and having our throats slit.

The Martha Washington is one of about a dozen gambling establishments along a two-mile stretch of 301 Highway in Waldorf. The Desert Inn, Don Owens' 301 Ranch, the Wigwam, the Star Dust Inn, the Frontier, the Spring Lake Hotel, and Howard's are all within walking distance of one another. At night, it's a pretty sight to pass by them and see all the multicolored neon lights flashing.

When I go to the restaurant to eat my supper, I'm fascinated to see how the establishment works. When you walk through the front door, the dining area is on the right. In the middle is a long bar and on the left is the gambling establishment. There's a big horseshoe-shaped counter that holds forty to fifty slot machines. On Friday nights and all day Saturday, just about every machine is occupied.

It's fascinating to watch how the workers never stop moving. Busboys clear tables just in time for the next family or group of people to sit down. As one slot machine is abandoned, someone else comes along and occupies it. The constant clanging of the change machines, the rattling of plates and saucers and glasses, and the loud cries of winners and those who came close fill the air and make the atmosphere exciting.

Michael and I eat our meals for free and get to order whatever we choose from the menu. There's a pretty waitress named Francine who treats us like we own the place. I know I'm too young for her, but she makes me feel like Mack the Knife when she winks at me. She says, You look handsome and sharp with your shirt sleeves rolled up like Charlie the bartender. I say, Thanks, and I'll bet you get a lot of tips as pretty as you are.

She says, Are you flirting with me?

I say, I sure am.

Two months and I'm busing tables in the restaurant all day on Saturdays. When I need extra money, I steal tips from the waitresses who are too stingy to pay me for working so hard. I watch to see where the customers leave their tips on the table and as soon as they leave, I clear the table before the waitress arrives. If a customer leaves four ones, I take two and leave two. I never steal from Francine's tables because she is one of the only waitresses who looks out for Michael and me.

I'm no damn dummy either. I make it a policy never to take money and put it directly into my pocket because there's always a chance that someone's watching. Instead, I place the bills directly into the plastic tub I use to collect the dirty dishes and then remove the money before I arrive at the dishwashing station in the rear of the kitchen. Cleaning off a table of dirty dishes becomes an art to me. I learn to remove a handful of plates and saucers in one swift, graceful movement without anyone seeing the money disappear at the same time.

My crimes get bigger and bigger and the more I steal, the more excited I become. Charlie the bartender tells me to walk through the casino and pick up empty bottles and glasses. I enter the change boy's perimeter inside the horseshoe so I don't disturb the customers. I look ahead to see which bottles and glasses are completely empty and which ones are almost empty. When I'm not sure if a customer is finished, I say, May I take this, sir, or ma'am? The ladies smile and I smile back.

There are rows of plastic cups filled with coins inside the change booth perimeter. There are five-, ten-, and twenty-dollar nickel cups; ten- and twenty-dollar dime cups; and five-, ten- and twenty-dollar quarter cups. The change boy makes these cups up ahead of time so he doesn't keep customers waiting when he gets busy. With agile fingers I learn to move my hands over the quarter cups and lift three quarters from each cup in less time than it takes the change boy to click off five dollars worth of quarters from his machine and turn around to pick me up in his view.

Young man, a lady says. You can take that glass away.

She has a fresh drink beside her slot and an empty glass. I pick it up and she says, Say, can you give me a good tip on a hot machine, darling? She's a glamorous-looking lady. She has black and silver hair that's rolled in a French twist just the way Moma wears her hair. She's wearing red lipstick and nail polish, black high-heels and a black dress that fits her in all the right places.

I've been around slot machines long enough to know that one machine isn't any more likely to hit than the next one. But I'm obsessed with girls, and it doesn't matter that this one's at least twenty years older than me.

I lower my voice to a whisper and say, I'll find out for you, ma'am.

A few minutes later I return and tell her as seductively and conspiratorially as I know how that the quarter machine on the end is due to hit the jackpot. The lady smiles at me and says, You're a doll. Then she winks and I want to die. Moma says I could lie to the pope and get away with it, so I tell her that the slot is sure to pay off sometime that afternoon.

She gathers her drink, purse, and cup of coins and moves to the stool in front of the slot I pointed out to her. I watch her skirt ride up her thighs as she climbs up onto the stool and I get a hard-on. Before I walk away she says thank you and hands me several quarters.

You're welcome, ma'am. I'll come back and see how you're doing a little later.

You can bring me luck, she says.

Several times that afternoon, I walk over to her to see how her luck is going. She says she's come close twice to winning it all and she's having a great time. She wants me to stay beside her and bring her luck, but I can't. I have tables to clear.

Each time I come back to her, I stay a little longer. I smell her perfume and fantasize about touching her. When my arm brushes against hers, I get another erection.

That evening I'm delivering ice and newspapers to several of the guests in the hotel. I knock on the door and say, Bellhop! The lady from the restaurant opens the door. I'm ecstatic and my heart is pounding in my chest.

My goodness. What a surprise, she says. I walk into her room and set the ice bucket on the dresser. As she's closing the door she tells me I sure do have a lot of jobs and that's when the natural-born liar comes out of me.

I tell her, I work two jobs to help my mother support my brothers and sister. My no-good father left us when we were little kids, and then we had a no-good step-father.

She says, That's so sad.

Not really, I say. I like to work.

How old are you?

Although I'm only fourteen, Sherry Murphy tells me I can easily pass for sixteen. She says I'm tall and very handsome.

I'm sixteen going on seventeen, I say.

She walks over to me and hugs me like Aunt Alice would. She says, That's so very sad. I hug her back and hold on to her tightly. I can smell her perfume and the alcohol on her breath and I get the biggest hard-on. She pulls away. I'm standing there ogling over her like she's the goddamn Queen of Sheba dressed in a black silk nightgown.

Did you hit the jackpot, ma'am?

She lights a cigarette and waves it. No, but I came out forty dollars richer thanks to you, she says. Here, let me share my winnings with you. She takes out her wallet.

Oh, no, ma'am. I can't take that. She has a twenty-dollar bill in her hand.

Why not? You gave me a good tip. I insist that you take it.

She folds the bill and puts it in my shirt pocket and I want to glue myself to her.

Thank you, ma'am. Maybe I'll see you again.

I don't know, she says. I'm heading for home early in the morning.

Do you live far away?

Dover, Delaware, she says. Do you know where Delaware is?

Yes, ma'am. Dover's the capital, right? I know all the capitals. I never knew anyone from Delaware before. We almost went to Delaware on vacation once, but we ended up in Ocean City on account of our stepfather knew the motel owner and got a discount.

She says, You're a very nice young man.

Thanks. I guess I'd better finish making my ice deliveries, or I'll be out of a job, I say. It was nice meeting you. You sure are beautiful.

She says, You're quite handsome yourself.

When we say good-bye at the door, I already know I'm going to see her again and maybe she'll let me stay the night with her. Maybe she'll even give me her phone number and I can call her every week.

For the next two hours, I stay busy delivering ice and escorting new guests to their rooms. The whole time I can smell the lady's perfume and all I can think about is seeing her again. I'm so excited that I almost piss my pants. Mr. Jamerson, the night clerk, tells me if I'm feeling sick I can take off early. When it's ten minutes to ten, I say, I'll leave now then.

At ten o'clock, I knock on the lady's door. When she doesn't answer, I knock three more times. Maybe she's in the shower. I try to open her door, but it's locked. Five, ten, fifteen minutes later, I'm knocking like a drunk. She doesn't answer. Finally, I turn away and start down the highway for home.

After walking a mile, I turn to face the traffic and stick out my thumb. Tears are streaming down my face.

Chapter 8

On the last Monday of eighth grade, Sister Isidora gives me the shaft. She calls my name over the PA system and tells me to report to her office. I walk in and the first thing I see on her desk is my final exam in math at the top of a pile of papers. There's a big F scrawled at the top of the page. My heart starts to pound and my hands get sweaty like they always do when I'm in trouble.

Patrick, you're a smart boy, she goes. But you don't apply yourself. You've missed too many days this school year and you completely failed math and science.

Then she looks at me like she's really goddamn sorry she has to say what she's about to say.

I cannot promote you. You're going to have to repeat the eighth grade.

I tell Moma, It's the math. I failed because Sister Isidora goes too fast. I can't learn the way she teaches, Moma.

Moma says, You should have stayed with the tutor. Your grandfather's going to be devastated. And don't expect me to tell him. You'll tell him yourself.

That Sunday when I tell my grandfather he says, Pat, you missed a lot of days and Sister Isidora tells me you rarely turned in your homework. Son, you shouldn't be working at night if you're behind in school. Do you want me to get you a tutor?

I say, No, sir, we tried that. I'm just not good at math, DaDa.

He says, Son, yes, you are. You just have to apply yourself.

Yes, sir, I say. I'll do better next year.

And that's the end of the conversation. I can tell by the look in his eyes I've let him down.

The next Friday, Michael and I are supposed to spend the weekend on Maple Knoll. I tell Michael I'm not going and he yells at me. Pat, if you don't come, DaDa and Vera are going to be mad as hell at you. They're taking us shopping on Saturday. Now you'd better get ready and come along.

But I don't. Instead, I go to the Friday night dance at the La Plata Fire House to meet up with Colleen O'Donnell. The Executioners are playing, and they are one of the hottest rock 'n' roll bands in Charles County.

Colleen and I sit in a corner and make out between dances until my cousin Andy Mills gets in a fight and knocks a boy on his ass right in front of us. The chaperones don't see the scuffle, but they come and tell Colleen and me to put space between us. Colleen's practically sitting in my lap. She gets up and says she wants to find her girlfriend, Jenny Lou Zhong.

I ask Andy what the fight was all about. He says the boy was running his mouth about how tough he was and Andy thought he was challenging him. Then he says, Look, Pat, you dumb ass. You just lost your girlfriend.

Colleen and Jenny Lou are standing in front of the bandstand talking to Jimmy Tree, the lead singer of the Executioners. Jimmy is in his early twenties and he looks like a movie star. He has the greatest voice, too. He can sound like Jim Morrison one minute and John Lennon the next. Just about every girl at the dance who's doing it would drop her panties in a hot second to be with Jimmy Tree.

I say, Wrong, smart ass. He's after Jenny Lou.

Andy says, You going steady with Colleen?

No, we just talk on the goddamn phone all the time.

Wanna bet I can pull her?

No, Andy. Get your own goddamn girl.

The band is on break and Jimmy Tree is leading Jenny Lou to a room behind the bandstand. Jenny Lou is a pretty Asian-American girl who goes to La Plata High School. She's a senior and has a reputation for putting out.

I walk up to Colleen and take her hand in mine. She says, I'm thirsty. Buy me a soda. And he wants to talk to you.

I say, Who? She says, Jimmy Tree.

About what? I don't even know him, Colleen.

I don't know. He said he'd be right back.

When Jimmy Tree and Jenny Lou return I introduce myself and tell him how great his band sounds. He thanks me and says, Let me talk to you for a minute. He puts his arm on my shoulder and leads me to the side of the bandstand.

He says, I want to take this girl Jenny out after the dance, but she's staying the weekend with her cousin Colleen.

Yeah, I say, and neither one of them will leave without the other.

Why don't you and your girl come with us?

Where are we going?

He lowers his voice. Ever been to the gravel pit?

No, but I've heard about it.

Well, that's where we're going. And after that we'll take them to the Desert Inn.

Jimmy walks over to Jenny Lou and whispers into her ear. Then he jumps up on the bandstand and Jenny Lou whispers into Colleen's ear. She looks over at me with a scowl on her face.

I smile back at her and think, Holy shit! I'm in like Flynn. There isn't a boy in the fire hall who wouldn't give away his sister to be going on a double date with Jimmy Tree of the Executioners. Not only is he a well-liked guy, but he happens to own the cleanest sky-blue '64 Chevy Impala convertible in the entire state of Maryland. I want to walk over to Andy and Keith and the other boys and rub it in their faces and tell them what a dumb ass I am now, but Colleen stops me dead in my tracks.

She says, You've got another thing coming if you think we're going all the way just because we're going to be in the backseat of a car.

Christ, Colleen, you promised. You said the first time we're alone.

Yes, and I can change my mind if I want.

After the dance I help Jimmy Tree carry his equipment to his car. The parking lot is full of boys and girls who are drinking beer and making out. I pass by Andy and the other boys. I'll check you guys out later, I say.

Colleen and I climb in the backseat. Jimmy slides a Mamas and the Papas tape in his eight-track, cranks up the volume, and smokes the tires as we pull onto the highway. This is my first real date in a car and I'm feeling ten feet tall. I put my arm around Colleen and kiss her while the Mamas and the Papas sing "California Dreamin'."

When we pass the Martha Washington, I tell Colleen that's where I work and that's where I'm supposed to be tonight, only I took off so I could be with her. She's not impressed, but she should be. When you're fourteen and you're clearing thirty-five bucks a week, that's a pretty goddamn big deal by anyone's standards.

Colleen says, Aren't you glad you took off?

What do you think?

Well, you should be. And then she leans over and kisses me.

When we get to the gravel pit, Jimmy drives to a spot away from the other cars. He and Jenny Lou get out and Jimmy takes out a blanket from his trunk. Then the two of them disappear.

Colleen and I lie on the backseat and make out until she starts crying. What's wrong? I ask.

She says, I'm sorry. I'm on my period.

I say, So what? Can't we still do it?

She says, Do you want me to bleed to death?

Later we stop at the Desert Inn to get something to eat and I feel like a heel when we walk through the front door. Kids we know who were at the dance are staring at us like we're some kind of big-shot movie stars or something. We get a booth in the corner and Jimmy shows he's got more class than any guy I know. He asks Colleen and me all sorts of questions. Who are our favorite bands? What are our favorite songs? Where do we go to school? What are our parents like? How many brothers and sisters do we have? Jenny Lou doesn't take her eyes off Jimmy the whole time we're sitting there.

After we take them home, Jimmy asks me where I live and I tell him he can drop me off anywhere on Washington Avenue. Jimmy says, I can't just drop you off on the side of the road at twelve o'clock at night. Your parents will have the law out looking for you. I tell him no they won't and I don't want to go home yet because it's too early.

He says, Then let's ride around for a while.

For the rest of the night we drive all over the county listening to music and talking about his band and other rival bands. I try to impress him with my knowledge of music and the names of the members of the Tempests, the Suburbans, and the Warringtons. I tell him I grew up with Johnny Murphy, who plays rhythm guitar and sings background vocals for the Suburbans, and I was present at his house the day his parents gave him his Fender Stratocaster.

I also personally know Johnny Frere and Jimmy Simpson, the two lead vocalists of the Tempests. They are seniors at Archbishop Neale School. The Tempests are a real smooth group. They wear red glitter-covered sport coats and black ties, and they play lots of surfer music mixed with songs by the Drifters, the Four Seasons, and Hank Ballard and the Midnighters. They're always booked up but they only play during the holidays because a couple of their members went off to college this year.

Jimmy says, How would you compare our band to the other bands in the county?

We both agree that his band's biggest competition comes from Johnny Murphy's band, the Suburbans. They don't have a lead singer with the range and quality of Jimmy Tree's voice, but they have three-part harmony in their songs and their stagemanship is second to none. They also play more slow songs than most other bands and that's what a lot of kids want to hear when we go to dances.

Then there's the Warringtons, a band from Indian Head, Maryland. They feature a wild young drummer named Dale Belnap and a raspy lead singer named Kenny Rabey, who I also know personally. The Warringtons play a lot of Rolling Stones songs and they always draw a mob of hooligans from Lackey High School wherever they play, I tell him. My cousins Andy, Jimmy, and Bobby Mills have beaten the crap out of the toughest of these hooligans at one time or another.

I say, Your band is known for having the greatest lead singer in all of Maryland and D.C., as well as for Pete Brown's lead guitar licks. There's no one around who can sing the Righteous Brothers' "Unchained Melody" or Roy Orbison's "Pretty Woman" the way you do.

He says, I really appreciate that.

At five in the morning, we stop at Danny Ferris' all-night diner to get milk shakes. I start to tell him about my family and my lousy stepfather and how I have to repeat the eighth grade. Then he tells me about his family. He still lives at home and he doesn't get along with his father either. He avoided going to Vietnam by joining the National Guard, and he has to pull guard duty every week at a secret missile base in Waldorf. His two loves in the world are music and girls, he says.

Mine, too, I say.

When the sun comes up, Jimmy drops me off at the end of Kline Drive. He says, You wanna go to Georgetown with us tonight? We're going to see the English Setters play.

Holy shit! I heard their advertisement on the radio, I say. I'd love to go. I'll just have to take off from work early. Thanks a lot, man.

That night Jimmy picks me up in front of the Martha Washington with his drummer, Ronnie, and another boy named Rex. We drive into D.C. and right past the White House. The lawn is flooded with light and all the rooms are lit up on the first floor. I swear I see President Johnson staring out the window. He's probably thinking about what he can do to win the war in Vietnam. My grandfather says there's no harder job in the world than being the president of the United States of America.

We continue up Pennsylvania Avenue until it merges into M Street and then we cross a little bridge. Jimmy says, Welcome to Georgetown, fellows.

We're in bumper-to-bumper traffic and I have my head stuck halfway out the window looking at all the long-haired people gathered around the sidewalk vendors who are selling everything from psychedelic t-shirts to leather sandals, volcano lamps, posters, Indian jewelry, and live monkeys. It's the most exciting goddamn thing I've ever seen.

Red and neon signs flash over the doorways of the nightclubs and coffee houses and the live, hard-driving sound of electric guitars spills out into the streets and saturates the warm night air.

I can't believe I'm in Georgetown, home of the famous Peppermint Lounge nightclub, and the East Coast mecca for musicians and draft dodgers and an entire pop culture.

We turn up Wisconsin Avenue and find a parking space in front of a Little Tavern. Jimmy says they have the best hamburgers on the East coast and maybe we'll eat there later. We walk back down to M Street and stand in line out in front of the Crazy Horse nightclub. When we get to the door, Jimmy gives the guy a twenty-dollar bill and tells us we can pay him back later. The English Setters are playing the hottest song of the summer, Paint It Black by the Rolling Stones:

I see a red door and I want it painted black
No colors anymore I want them to turn black
I see the girls walk by dressed in their summer
clothes
I have to turn my head until my darkness goes

At the end of the song they stop on a dime and go right into Taxman by the Beatles. We make our way to the front of the stage. The English Setters are dressed in Nehru jackets and knee-high moccasins. They have long hair and glassy eyes and the lead singer looks like George Harrison of the Beatles. They have the hottest and loudest sound I've ever heard. We stay until they play their last song and then we don't shut up talking about them until we reach the Junior Hot Shoppes in the Eastover Shopping Center.

For the rest of the summer, I hang out with Jimmy and his band. I learn how to set up their equipment and operate the mixing board, blending Jimmy's voice with the right amount of highs and lows. Sometimes Ronnie the drummer lets me sit in on a song and I don't miss a beat. When the band does Pretty Woman, I sing the background harmony with Jimmy. He says I have a strong tenor.

One night I almost catch the clap. We're in Georgetown and I pick up a pretty girl who is panhandling on the corner of M Street and Wisconsin Avenue. She's hungry, so I take her to the Little Tavern and buy her a hamburger. Later we're making out in the backseat of Jimmy's car when she says, Do you have a rubber? I tell her no, but I promise I won't get her pregnant.

She says, That's not it. I've got the clap.

I don't exactly know what the clap is, but I know I don't want it by the way she says, I've got the clap. I pull up my pants and tell her I don't know where I can get a rubber at this time of night.

Moma's mad as hell. My grandfather and aunts are on her back because I've missed Mass and my weekly visits to Maple Knoll for three straight Sundays. Moma says she doesn't know what to do with me. Sometimes I stay out all night and don't come home for two or three days. I'm only fourteen and I need more supervision, she says.

But I hate being at home. When I borrow Jimmy's band equipment to start my own band, Max throws a fit. Melvin Brown, Bernard Briscoe, and I are practicing on the carport when Max comes home from work.

He stumbles over the microphone cable and says, Who in the hell said you could start a band on my carport?

Moma did.

Well, I say you can't!

I throw down my drumsticks and follow him in the house. He says, You listen to me. I don't want any of your goddamn nigger friends around my house.

Moma says, Leave them alone, Maxie. They're not bothering you.

Max is a hateful son of a bitch. Get them out of here, he says, and that's all there is to it.

Two weeks later, Melvin and Bernard quit the band and join Paul Wills' band. I say, You mean Paul Wills who lives off Washington Avenue? That's the one. Sometimes Moma drinks with Paul's mother, Midget, who irons all our clothes every week. Once, after we all went to a farm outside of town to pick fresh kale and strawberries, she and Moma sat on Midget's porch drinking liquor while Paul and his brothers and sisters and I played Red Light, Green Light. That's when I heard Paul singing, A Change is Gonna Come, by Sam Cooke. He has a sweet, soulful voice.

Melvin and Bernard are great musicians and they can both sing and play different instruments. I can't be mad at them for quitting. I know they're going to be famous one day. They tell me if I ever need any help to just call them. That's the kind of fellows they are. We've been friends since we started the first grade together at Archbishop Neale School.

A couple weeks later, I start another band. I move to rhythm guitar and lead vocals. Eddie Cox, a classmate of mine, plays lead guitar; Ed Cooksey plays bass; and my little brother Huck plays drums. We sound pretty lousy. Huck has been playing drums since he was three and he is quite a sensation. He can listen to a record one time and then play the original beat including all the rolls and accents. He is by far the best musician in the band. Before we break up, we play at Judy Hayden's birthday party and all the girls think Huck is the cutest little thing.

At home, Moma nags me. She says, You'd better buckle down in school this year. I tell her I know all the subjects but math, and I've got all year to catch up.

You're not going to get anywhere with that kind of attitude, she says. And you'd better start going to see your grandfather on Sundays with your sister and brother.

When I miss three days of school in September, Sister Isidora calls my grandfather and the juvenile authorities. Moma has to take me to the Charles County Courthouse to see Mr. Buffington, the probation officer. Mr. Buffington tells me about the importance of studying hard and getting a good education. He tells me I need to listen to my parents and work hard to get along with others.

On the way home I tell Moma it was stupid how he talked about everything except skipping school. Moma says, Don't be a smart aleck or you'll have to go back and see him again.

A week later I'm back in his office with Francis Flynn after we're caught shoplifting in Hecht's department store. The security lady at the store calls our mothers and then calls juvenile services. This time I have to go before the juvenile judge, who places me on probation. Now I have to report to Mr. Buffington's office once a week after school.

At home, Maxie acts like he's won the goddamn Kentucky Derby. He looks at me like I'm a full-blown criminal and I hear him tell Moma, I told you that boy's headed for reform school. Moma sips her beer and tells him to shut his mouth. He laughs at her and says, Sure, ToTo, make me the bad guy.

On Sunday, I visit my grandfather for the first time in a month. My Aunt Vera tells me he's out in the shed stripping tobacco and he's waiting for me. When I walk through the door we shake hands and he tells me to sit down.

He says, Son, I'm not going to preach to you. I just want you to think about some things. It hurts us all to see you wasting your potential. We want to see you make something out of your life, son. If you'd just take the time now to study hard and apply yourself, later in life you'll be glad you did.

Not once does he raise his voice or scold me. I tell him I'm caught up with the math and I'm ahead of everyone else in my class in all the other subjects on account of it's my second time around.

He says, I know, son, but you've also got to start listening to your mother and Maxie. I don't tell him how mean and hateful Maxie is because I know I'm supposed to be listening and not talking.

He asks me to please buckle down and do well and not hang around with other boys who are a bad influence. I say, I'm trying awful hard, DaDa. He says, I know you are, son.

For the next three weeks I go to school every day and do all my homework. I come right home after school and tell Moma I'm turning over a new leaf. I cut the grass and pull weeds from her flower beds and play baseball with Michael and Huck and boys from the neighborhood. When the Martha Washington changes owners, I quit after the new owners tell me they only need me on weekends.

But two weeks later, I get a new job at Howard's restaurant busing tables four nights a week. Howard's is one of the finest restaurants on the strip, and they have the prettiest waitresses I've ever seen. They all tip me generously and I'm making more money than ever before.

Some nights I help in the kitchen. I learn to deep-fry chicken and crab cakes and onion rings; I cook steaks on the grill and toss a chef's salad.

Sometimes I help Leroy and James Proctor, two albino brothers, wash the pots and pans. Leroy and James have worked at Howard's since they got their worker's permits. They're both in their late teens and are valued employees. Without being phony, I let them know from my actions that I consider them my friends. When we go on our lunch breaks we hang out together and smoke cigarettes. Sometimes we page through the girly magazines that James keeps under the front seat of his purple Ford Fairlane.

In my second week, Leroy waves me to the back of the kitchen as if God had just told him something terrific. He says, Eileen the waitress is crazy about you. I push him jokingly and tell him he's as funny as a condom machine in a maternity ward. He says, No, man, I'm serious. She told me.

Leroy is a practical joker and I can't tell if he's really serious or setting me up.

What did she say?

She said you're a doll.

Eileen is gorgeous. She has black hair and wears red lipstick, and her black-and-white waitress uniform cups her curves in all the right places. What I like most about her is that she treats me like an adult. One day she gets her hair cut and says, Does it look OK? Or did it look better when it was longer? I tell her she looks beautiful. She smiles and thanks me.

When she sits down to eat, I wait on her. I tell her how I'm repeating the eighth grade and how Moma and Max fight all the time. I tell her about my siblings and how much I love my little brother, Huck, and about my girlfriend, Colleen, and my best friend, Jimmy Tree. She tells me that her father was an alcoholic too. She was married once. She gave her husband the boot when she caught him cheating.

I say, Why would any man cheat on you?

She says, He was a dog.

Two days later, I come to work in a rage. Eileen says, What's wrong, doll? What happened? When I start to cry, I turn away from her and walk into the storage room. I'm crying and shaking like a goddamn baby when she walks in behind me. She takes my hand in hers and says, Pat, tell me what's wrong.

I stop crying and tell her. When I came home from school to change clothes, I found my stepfather choking my mother. I cracked him across the back with Moma's antique wicker chair and ran out of the house.

Oh, no, she says. Is your mother all right?

I don't know. I didn't stick around to find out.

We need to call her and make sure she's all right.

I'm going to kill that big son of a bitch one of these days, Eileen, I say.

She stays by my side as I call home. After five rings Moma answers and tells me she's all right. Max left the house and she's going to her sister's, Aunt Anna Lee's. I tell her I'm not coming home tonight and she says OK, but be careful.

Eileen says, Where will you stay? I tell her I'll probably sleep in Jimmy Tree's car. He's pulling guard duty all night at the missile base.

She says, No, you're coming home with me.

Later when I'm on my dinner break and smoking a cigarette, I thank God for the antique wicker chair and I tell myself, *Holy shit, you've done it, boy! You're going to be with a real woman.*

For the rest of my shift all I can think about is being alone with Eileen. I picture every love scene from every Elvis Presley movie I've ever seen and I recall how confident and sexy Elvis always is. I'll be the greatest emulator.

When we get to her trailer, Eileen turns on the television and tells me to relax while she takes a shower. The whole time she's gone I imagine lying beside her and kissing and touching her. I'll act as if I've done this a hundred times before.

Several minutes later, she comes out of the bathroom wearing a terry-cloth robe. She hands me a towel, a new toothbrush, and a robe that matches the one she's wearing.

She looks beautiful. I'm shaking in my shoes. She says, Go take your shower.

I brush my teeth in a hurry and take a quick shower. The whole time I'm thinking about how I'm going to act when we get into bed. When I walk into the living room, I'm wearing the bathrobe and my clothes are folded neatly over my arm.

Eileen turns the television off and says, Do you need anything before we go to bed? I tell her I don't think so. I follow her down the hall and into a small bedroom with a single bed. Eileen takes my clothes and hangs them in the closet. She pulls the sheets down.

I'll get you up in the morning in time to fix your breakfast before I take you to school, she says. I tell her I usually don't eat breakfast, but she says I'm not going to school without eating first. Then she stands right up against me and kisses me on the cheek. Good night, she whispers.

I want to ask her if I can sleep with her, but I've got too much goddamn class. I'm so disappointed I want to die. I say good night back and when she leaves I take off the robe and crawl into bed.

I start thinking about the way she looks at me at work and I'm confused. Why does she let me put my arm around her waist when no one's around? And why does she wink at me all the time and call me doll? Why in the hell is she leaving me alone? I start touching myself until I'm throbbing and I think about going into her room and getting in bed with her. But I don't. I've got too much goddamn class for that.

Two nights later the restaurant's ice machine breaks, and Eileen sends me over to the bar to get several buckets of ice from their machine. I'm standing behind the bar like I'm the bartender and I feel ten feet tall. That's when I notice a half-open drawer under the cash register. I look inside and it's filled with stacks of fresh green money. They'll never miss one stack! I fill the first bucket and look over my shoulder. When the bartender walks away I slide my long, skinny fingers into the drawer, pull out a packet of bills, and drop it in the empty bucket, pushing the drawer almost closed on my way out. Then I cover the money with ice and walk away, as inconspicuous as a cat burglar.

In the storage room I dig the money out of the ice and shove it down the front of my pants. Then I go and empty the buckets of ice into the dining room ice machine. When I walk into the men's room and into a stall, I'm shaking like a drunk and about to throw up the turkey and mashed potatoes I had for dinner all over my clean white shirt and green money. I sit on the toilet and count the money and Holy Mary, Mother of God! There's fifty twenty-dollar bills in the stack. I do the math. It's a thousand dollars! I've never seen so much money!

I put it back in my underwear and I'm still sick. I tell my boss I want to go home.

The next day I quit my job.

It's my first grand larceny and I'm sure I've gotten away with it until I get home from school on Friday and meet the state police detective who's sitting in our living room. He tells Moma and me he's investigating the theft of a thousand dollars from Howard's restaurant four days ago.

The detective goes, The head waitress told us that the busboys never go in the area where the money was taken, but I still need to ask you some questions. Moma sighs in relief. I try not to sigh. Instead, I look at him like I'm really hurt that I have to be questioned like a goddamn criminal.

Did you see anything suspicious on Monday night?

No, sir.

Did you see anyone in the bar area who didn't work there?

No, sir.

He turns to Moma and asks her if she'd mind driving me to the Waldorf Hotel to Room 212 where another detective is waiting to give me a lie detector test. I don't have to take the test, he says, but every employee who was on duty Monday night is being asked to do so.

Moma says, Pat, do you want to take the test?

I don't care, Moma.

Moma lets out another sigh of relief.

On the way to Waldorf I'm sweating like hell and thinking, Jesus fucking Christ! I'm going to prison now. When we get there and I walk up the steps, I tell myself I'd better stop acting like a guilty criminal. Then I remember that Eileen lied about me not being in the bar area, and I feel better.

The detective is standing in the doorway waiting for me. He's real shrewd. He offers me a seat and then asks me what I learned in school today. What sports do you play? How do you like school? How do you get along with the nuns?

After he did his nice fellow routine, he says, Do you know why you're here? How long did you work at Howard's before you quit? Why did you quit? When I answer his questions he goes, OK, I'm going to hook you up to the machine now. Then I'm going to ask you a series of questions. I want you to relax and try not to move around too much.

He hooks wires up to my fingers and around my chest. The whole time I try to be cool and calm, but I'm scared to no end. When it's all over, the detective thanks me for coming and tells me I can leave.

We never find out what the outcome is and Moma says that's proof of my innocence. Except for Jimmy Tree, I don't tell a soul about the money. Jimmy's transmission is shot so I buy him a new one for four hundred dollars. I also buy a nice used set of pearl-colored Ludwig drums for Huck. I tell Moma they belong to Jimmy. With the rest of the money, I buy clothes and records and treat my friends when we go out.

Chapter 9

On the last day of school I thank Jesus Christ I'll never have to set foot in Sister Isidora's classroom again for as long as I live.

Sister says, See what you can do when you apply yourself just a little, Patrick? You earned a B in math. You're on your way to high school, Mister. Congratulations. I say, Thank you, Sister. But inside I'm thinking, Good riddance, you old witch.

Two weeks after school's out, I get a job as a bellhop at the prestigious Waldorf Hotel. Because of my experience working at the Martha Washington and because the manager knows my grandfather personally, I'm made the goddamn head bellhop on the evening shift after my first week. I have to see to it that the other bellhops do their jobs right and fill in wherever and whenever I'm needed.

I'm the best bellhop they ever had, too. I keep the other boys on their toes and threaten to have them fired whenever one of them refuses to listen or gets lax on the job. When a boy who started the same day I did gets the idea of breaking into one of the rooms, I tell him he'd better not do it when I'm around.

Eventually, I find the master key to all the rooms hidden in the main office. Jimmy stops by one evening and takes the key up the street and gets a copy made. Then I wait until none of the other boys are around and become a professional thief. I enter rooms when the occupants go to the pool or to the restaurant or casino. When I come across wallets and envelopes filled with money, I only take a few twenties and tens. Sometimes I take bracelets and rings, but I never get greedy.

Every Saturday, Moma tells me I should go to confession because I haven't gone in a long time. At first I think she knows everything. I say, I haven't done anything, Moma. She says, What are you talking about? Father Danvea has called here a dozen times for you. You should go to confession and then visit Father.

Ah, hell, Moma. God already knows my sins and Father just wants me to go caddy for him.

Moma says, Well, all you do is go to work and stay out all night. You're never home anymore. Why don't you take a boat ride with Huck and Mon Wink today? Mon invited you to go along.

I gotta work this afternoon, Moma.

Mon Wink is a friend of our family and he's always taking Huck somewhere on Saturdays. He has a speedboat that he keeps down at the Port Tobacco Marina. When we were younger, Michael and I went boating with Mon almost every Saturday. We'd take turns holding Huck on our lap as the boat bounced up and down on the water, and Huck would laugh and scream like a monkey when he got splashed by the waves. I always had fun on these trips, but now I'm having more fun working and being on my own.

At work that afternoon, an elderly woman checks in alone. She's wearing diamonds on her fingers and ears. I'm sitting in the restaurant finishing my dinner when I see her come through the front door and head for the casino. I'm in her room ten minutes later and find a treasure of jewelry stashed in a blue velvet box at the bottom of her suitcase. I see a heart-shaped pendant with tiny diamonds around the border hanging on a thin gold chain. It's beautiful and it's the only thing in the old lady's room that I take.

The next Monday I call Colleen on the phone and I'm sadder than the little boy in *Old Yeller*. She says, What's wrong, sweetie?

I tell her we had to go to a funeral, our Uncle Mon died last week. Then she says how sorry she is and that she lost her grandmother two years ago and so she knows what it's like to be sad over losing a relative. I tell her that our uncle left my brothers and me his speedboat that he kept at the Port Tobacco Marina and would she like to go out in it sometime. She says she'd love to.

I say, How about the day after tomorrow? There won't be that many boats on the water on a weekday, and we can go all the way to Cobb Island if she wants.

I can't wait, she goes. What time should I be there? I tell her by noon and to bring some sandwiches for us to eat.

Mon works all day for the State Roads Commission, so I won't have to worry about him showing up. I also know there's a spare key to the boat in the side panel near the steering wheel. The key is attached to a screw that goes through the mouth of a six-inch-long wooden fish.

On Wednesday morning, I wake up early and scrounge through Moma's closet until I find a small white gift box. I place the necklace I stole between the two sheets of cotton inside the box. After breakfast, I place the gift box in my back pocket and hitchhike the six miles to the marina.

When I come over the hill and down the road that leads to the marina, I see Colleen sitting at the end of the dock smiling coyly, her long tan legs dangling in the water. She's wearing a pink two-piece bathing suit and a pair of cut-off jeans. Beside her is a small Styrofoam cooler.

She says, Hi, gorgeous. You're late. My mom almost wouldn't let me sit here waiting for you by myself.

I had to hitchhike, I say, and I'm only fifteen minutes late, for crying out loud. So what are we waiting for? Let's go, girl.

I escort her down to the slip where Mon's boat sits and she jumps on board. I hand her the cooler and toss the ropes to her as I untie them. Then I jump down beside her and find the spare key in the side slot. We stop at the marina and fill the gas tanks and then we set out for Pope's Creek.

There are only a couple of other boats on the water, but I'm still careful not to go too fast. Once I open the throttle all the way and we bounce along the top of the waves. I know where all the buoys are and I'm careful to stay away from them. I know all too well what can happen if a boat steers on the wrong side of a buoy.

Once when we were with Mon, we saw a boat moving along at full throttle as it pulled two skiers. Instead of watching where he was going, the driver was looking back over his shoulders at the skiers. The boat went between the buoy and shoreline and rolled right up on a sand barge and turned over. The people in the boat were lucky they weren't killed, Mon said. The two girls who were skiing let go of their ropes and Mon circled around and picked them up. They were high school girls and they were real pretty.

On the way to Pope's Creek, I slow down when we get near Chapel Point. I say, Let's see what's left of the place, Colleen.

When we were children, both of our families spent many summer days swimming and roller skating here. We both have lots of happy memories of the place.

I get as close as I can to the shoreline, shut off the engine, and drop the anchor in the sand. The first thing we see is a jungle of green ivy crawling all over the support beams and canopy of the dilapidated roller rink.

My mind is flooded with images of things that once were: the mechanical horse and helicopter I rode over and over until my last dime was gone; the big Wurlitzer jukebox that never stopped playing all day and night; the thick milk shakes and delicious hamburgers the pretty college girls sold at the windows; the round white tables and chairs that were once spread out around the veranda where all the kids used to jitterbug; the shady roller rink with its smooth wooden floor and smells of sweat and leather skates; and the summer breeze cooling our faces as we skated around the rink as fast as we could.

We walk behind the old dressing rooms and I show Colleen where I once saw Jimmy Simpson of the Tempests holding his girlfriend in his arms and kissing her and how I cried later because I wanted a girl of my own to kiss. I look at what is left of the beach and I recall the first time I saw my cousin Mary Beth in her bathing suit. She was the prettiest girl on the beach and I was so proud that she was my cousin.

By the time we finish sharing our favorite memories, I can hear the songs in my head that played on that big jukebox back then—The Duke of Earl, by Gene Chandler; Poetry in Motion, by Johnny Tillotson; Poison Ivy, by the Coasters; Little Darlin', by the Diamonds; and The Wayward Wind, by Gogi Grant, to name a few.

Colleen says, I don't like it here anymore. Let's go.

Yeah, me neither, I say. It's kind of creepy. Let's ride down to Pope's Creek.

When we get there, we tie the boat up at the dock behind Robertson's, one of three crab houses located only a couple hundred feet apart and right on the water.

The other two are Captain Drinks' and Captain Pete's.

Kids and their mothers are fishing on the docks. We look around for people we know. I see Earl Brown working on a boat beside his father's restaurant, Captain Pete's. Earl's older brother, Pete, plays lead guitar for the Executioners, and sometimes Earl comes to the dances when his brother's band is playing. He's a pretty tough fellow, too. Once he picked a fight with three boys from Lackey High School and was kicking their asses even before his brother jumped in. I stop and talk with him while Colleen goes inside the restaurant to use the bathroom.

I ask him how far down the river is Cobb Island and he tells me. Then he says, Who's the girl?

Ah, you don't know her, Earl. Her name's Colleen.

I'd sure like to know her.

Ain't it the truth? I say. What boy wouldn't?

Colleen decides she wants to go swimming so halfway to Cobb Island we turn around and head back to Chapel Point. I steer the boat toward the shoreline, turn the motor off, and drop the anchor over the side. Colleen dives into the water and swims out several yards before she surfaces.

She says, Get in and save me. I'm drowning. I swim to her and dive under the water, bringing my head up between her legs. I grab a hold of her feet and propel her up out of the water. We race back toward the boat until we can feel the thick seaweed dancing against our legs. It's a creepy feeling.

We swim and play for a while longer before I climb back into the boat to eat a sandwich. Mon has a bunch of life preservers stored up in the bow, and I get them all together and make a cozy bed. When Colleen climbs back into the boat, I take her hand and try to lead her up to the bow. She breaks away and says she's thirsty. When she drinks half the soda, I say, Colleen, let's get out of the hot sun for a while. I take her hand again and this time she follows me up to the bow and sits down on the makeshift bed.

We start making out and just when she puts her arms around my neck, I pull away and I'm so damned excited I start to stutter. I-I have something, I have something for you, Colleen. I reach my hand down into the side panel where Mon keeps his spare key and pull out the small white box.

She takes the box in her hands and I watch the expression on her face when she peels the top layer of cotton back and sees the necklace.

Oh, Pat, it's beautiful! she says. She's ecstatic.

I say, It should be, Colleen. I had to work a whole goddamn month to pay for it.

She blushes and beams with joy as she puts the necklace around her neck. Then she throws her arms around me and kisses me. We lie back on the soft life preservers and kiss passionately. When I shove my hand down inside her bikini, she almost manages to toss me off her.

When we arrive back at the marina, Colleen kisses me good-bye and says, When can we go boating again? I tell her I don't know, that my brother Michael gets to use the boat too, and I'll let her know.

But I never get the chance to take her out again. The following Monday, one of Buddy Garner's deputy sheriffs picks me up and takes me to juvenile services in the county courthouse. Sheriff Garner is there to question me in front of Moma and my probation officer, Mr. Buffington.

Before he starts, I say, Why am I here, Mr. Garner? I didn't do anything.

He says, We have information that you and a girl took Mon Wink's boat without permission last Wednesday, son, and that's a crime.

It wasn't me.

Come on, son. The dock attendant who sold you the gas identified you. He knows you and your brothers by name. Now are you calling him a liar? Who was the girl with you?

I refuse to tell him.

He tells Moma that Mon would never have known I'd used his boat except for my own stupidity. I had mixed the wrong ratio of oil to gas in one of the tanks and when Mon took the boat out over the weekend, the motor started to smoke like a stopped-up chimney. I had also damaged the propeller when I brought the boat close to the shoreline where we went swimming. Seaweed had wrapped around the propeller and worked its way into the shaft and bearings.

Mon agrees to drop the charges if Moma pays for the damages I caused.

On the way home, Moma's crying. I don't know what's wrong with you, Pat, but you'd better settle down and start listening to someone. You're gonna wind up in trouble and I'm not gonna be able to get you out of it. Sometimes I think you're losing your mind. I really do.

But do I listen? Hell, no. I hang out with Jimmy and my other friends day and night and come and go as I please. I go to work and get off at eleven or twelve and then stay out the rest of the night. We go to all-night drive-ins and pick up girls in Georgetown. Home is the last place I ever want to be. The only time I feel loved and needed is when I have a girl in my arms. It's the greatest feeling in the world, and it's all I think about.

Home is a battlefield for Moma's and Max's private war. The only things they have left in common are liquor bottles and personal slings and arrows. Max has sold his bar and grill and, along with his important job at the Naval Ordinance Station, he works as a rent-a-cop at Aqua Land, a combination casino, bar, and amusement park located right on the Potomac a few miles downriver from Pope's Creek. Max comes home from Aqua Land with black eyes and cuts and bruises on his face and hands.

At two in the morning one Sunday, I'm sitting in the kitchen eating a sandwich when Max walks in through the carport door. I can tell by his heavy footsteps that he's drunk. He staggers into the kitchen and leans against the counter, staring down at the floor and bobbing his head back and forth the way drunks do. I start giggling. I want to get up and boot him dead in his ass. He starts to babble and pulls out his .38 service revolver. He twirls it around his finger like a goddamn Wild West gunslinger. He says, Boy, you're sitting on my last nerve.

I laugh at him. What's that mean, Maxie? That doesn't make any sense. How can I sit on your nerves?

Don't get smart with me, boy.

He goes to sit down and falls on his ass. I laugh like hell. You're drunk, aren't you, Max? I say. You're as drunk as old Ham.

He starts to get up. I'll show you who's drunk, boy. He's still holding the goddamn gun in his hand as he pushes himself off the floor with his other hand. I start to get nervous. It's not that he'll shoot me or anything, but what if we lock horns? What if the gun goes off? What if he shoots himself?

He gets up and he's moving toward me. I whirl around and run as fast as my ass can go and out the side door. I run up the street and into the neighbor's yard. I hear gunshots. Max, that crazy son-of-a-bitch, is standing in our front yard firing his gun into the air.

Pow! Pow! Pow!

When the gun's empty, he staggers back inside the house, and I head for my tree house in the woods where I stay for the rest of the night.

The next day, Jimmy comes and gets me and it's two weeks before I come home again. Moma warns me that the sheriff's department is looking for me again. Mr. Buffington's been calling the house every day, she says. She's supposed to take me in for a conference. My grandfather wants to see me too. Moma says, Pat, if you don't go with me to see your probation officer today, they're going to put you in Boys' Village.

Moma, if everybody's been looking for me, why didn't they come to my job? I've gone to work at the Waldorf every night.

Moma doesn't answer.

Mr. Buffington wears a crew cut and reminds me of a traveling salesman who once came to our house. He's nice enough. He never says anything like, You've really screwed up this time, son, or, You're in serious trouble this time, young man. Instead, he tells me it's good to see me and how have I been doing. Fine, I say. I'm working and staying out of trouble and everything's fine.

He says, apologetically, The judge wants to see you and your mother today. He turns to Moma. Mrs. Bair, after talking with you this morning, I scheduled an appointment for you and Pat to see Judge Diggs this afternoon at three o'clock. Now, Pat, it's extremely important that you be there.

Moma says, Don't worry. He'll be there.

The last place I want to wind up at is Boys' Village. I don't personally know any boys who have spent time there, but Jimmy and I pass the place every time we go to his house. And every time, we see platoons of boys, marching around like goddamn soldiers and others working in the fields with their shaved heads and khaki uniforms.

When I stand before Judge Diggs, my knees are knocking. He has snow-white hair and looks to be about my grandfather's age. And he's as serious as my grandfather when he speaks. Son, tell me what's going on in your life.

I say, What do you mean, your Honor?

He says, Mr. Buffington tells me you won't listen to your mother.

I listen, your Honor.

You do? Does your mother allow you to stay out all night and come and go as you please, son?

No, your Honor, but I have to work and I play in a band.

The judge starts reading some papers on his desk. He says, Mrs. Bair, I understand Pat's grandfather wants to see him and will in fact be seeing him this weekend. Is that correct?

Yes, your Honor. He'll be visiting with his grandfather on Sunday.

That's fine. I'm going to give you and his grandfather a chance to straighten him out, to help him, before I do. Son, I don't want Mr. Buffington to have to bring you here again. Do you understand?

Yes, your Honor.

Because if he does, I'm going to personally drive you up to Boys' Village myself. All right?

Yes, your Honor.

All the way home I'm mad as hell at Moma because she knew what was going on and didn't tell me. And how did the judge know that DaDa wants to see me anyway, Moma? But Moma won't talk about it. All she says is, You have to go see your grandfather.

When I walk into my grandfather's parlor on Sunday morning, he's sitting in his big green recliner talking with Aunt Alice and Aunt Vera. After I hug and kiss them and shake my grandfather's hand, I sit on the edge of the couch facing DaDa.

He says, Son, we know you're not getting along with Maxie and we know the situation at home is not good for you. The Sisters don't want you back at Archbishop Neale next month and we don't want you attending public school down in La Plata. Your aunts and I have spent the past week checking into several fine boarding schools and we've found one that we think you'll like. It's actually a private home, son, and it's up in western Maryland. We want to drive up there and visit the place with you some time this week.

99

Aunt Alice hands me a brochure but the words are all a blur, I'm so goddamn furious. I haven't done anything to deserve this shit! There's not a fuckin' thing wrong with me. And what gives anyone the right to send me away to school?

I want to say all of this and more, but I don't. I respect my aunts and grandfather way too much to lose my temper in front of them. After more discussion and mild protest, Aunt Vera says, Pat, this Saturday why don't we all drive up to visit the place? If you don't like it after you've seen everything, we'll keep looking.

All right, I say. But what's the name of this place?

Aunt Alice says, Pat, read the brochure. It's called Bowling Brook Home for Boys.

Chapter 10

Bowling Brook Home for Boys is a two-hour drive from Waldorf. When we get to Frederick, we turn off the main highway and drive a mile or so before we see a sign that says, Welcome to Middleburg. There's a single building in the town, a combination post office and general store with two old Texaco gas pumps out front. The building stands on a lot between a row of small country houses with flower boxes in the front windows and vegetable gardens on the side or in the back of each house.

A hundred yards later, we drive past a wide green field on the left side of the road closed in by a fence made of smooth white boards. We see several horses grazing and galloping about the vast green pasture. My grandfather, who's sitting in the front seat, tells Uncle Leo to slow down so everyone can enjoy the view.

The fence runs parallel to the road for at least two hundred yards before it turns in and runs alongside the blacktop driveway we pull into. At the entrance of the driveway a sign with big black fancy letters reads: Bowling Brook Home for Boys.

Aunt Vera and my cousin Lucy are awestruck by the sight of the colossal white mansion that stands about fifty yards off the main road, with its spacious lawns that seem to roll out like a giant green carpet in front of the house. There are ubiquitous beds of orange and yellow and purple and red flowers rising from circles and rectangles of fresh black mulch. Aunt Vera says, Daddy, is that a New England colonial?

DaDa says, It is indeed, Vera.

To the right of the house I can see, beyond a labyrinth of box hedges, a basketball and tennis court and beyond them a large oval track with a single rail around it. Cousin Lucy nudges me in the ribs and points out the window to our left. Look at the horses! she says. Aren't they just splendid?

Beyond the fence that runs alongside the driveway, we see several magnificent-looking horses running in pace with our car. There are dozens of other horses in the field.

I immediately think of Marianne and how excited she would be if she were here to witness this spectacular view. Uncle Leo pulls into a parking space behind the mansion. Uncle Percy, who has followed us in his car with Aunt Alice, Suzie, and Michael, pulls in beside us. When we get out, we're greeted by the superintendent of Bowling Brook, Dr. Tom Harrington. He's a tall, handsome man with a deep voice. As soon as we shake hands, I know I'm going to like him.

He looks me right in the eye, without a hint of authority or self-promotion, smiles at me and says, Pat, welcome to Bowling Brook.

There's a bunch of small talk about how easy it was to find the place and how splendid the scenery is, and then Dr. Harrington takes us on a tour. He points out the little yellow cottage that's off to the side of the mansion where he and his wife and fifteen-year-old daughter live. Then we follow him inside an authentic log cabin behind the mansion. This is the boys' cabin, he tells us, a place where they can come to be away from others or just let off some steam. The room also has a big fireplace, table tennis, some wrestling mats, and a punching bag.

We walk around the grounds admiring the hedges and flowers. Dr. Harrington explains that there are actually two Bowling Brooks—the Bowling Brook Home for Boys and the Bowling Brook Thoroughbred Horse Farm. A few Kentucky Derby winners were born at Bowling Brook, he tells us.

We walk over to the oval track and Mr. Harrington says that every morning the boys can look out their windows and see the trainers exercising the horses. He says it's really special to see these magnificent horses up close.

It's a beautiful August day and the sky is a sheet of solid blue. Dr. Harrington asks us if we want to see the stables and everyone says yes. On the way he tells us that the entire four-hundred-acre estate is owned by a philanthropist by the name of Thomas Richardson III. Mr. Richardson is retired and lives in Baltimore. He says that because of insurance reasons, the stables are off limits to the boys. I'm disappointed to learn that riding these beautiful horses will not be part of the deal.

We're walking down a long wide lane bordered by huge trees and high white-washed fences on either side. Right beside us we see a chestnut horse trotting alongside the fence with her newborn colt that's throwing its head this way and that way and kicking up its little hooves.

When we reach the stables we walk inside a short distance and watch as the trainers and stable hands walk horses to and from their stalls. The place is immaculately clean. It smells of leather and grain and fresh hay. I'm standing there taking it all in when my brother Michael hangs his arm around my shoulder. This place is really nice, isn't it, Pat?

Yeah. It sure is.

He says, I wouldn't mind living here myself. You think you're gonna like it?

I can tell he's excited and really impressed by the place and he wants me to be happy. No matter how many times I've embarrassed him by my actions around other boys and nagged him to let me tag along with him and his friends when we were growing up, Michael has always been the greatest brother a fellow could have. Standing there, I feel closer to him than ever and I want to cry.

I look down the center aisle of the stables and see a small circle of light at the other end. It seems like two hundred yards away and all I want to do is run there and through the light. I feel overwhelmed by everything that's happening and just want to be alone.

Michael says, So what do you think, Pat?

It's OK, Mike, I say. I think I might like it here.

On the way back to the main house, all my relatives ask me the same question. Pat, do you like the place? And I think, What boy in his right mind wouldn't? But deep inside what worries me the most is that I know I'm going to be awfully homesick.

When we enter the white mansion, my first thought is that the place looks like a museum. Every room but the kitchen has a fireplace in it and there are antiques everywhere. Aunt Vera points out the Queen Anne writing table in one of the hallways and tells Aunt Alice that you'd pay an arm and a leg for it.

The living room is furnished with two oversized wing chairs, a couch, a butler's tray table, and a Queen Anne desk and secretary bookcase that looks just like the one my Great-Aunt Fanny gave to Moma. The wooden floors are finely polished and shined and are accented by a large multicolored Persian rug with fringe around the border. In the main hallway stands a magnificent grand piano, the wood polished so high you can see your reflection in it.

In the study, pictures of the great presidents hang on the walls in ostentatious gold frames. Along one wall are several writing desks, each one furnished with a small gooseneck lamp and desk blotter. Along another wall are bookshelves filled with encyclopedias, dictionaries, and novels. Behind the study, in the rear corner of the house, is the dining room. There are three long maple-top tavern tables and several chairs and a side bar in the room.

The staircase leading to the second floor reminds me of Tara in *Gone With the Wind*. It's wide enough for three people to walk up or down side by side, and it has a smooth, shiny banister.

Once upstairs, we walk through seven large bedrooms. When we reach the bedroom in the very back corner of the house, Dr. Harrington tells me that if I decide to come to Bowling Brook, I'll share this room with a second-year boy from Baltimore whose name is Michael. It's the smallest of all the rooms, but the view is serene—a flower and rock garden just below the window that's outlined by a wall of privet and box hedges. Beyond that is a perfect overhead view of the exercise track. The room also has a long walk-in closet and I like the fact that right outside the door is a set of narrow, winding steps that lead directly to the back door of the house.

We end the tour on the first-floor glass-enclosed sun porch that serves as Dr. Harrington's office. When we're all seated, a very big black woman with silver and black hair enters the room pushing a cart on which are cookies and pastries and coffee and punch. Her name is Eleanor and she's the main cook. I like her from the moment we shake hands and I see the loving gleam in her eyes.

Dr. Harrington stands and introduces her to everyone. She says, How're you doing, young man? I'm real pleased to meet you.

I'm fine, ma'am, thank you.

Well, I do hope you decide to come back and stay with us. I really do.

Thank you, ma'am.

After she disappears Dr. Harrington says, Pat if you decide to return to Bowling Brook, you'll be living with twelve other boys whose ages range from twelve to seventeen. They come from all over the state of Maryland, and they're good boys who have just run into difficulties at home or in their communities, just like you. Since we don't have our own school, you'd be attending our fine public school right up the road called Francis Scott Key High School. Here at Bowling Brook we create a caring and stable environment where we help each boy build character and discipline, as well as communication and social skills. You'll be expected to perform daily chores around the house and grounds and to follow the rules and get along with the other boys. We don't believe in corporal punishment here, but we do hold each boy accountable for his behavior. You'll also be required to attend church every Sunday. Pat, do you have any questions?

Yes, sir. I say. What about going home on weekends and holidays?

He says, The boys go home at Thanksgiving and Christmas, and special weekend visits will come after a positive adjustment.

What about my record player and records? Can I bring them with me?

Certainly, you can. You can also bring your bicycle, your roller skates, and any other recreational things you own.

Then the room gets real quiet and everyone's sitting on the edge of their goddamn seat waiting to hear what I could possibly ask next.

What about calling home? Can I call my mother?

You can use the phone, Pat, every week unless you do something to lose your phone privileges.

I look out the window and then at my grandfather and I can't think of any other questions. After a long pause, DaDa says, Son, do you think you'd like to come back and stay?

I smile politely. I'm nervous. I look out the window and then back at my grandfather. Here comes the biggest decision of my life.

Yes, sir, I say. I'll come back.

Chapter 11

Two weeks later I return to Bowling Brook, arriving the same day my roommate, Michael Griffin, and several other boys do. I make it up to the room before Michael and take the bed near the window overlooking the flower and rock garden. I also take the dresser with the mirror.

Two minutes later, Michael walks in. After we shake hands and introduce ourselves, he says, You can keep the bed, but that's my dresser.

I don't want to start off on the wrong foot, so I clear my things off the top of the dresser with the mirror. We divide up the closet space, put our clothes away and arrange the room. Then we sit on our beds and talk until it's time for supper. We're both into music. He likes psychedelic music and owns a cardboard box full of albums by the Doors, Jefferson Airplane, Count Five, Cream, Steppenwolf, Spirit, Vanilla Fudge, and Jimi Hendrix. I dig these groups, too, I tell him. And then I show him my collection of records and albums by the Temptations, the Beatles, the Beach Boys, James Brown, Otis Redding, the Drifters, and the Marvelettes.

What are the girls like around here? I ask.

This is Hicksville, man, he says. Most of these girls are real stiff. They like country music and guys who chew tobacco. You'll see, man. The dudes are real rednecks. They wear penny loafers and white socks, and they all belong to a club called the Future Farmers of America.

When the dinner bell rings, we leave the room together, and I feel good about the prospects of a friendship with him.

Dr. Harrington and his family are seated at the head of the table. Before dinner is served, he stands and gives a welcome speech. He embarrasses me by asking me to stand so he can introduce me to everyone. I'm the only new boy to arrive today. He sounds off each person's name and all those eyes and faces are staring at me one after the other. Sandy, a big blond-haired, baby-faced boy who's a senior and the oldest boy in the home. David and Barry, both fifteen and in their third year. Eddie, a tall blond boy, who is fourteen and in his second year at Bowling Brook. Next is Denton, who's sixteen and has an I. Q. that Dr. Harrington says can't be measured. Everyone laughs but me. It's an inside joke, and I'm still an outsider. But I'm not dumb. I get the joke. Either he really is a genius or he's an idiot. Denton takes off his thick eyeglasses and rubs his eyes. I'm guessing he's a bright boy. Then there's Charlie who's thirteen but looks ten; and Ricky, a chubby boy with a perpetual smile on his face, who's sixteen and in his second year.

At the end of our table is an older couple—Mom and Pop Carson, the full-time houseparents. Pop is a high-spirited energetic man who greets several of the veteran boys at our table with a hug and a thunderous slap on the back. He's bald-headed and has a gravelly voice and a cherry red face. I like him from the start. Mom Carson doesn't get up when she's introduced. She's a large woman with a stoic expression and a face caked with makeup that doesn't hide the heavy wrinkles around her eyes and across her forehead. Her movements are slow and lethargic and there's something about her that I don't like. She seems cold and distant. A second lady at our table is named Mrs. Beamus. She's our house mother on Mom and Pop's days off. She's a pleasant middle-aged lady who reminds me of the lady who runs the Charles County library.

Dr. Harrington saves his family for last. Mrs. Harrington stands. She is tall and quite beautiful and could pass for the older sister of her fourteen-year-old daughter, Cindy, who's sitting beside her. Cindy, who has bright green eyes, golden blond hair, and a California girl's tan, doesn't get up when her father introduces her. Instead, she raises her eyebrows and frowns as though she's sitting in something wet and slimy. She's as cute as she can be, but I've been around enough girls to know that she's spoiled rotten.

The next night after the other boys arrive, we have a mixer. I meet the other new boys, Richard and Jimmy, who are both twelve and very frail. Then there's Kenny, who's sixteen, and Li, an Asian-American boy who stutters. Just when I think I've met the last boy, Pop Carson makes a big deal out of introducing Mark Franks.

Pop says, I want all of you new boys to meet our other senior and a true leader here at Bowling Brook, Mark Franks. Mark, would you stand?

This muscle-bound, pimple-faced boy stands up and Pop drapes his arm around him. This is Mark, fellows, and he's in his fourth and final year at Bowling Brook. Mark's the captain of the wrestling team at Francis Scott Key, he's a straight A student, a member of the debate and glee clubs, and one of the most popular boys in his class. He's a real help and asset to us all. Pop leaves no doubt that Mark Franks is the greatest thing Pop has ever discovered.

Dressed in a pair of neatly pressed blue jeans, Weejun loafers, and a light blue button-down shirt with a navy blue and red tie, Mark Franks smiles impishly as he waves his hand at us like a goddamn politician. From the moment I lay eyes on him, I know I don't like him. It's not because he dresses so cool or that he seems to have it made in the shade. It's the way he looks at all the boys like he's our goddamn principal or something.

But it doesn't take long to find out that Mark is everything Pop says he is. The first week in school, I watch Mark walk down the halls with a stack of books under his arms and three girls at his side. The girls are all fine-looking, too. During the school's first pep rally before the wrestling team's home opener, Mark is introduced as the returning team captain and by the sound of the cheers that go up for him, you would think that Casey was at the bat with two on and two out in the bottom of the ninth in a tie game.

Back at Bowling Brook, he's just as impressive. During evening chores he walks around with his clipboard, inspecting everyone's work. Hey, could you clean that pan a little better, son? he says. And, you missed a spot on the counter, youngster. Would you mind going over it again? During study period, he tutors the younger boys in math or English or whatever subject they need help in. He has everyone eating out of his hand.

I'm in my room listening to records when he walks in without knocking.

He says, So you like Motown, do you?

I'm listening to my new Temptations album and Eddie Kendricks is singing "The Way You Do the Things You Do." Before I remember the rule that says you're supposed to knock before you enter another boy's room, I remember how my own mother never even enters my room at home without knocking first, and I wonder if Mark Franks thinks he's better than my mother.

Hey, I don't mean to start off on the wrong foot, I say, but what about the knock, knock policy before entering someone else's room?

You're right, son, he says. And I apologize. It's just that I was on my way downstairs when I heard my favorite song playing, so I thought I'd stop in. He goes to the door and knocks on the wall. He's being a smart ass, I think. I ignore him.

Yeah, I say. I've got all the Tempts' albums.

He says, I've got some Motown stuff I'll bet you don't have. Why don't you stop around my room and I'll show you.

I'm kind of busy right now.

Well, I don't mean now, youngster. I mean some other time.

He starts to leave and I say, Hey, could you do me a favor?

What is it, son? I'm kind of busy.

Could you stop calling me those names?

What names?

You just called me youngster and then you called me son.

He looks at me like he just beat me in a hundred-yard dash. He says, Hey, come on. It's just a figure of speech. Don't you have a sense of humor?

If that's what it means to have one, I guess I don't.

Maybe you should practice getting one while you're here, he says. Every boy needs a sense of humor. It builds character.

He walks out of the room and I exhale a big sigh of relief. There's no goddamn way we're gonna be friends.

Attending public school is a gas. For the first time ever, I don't have to wear a tie and sport coat to school. I get to wear jeans and sports shirts and sneakers. And for the first time, I don't have to sit in the same classroom all day. Every period we change rooms and I have a blast walking down the halls checking out all the girls.

It doesn't take long before word gets around that I'm one of the new boys from the boys' home. It goes without saying that if you're from the boys' home, you're a troubled boy. The students are curious about me. I flirt every day with every girl I can. They're laid-back and unpretentious and they aren't used to slick, fast-talking boys. Unlike my roommate, I like these girls a lot.

The white boys are another story. They're farm boys who wear white socks, listen to country music, and talk about tractors and cows. I hate country music and wouldn't be caught dead wearing white socks with dress shoes, but what I despise the most about these boys is that they're as phony as a three-dollar bill. They play sports and laugh and joke and get along real chummy with the black boys. But in the lavatory when only the white boys are around, the Klan comes out of them. They say, Wanna hear a good nigger joke?

I don't feed into these racial jokes and slurs. Once a cousin of my grandfather's referred to old Ham as a good hard-working nigger and my grandfather exploded. He said, Henry, we don't use that word around here. My grandfather's spirit made an indelible impression on me that day.

I have my own comeback line whenever one of those white boys calls a black boy a nigger. I say, Now you know goddamn well you wouldn't call that boy a nigger to his face.

I don't have a single friend among these white fellows, and that's fine with me because I don't like being around phonies.

The day I try out for a spot in the percussion section of the high school band, I meet a black boy named Lonnie who's in the eleventh grade. During the audition, Lonnie's on the tenor drum next to me and I start asking him questions about the band director and the audition I'm about to have. He tells me to relax and play the cadences the man puts in front of me when my turn comes. Relax, hell! I can't read a lick of music. But I keep that to myself.

The band director hands out the same music to each of the drummers. When Lonnie's turn comes, I listen carefully to the cadences he plays and do my best to replicate them when my turn comes next. I know I'm just as good a drummer as Lonnie and the other boys I just heard play; the only thing they have on me is that they can read music.

When I pass the audition, Lonnie says, You've got balls, brother.

Why do you say that? I ask.

Because you can't read music, can you?

Not even a little bit, I say. We both laugh and slap each other's hand.

I say, Do you think the band teacher could tell I can't read music?

He says, It doesn't matter. You're in, my man.

From that day on, Lonnie and I hang out together every day at school. We trade albums. I loan him one of my Temptations albums and he gives me his Junior Walker and the All Stars album.

Lonnie has a sister named Diane who's in the tenth grade. She's a pretty brown-skinned girl who wears her hair in a bob. I tell Lonnie I've been checking her out and that I kind of like her. He says, Well, what you telling me for, man? Tell her yourself.

Instead of telling her, I show her. I start walking her to her classes and eating lunch with her. We talk about music and movies and the Vietnam War. We each know someone who's in Vietnam. She reads a poem to me from this black poet named Langston Hughes. The poem's about what happens when people's dreams get squashed. I really like the poem and after hearing her read it, the crush I have on her grows and grows.

I know about another interracial relationship in the school. Debbie Morant, a cute little blonde, is secretly going steady with Eddie Frazier. Debbie and I sit beside each other in every class and pass notes back and forth. She isn't like most of the other girls. She's real hip. She listens to soul music and hates boys who chew tobacco. She confides in me about her relationship with Eddie after she sees me hanging out with Lonnie and his sister. She says her father would kill her and skin Eddie alive if he ever finds out.

Diane and I hold hands when we walk down the halls and kids look over their shoulders when they pass. I give her my navy blue Peters jacket to wear. We both love it when we cause heads to turn.

The white boys belong to a club and wear shiny green jackets with the letters FFA (Future Farmers of America) inscribed on the back. On my way out the school door I hear the words *nigger lover* as I pass by a group of them. I glare at them in disgust; I can't tell which boy said it. These are big strong country boys, and I wouldn't stand a chance fighting any one of them let alone all of them. But I'm not afraid of them, and I stare them down.

Three weeks go by before I realize that Diane and I will never be together outside of school. And what the hell good's a girlfriend if you can never be alone with her? The boys from Bowling Brook have to have a chaperon at every social event we attend, and we're not allowed to go off in cars with other boys.

Diane and I almost get off alone at the Sadie Hawkins dance. We're leaving the gymnasium to occupy the backseat of Lonnie's car when the vice principal spots us and tells us we can't leave the building. For the rest of the evening, he keeps his hawk eyes on us. Every time a slow record is played, though, we antagonize him; we do the slow grind, a dance where you get as close as you can to your partner and the two of you grind your groins together.

Even though we can't be alone, Diane and I still hang out together between classes. I take pride in being with her and in being the topic of gossip among the mostly white trash.

But what I need more than anything is a girl to kiss and touch and be intimate with. Even though I'm getting along with everyone, I'm lonelier than I've ever been. When I call home, Moma says I have to hang in there and not let everyone down. I tell her how hard it is, being so far away from home and my friends. She says she knows, but it's not forever.

After two months the excitement I felt when I first arrived at Bowling Brook wears off, and I start feeling anxious and nervous again. When I go to Mass on Sunday, I pray for my family and the soldiers in Vietnam and then I ask God to help me find a girl who'll make me feel loved.

God answers my prayers a week later. I'm riding my bike up to the Middleburg general store and I meet a girl named Toni Hayden, a pretty-ass eighth grader with long brown hair and brown eyes. I buy her a soda and we talk until the sun starts to go down and I have to leave. I ask her if she has a boyfriend and she says no. I say, That's good and would she meet me tomorrow after school. She says she lives in the house beside the store and if I come back tomorrow maybe she'll see me.

I'm at the soda machine on the store porch the next day when she comes strolling by and walks into the store. She comes out two minutes later with a pack of Winstons and says they're for her mom. We sit on her front porch and talk until I have to go back to the home to eat supper.

When I return an hour later, she invites me into her house. She takes me to her bedroom where we listen to records and make out. I ask about her father and she tells me he drives a tractor-trailer all over the country and he's hardly ever home. One evening I see a man sitting at the dining room table when we pass through the house on the way to her bedroom. I ask her if that's her father and she gets mad.

No, he's not my fuckin' father, she says. He's one of my mother's boyfriends. Then she asks me if I have money for cigarettes. I offer her a Marlboro, but she doesn't want it. She and her mom smoke Winstons. There isn't much difference between the two, I tell her. She says there is too, but never mind. I take out my wallet and give her a dollar.

Here, Toni. I've got plenty of money. I don't care about the money. It's just that I've smoked my Aunt Harriet's Winstons before and they taste just like a Marlboro to me.

Marlboros are stronger. Wait here.

While she's gone, I hear her mother and the man walking up the stairs. They're almost whispering to each other and then a door closes.

When Toni returns, she's smoking a cigarette. She has a Royal Crown in her other hand and a *'Teen* magazine.

I spent the whole dollar, she says. Is that OK?

I don't mind, I say. Now why don't you come here?

We make out and I try to go all the way, but she won't. She tells me she has to get to know me better. She asks me how do I have my own money and do they give it to me at the home. I tell her that my mother and aunts and grandfather send me money every month. She says I'm lucky and kisses me until I'm so hot that I tell her she's gotta let me do it. She says, Jesus Christ, that's all every boy wants. We've only known each other a week. Is that all you think about?

No, it's not, Toni. I really love you, for Christ's sake.

I buy her practically everything that's sold in the Middleburg general store. Perfume. Records. Black leotards. Chocolate candy. Eye shadow. Nail polish. Every time, I buy her something, she gives in a little more. She needs ten dollars to pay off a black satin jacket she's had on layaway for two months, and I give her the money. I make it so she doesn't want to look at another boy. We're going steady now and I feel secure and loved. I want to be with her for as long as I'm at the home.

My roommate and I are in big trouble. It all started after school when I went into the walk-in closet to hang up my clothes. Michael was sitting on the floor breathing in and out of a paper bag. He saw me hovering over him and his eyes got real wide and then he burst out laughing like a goddamn hyena. He pulled the bag away from his face and pushed it toward me. Here, man. Breathe, he said.

I took the bag, put it up to my mouth and took a good whiff. It smelled like model airplane glue, which is just what it was. I breathed in and out until I started getting lightheaded and the skin on my face and scalp tingled. Then I heard a train roaring through my head and passed the bag back to Michael. That's all there was to it.

Now we're sitting in Dr. Harrington's office and the top of his desk is covered with crumbled-up paper bags. I can smell that stinking odor that made me so dizzy and gave me the worse headache I ever had, and I start feeling nauseous again.

Dr. Harrington has a scowl on his face. He says, Mrs. Beamus found these bags buried in the back of your closet. Both of you are on house restriction for the next two weeks. You'll both do all the upstairs chores and you're not to use the phone.

Then he tells us about how sniffing glue causes irreversible brain damage. The way he describes how your brain cells get destroyed scares the hell out of me. He says there's a part of our brain that no longer has any nerves, so it can't send signals to the rest of our brain because that part is dead.

I look at him as if to say, What in the hell makes you think I was doing it? You weren't there. But somehow I know he knows. He warns us that if we ever do it again, there will be serious consequences. Maybe they'll send us home or place us on house restriction for two months and give us all these stupid chores to do. All I can think about is how much of my brain has already died. I have no intentions of sniffing glue again.

We can't leave the grounds for two weeks. I call Toni on the telephone and tell her to meet me behind the row of box hedges outside my window after school. She does and we disappear into the tunnel I made inside the hedges. In the evening, I do my chores and then sneak into the pantry with the telephone.

I call Moma and Max answers. He says, Your mother's not here. And then he hangs up before I can tell him I got all As and Bs on my first report card and ask who's coming to get me for the Christmas holidays. What a goddamn idiot he is.

But nobody is coming to get me. Instead, Pop drives me to the Maryland School for the Deaf and Dumb in Frederick where I catch a ride back to La Plata with Mr. Carl Bowie, who's coming to pick up his ten-year-old son Gregory. Mr. Bowie owns the only grocery store in Port Tobacco and Moma's been buying fresh fish from him for as long as I can remember.

On top of being deaf and dumb, Gregory's like a stick of dynamite. Before starting down the highway Mr. Bowie says, Pat, he just might get a little restless on the ride. That's the biggest understatement I've ever heard. The little boy crawls on my lap and stares a hole right through me before he slams his head against my face. The helmet he's wearing smacks me right in the goddamn nose and it starts bleeding. Then he takes off out of my lap like a jackrabbit, banging his head against the window and flinging his arms wildly.

Mr. Bowie tells me to grab hold of him and put him back on my lap, but the boy won't let me. He claws and scratches my arms with all his might and makes the most God-awful whines and cries I ever heard coming from a human being.

Now there's blood trickling down my forearms. They look like I ran through Aunt Fannie's briar patch. Mr. Bowie doesn't know I'm bleeding until he turns around to get Gregory's attention. He pulls the car over to the side and takes out a box of tissues from the glove compartment.

He communicates with Gregory in sign language and Gregory seems to go into a trance. He's calm and cool and I'm thinking, it sure as hell wouldn't hurt to ask how I'm doing.

Halfway to Baltimore, Mr. Bowie stops at a Dairy Queen. Gregory just loves ice cream, he says. I always stop here when I bring him home. Would you like some ice cream, Pat? Yes, sir, please, I say. Chocolate would be good.

Before we get a hundred yards down the road Gregory has ice cream all over the backseat, on both of the side rear windows, and my pants and shirt. I ask Mr. Bowie how he gets along when it's just Gregory and him in the car. He smiles and says, It's not hard at all.

By the time we reach Waldorf, Gregory is back in my lap and all his little muscles are relaxed. He has his head against my shoulder and he's fast asleep. Watching his little chest rise and fall with each breath, I remember how I used to hold Huck while he slept. Suddenly, I feel sorry for this little kid who's so helpless and innocent.

When I arrive home, no one's there to greet me or say, Welcome home. My sister, Suzanne, says Moma's running errands and getting her hair done. She asks me what public school's like. I tell her it's nothing like Archbishop

Neale and everything they're teaching in the ninth grade I learned in the eighth grade. Then we don't say another word to each other for the rest of the time I'm home.

Max walks through the living room and I try to be nice to him. I say hello, but all he says is, Um-hmm. When he leaves the house, Huck comes running into my arms and hugs me. While I'm hugging him back, I remember all the times I thought of him and longed to see him again, and I'm so happy to be home. He wants to go outside and pass the football around. He's grown two inches since I've been away and he's gotten faster. He has great eye-hand coordination and doesn't drop a single ball.

Moma's home from shopping and she's not happy. She seems glad to see me, but I can tell she's been crying. I ask her what's wrong, but she won't tell me.

She says, I got your favorite ice cream. She hands me a half gallon of Breyers peach ice cream. I put it in the freezer and sit at the kitchen table to watch her put the groceries away. Why were you crying, Moma?

She says, Pat, you don't need to know everything. I'm fine. Now tell me all about school and what the boys' home is like.

It's all right, Moma. I just hate being so far away from home. I got all As and Bs, and I haven't been in a single fight. I have a girlfriend, too, named Toni who lives up the street.

That's real nice. Is she cute?

Yeah.

Did you thank Mr. Bowie for bringing you home?

Yes, ma'am.

Moma lights a cigarette and says, I've gotta get supper on. Your brother's bringing his girlfriend home to eat with us. Why don't you go look in the top of my closet? I got a new album for you. It's part of your Christmas present.

The album is the Beatles' *Sgt. Peppers Lonely Hearts Club Band*! I play my favorite song over and over on Moma's new stereo in the living room.

It's getting better all the time
I used to get mad at my school
The teachers who taught me weren't cool
You're holding me down, turning me round
Filling me up with the rules
I have to admit it's getting better
A little better, all the time

When Michael and Betty Lou walk through the door, I'm singing from the top of my lungs, *It's getting better all the time.* Betty Lou grins at me and she has the most beautiful smile. Michael says, Welcome home, Pat. He shakes my hand, then gives me a big hug. He says, Entertain Betty Lou while I go change clothes.

Michael and Betty Lou have been going steady ever since she transferred to Archbishop Neale from Our Lady Star of the Sea in her freshman year. She's the prettiest and classiest girl in Michael's eleventh-grade class. I ask her how things are going at school and she tells me about some of my old classmates. She was appointed captain of the cheerleading squad for the varsity basketball team this year, and Michael's one of the stars on the team.

They're the perfect couple. Instead of being happy for them, I get depressed seeing how normal and together my brother's life is compared with mine. He's the nicest guy in the world and it makes me sick.

After supper we go to the Christmas dance at Sacred Heart Church. Though it's good to see my old classmates and friends, I feel out of place. I can't help but think about all the things I've missed out on while I've been away and how I'm not a part of their lives anymore. Even though everyone's nice to me, I still feel like a goddamn criminal or some kind of alien.

On Christmas Eve, Michael, Suzie, and I visit Maple Knoll and I do a great job of hiding my discontent. I tell everyone how wonderful Bowling Brook Home for Boys is and how well I'm getting along with everyone. They're all proud of me, they say, and glad that I'm happy.

We get lots of expensive gifts. I get a new three-speed bike with a banana seat and high-rise handle bars, a bottle of Canoe, Weejun penny loafers, a tweed winter coat, dress shirts and pants, ties, sweaters, and underwear, and a fresh-from-the-mint twenty-dollar bill from my grandfather and each aunt and uncle. I give an Academy Award performance in thanking everyone and pretending I'm as happy and normal as Michael, hoping that my relatives will see the change in me. All they do is tell me to have fun and keep up the good work. Then my aunts hug and kiss me until I want to cry like a goddamn baby. It's the saddest Christmas I've ever had.

Chapter 12

Two days after Christmas vacation, my roommate runs away. I'm pissed off because he didn't tell me ahead of time so I could go with him. Dr. Harrington searches Michael's dresser and belongings looking for clues, He says, Did you know he was leaving? Don't lie. When I say no, he says he doesn't believe me.

I say, My grandfather told me it was wrong to squeal on my brother. I wouldn't have squealed on Michael even if I did know.

Do you know where he may have gone?

If I was to run away, I'd go home, sir. Maybe you should call his mother.

Three days go by and no one hears from him. Pop comes into my room and says I have to move in with Jimmy and Richard.

I say, Like hell, I will, Pop! This is my room.

Pop says I have ten minutes to get my belongings together and move.

I go to Dr. Harrington, but he refuses to overrule Pop's decision.

I say, But they're three years younger than me and we don't have anything in common. It's not fair.

Dr. Harrington says life isn't fair, and I have to do what I'm told.

Later I tell Eleanor how much I hate being at Bowling Brook and how all I want to do is go home. She takes my hand in hers and says, Life's hard sometimes, Pat, and sometimes we have to do things we don't want to do.

You just need to do what I do and take it one day at a time. That's all you can do, son.

Eleanor's advice doesn't make me feel any better. Later, after the whole house is asleep, I sneak down the back steps and into the pantry to be alone in the pitch-black darkness. Among the spices and flour and dust, I sit on the floor crying and wrestling with an awful loneliness. Conversations and memories of home pass through my mind like a bad dream. *Moma, Moma! Where are you? Not now! Not now! Can't you see I'm busy? Here's a new kite. Go and fly it! Be good. Be good. Step on a crack, break your mother's back!* Now *I'm alone and I wanna go home.*

The longer I sit with myself, the more urgently I want to run away.

The next day we're playing touch football on the front lawn. Right in the middle of the game, Toni comes walking up the street shaking her tail and waving at me. I get excited when I see her and want to show off because she's my girlfriend. I sneak up behind Jimmy and yank his sweat pants down to his ankles and his underwear comes with them, exposing his privates to everyone. Toni points and laughs and so does everyone else. Jimmy starts crying and says he's going to tell. I say, I'm sorry and don't be a baby, and then I walk Toni home.

But you can't always say you're sorry and expect things to be hunky-dory. I'm playing records in my bedroom that night when Pop walks in and says to come with him.

I follow him down the hallway and I hear footsteps behind me. When I look over my shoulder to see who it is, Mark Franks shoves me and says, Turn around and keep walking, punk. Pop is walking faster now and I'm confused about what's going on. He starts up the third-floor stairs to the attic, a place that's off limits to us boys.

At the top of the stairs, he takes out a long key from his shirt pocket, unlocks the door, and disappears into the darkness. A few seconds later, a dim light comes on and swings back and forth over Pop's head like a gallows. Mark pushes me into the room and Pop tells me to sit down in the chair he sets in the middle of the floor. Then he closes the attic door and leans against it.

Mark stands there staring at me like he's some kind of goddamn monster. Neither of them says a word. I turn to Pop and say, Pop, what's going on?

Mark says, Shut up. I'll tell you what's going on. You just pretend like Pop's not here. All the time he's pounding his fist into the palm of his hand. He says, You know what I hate worse than a lying, thieving punk?

What are you talking about? I didn't steal nothing.

Shut up and listen! I hate a punk-ass bully.

Then he smashes me in the face before I can blink twice. The first blow comes so fast and hard that it almost knocks me out. When he hits me again, I see stars and flashing lights.

I try to leap out of the chair, but Pop holds on to my shoulder. I look up into Pop's eyes and they're bright and round and there's a weird smile on his face.

Move again and you'll get it worse, Mark says. He hits me several more times. Most of the punches land right on my eyes.

He hits me again and again and then says, How'd you like me to pull down your pants in front of everybody, punk? And then he hits me again.

Blood is pouring from my nose and lip. I cry out to Pop, How can you let him do this, Pop! But Pop doesn't answer. He just stares at me with this strange shit-eating grin on his face.

I'm so full of rage now that I can't feel the pain of Mark's blows. He continues to hit and slap me, and all I can do is sit there like a beaten dog. When I fall out of the chair, Pop says, That's enough, Mark.

Mark says, Let that be a lesson, punk! If you pick on Jimmy again or any of these boys, you know what you've got coming.

I spit blood and words out of my mouth. I never picked on anybody. We were playing football. All I did was pull Jimmy's pants down. Everyone laughed.

Well, it's not so funny now, is it, punk? Then Mark Franks says to Pop, Let me by. He opens the door and runs down the steps.

Pop tries to help me off the floor, but I push his hand away and get up on my own. I slide my arm along the wall as we descend the stairs, and then I disappear into the bathroom. I sit on the toilet and kill Mark Franks over and over. I imagine his cold, dead eyes dangling from their bloody sockets; a big hole in his chest revealing the last slow beat of his heart; and his dick ripped out of his groin.

A half hour later I look in the mirror and both of my eyes are black and blue and swollen. I still hear bells and when I close my eyes I see a thousand stars. I'm shocked like hell because how could Pop let this happen? He's supposed to be my surrogate father. It's his job to look after us. Dr. Harrington will fire him when he finds out. But it doesn't matter. There's no way I'm going to stay in this home.

The next morning when I don't come down for breakfast, Dr. Harrington walks into my room. He says, You'd better get up and get dressed for school, Pat.

I look at him like he's lost his mind. I say, I'm not going to school looking like this. Look at my goddamn eye.

It doesn't look that bad. It looks like you got into a fight and lost. Isn't that what happened?

Is that what they said? Is that what they said? Goddamn, it wasn't no fight, Dr. Harrington! Pop let him do this shit to me. I swear on the Blessed Mother. I can't even see out of my left eye, Dr. Harrington!

Well, you're going to school, and that's all there is to it.

I hate Dr. Harrington for not believing me. I hate Pop for letting me get beat like a dog and enjoying it. And I hate the bastard Mark Franks most of all.

Two, three, four days go by and I withdraw from everyone. I wear sunglasses everywhere I go to hide my rage and swollen eyes. When I come home, I go straight to my room and the only times I leave it are at meals. Once Sandy knocks on the door and asks to borrow my Sgt. Peppers album. Sandy's a nice fellow. I give it to him and he says, Thanks and how's everything going? I say, Good. See you later.

At Mass on Sunday, I pray to Christ to forgive me for my sins.

Two weeks after the vicious beating, I smuggle a Louisville slugger from the log cabin up to my room. I put the bat under the covers and wait until I'm sure everyone's asleep. When they are, I get out of bed and put on my Chuck Taylors.

I know every crack in every floor board and make my way down the hall without the slightest stir. When I enter Mark Franks' room, he's sleeping on his side facing me. A shaft of moonlight illuminates his face and for some time I stand over him watching him breathe. As I'm about to bash his head open, it comes to me that the boy in the bed is not the same Mark Franks I know at all. There aren't any tendrils bulging from this boy's neck, no mocking scowl or angry lines of meanness on his face, no devilish grin.

For a couple of more minutes I stand there listening to the calm and steady rise and fall of his breathing. I raise the bat over my head, holding it with both hands, and practice bringing it down slowly to the top of his forehead. I do it two more times and suddenly the rage and hatred that had possessed me to want to kill him dissolves. Knowing that I have the power to split his head open like a watermelon, to hurt him far more than he hurt me, is revenge enough.

Three days later, Mark Franks is gone. Pop tells us at supper that Mark's father died and Mark has gone home to be with his family. After he's gone, I'm even more difficult to get along with. I continue to give everyone the silent treatment, and I do a half-ass job of doing my chores when I do them at all. Pop says for me to clean the back stairs and I tell him to go to hell. Every evening after supper I ride my bike to Toni's house and stay until Mom Carson calls for the third time to tell me I'd better get back to the home pronto.

In early February, I'm sitting in advanced English class when I'm summoned to the guidance counselor's office. When I walk into the room, Mr. Buffington, my county probation officer, is sitting in the chair. Mr. Buffington is not smiling when he greets me, and the first thing I think is something bad happened at home. No, it's not that, he says. He's come to take me from Bowling Brook.

He says, Dr. Harrington informed us that you're not getting along with the other boys, Pat, and he says you're making everyone anxious.

I say, Thank the Blessed Mother, Mr. Buffington. If you only knew how much I hate that place and what a bunch of hypocrites they are. They almost killed me, they really did. I'm glad to be going home and I promise you I'll turn over a new leaf, sir.

You're not going home, Pat. The environment there is no place for you right now. I'm taking you to the Maryland Children's Center in Baltimore. I'll tell you all about the place on the drive up.

The Maryland Children's Center! You don't have to tell me about that place, for Christ's sake, Mr. Buffington, I already know! My roommate at Bowling Brook was there and he said it's a goddamn crazy house. It's an institution filled with violent boys. I'm not violent and I'm not crazy, Mr. Buffington.

I know you're not crazy, Pat. It's not that bad a place. You'll only be there for thirty days.

Well, it's not fair, Mr. Buffington. I haven't done anything to deserve being put in an institution. And whose idea is it anyway?

It was Judge Diggs's decision, Pat.

Well, he can go to hell for all I care.

On the way back to Bowling Brook to get my things, I give Mr. Buffington the silent treatment.

After I pack my belongings, I go down to the kitchen to say good-bye to Eleanor. She's sitting at the island counter peeling potatoes and crying. When she sees me, she stands and gives me a big hug. I thank her for all the special meals she cooked for me and for the times she sat and listened to my problems. When it's time to leave she hugs me again and says, Be a good boy, son. Then she turns away.

On the drive to Baltimore Mr. Buffington says I'm being committed to the children's center for a psychological evaluation. I'll be there for thirty days and after that he doesn't know what will happen. He tells me to be good and cooperate with the doctors and all the staff.

I ask if my grandfather knows they're putting me in an institution for a goddamn psychological evaluation. When he says yes, my heart sinks and I want to vomit.

Chapter 13

Mr. Buffington doesn't believe me when I tell him my old roommate, Michael, was once at the Maryland Children's Center and said they restrain boys in leather handcuffs. He says my roommate was exaggerating. I say, Was he exaggerating too when he personally witnessed a boy getting gang-raped? Mr. Buffington says he never heard of such a thing happening.

I say, Do you think they'd televise it all over the goddamn state?

Mr. Buffington tells me to calm down and that everything's going to be just fine.

From the outside, the Maryland Children's Center looks like any other new brick building. Inside, it's a fortress. We walk through two sets of electronic doors before we reach the processing area. Mr. Buffington tells me he'll be calling every week to see how I'm doing. Just do everything they ask you to do, Pat, and I'll be back to see you in thirty days. Then the electronic door slides open and Mr. Buffington disappears down the hall.

I'm too goddamn mad to say good-bye to him.

This is the first time in my life that I know I'm afraid. I take a seat on the bench beside two boys who are both smaller than I am. Though I'm terrified at the realization that I'm now in a state institution, I'm determined not to show it.

After a few minutes, a black man with a big barrel chest tells us to come with him. We enter a shower room and the man tells us to take off our clothes and stand under one of the showerheads. I make it a point not to look at the other boys and to keep my eyes straight ahead just like I saw a prisoner do in a movie. The man sprays me with a foul-smelling chemical. It kills lice, he says.

But I don't have lice, I complain.

It doesn't matter. Being deloused is required.

After we shower, the man gives us each a pair of navy blue pants, a white shirt, and a bedroll and tells me to sit on the bench out in the hall.

A short while later, a tall yellow-skinned lady comes out of an office down the hall and says my name. I go into her office and she asks me a parade of questions about school, my family, and my religion. Then she tells me the reason I'm here. She says, Sometimes boys and girls have a lot of anger and pain inside them.It's our job to try and find out why so we can help them, she says. We have some children here who've had some tragic experiences and are left with emotional problems. Some have broken the law while others, like you, just seem to have difficulty getting along with other children.

I start to ask her how she knows so much about me until I see a blue file in her hand that I recognize from Dr. Harrington's office.

The lady says, The staff cares very much about every child here. We want to help you. While you're staying here at the center, all we ask is that you cooperate with us and try to get along with the other children. You'll be staying on Ward B with boys who range from ages thirteen to fifteen. Do you have any questions?

When can I call my mother?

Phone calls are not allowed, but your family can visit on weekends. You'll have to write and let them know.

I want to ask her if there are many fights on Ward B and if the answer's yes, I want her to know I'm not going to let anybody push me around or hurt me. But I don't. She's a nice lady and I don't want to make a bad impression.

She says, By the way, my name's Dr. Melton. Why don't you let me show you around the place?

The hallways and rooms we pass through are freshly painted in shiny white or light blue and trimmed with bright red, yellow, blue, and green geometric patterns—triangles, squares, rectangles and circles. The place smells like Pine-Sol.

After she shows me the gymnasium and dining room, we walk down a long corridor until we reach a heavy metal door that says Ward B on it. Dr. Melton unlocks the door and leads me to an office inside. There are two large windows in the office and as I look through one of them, I can see several boys standing around a pool table and others sitting at a table playing cards. Fear overcomes me once again and my stomach turns over and over.

I suddenly remember my English teacher back at Francis Scott Key and a passage she shared with the class from Lewis Carroll's *Alice in Wonderland:* Down here we got our act clean yesterday, and we plan to start getting our act clean tomorrow, but we never clean up our act today.

As I stare through the glass, my heart is beating fast and the butterflies are fluttering in my stomach because I'm afraid, but I know I have to face it now. I tell myself that everything's going to be all right. I'm not going to let anybody hurt me.

The ward supervisor, a friendly old man with a long and wrinkled neck and a crooked smile, reads the rules to me, then tells me to go out in the dayroom and relax until it's time for supper. I stand and swallow hard. I tell myself I have my act together. I will wear the countenance of a wild and angry boy for as long as I have to.

I sit on a vacant bench in the dayroom and look around the room like I haven't a care in the world. I let my breath out when I see that these boys look just like any other boys. They're not the freaks I'd imagined they would be. They aren't so tough-looking after all.

Two of the biggest boys in the room are trash-talking to the boys who are shooting pool. I watch them indifferently as I reach my hand into the cardboard box containing my personal belongings and pull out a pack of cigarettes. I fire up a Kool and blow two perfectly round smoke rings into the air.

It's the trash-talkers' turn and the first shooter scratches. The small boy makes three balls in a row and then misses. The second trash-talker takes his turn and runs the table. The smaller boys turn over a handful of cigarettes. The trash-talkers say, Any other suckers wanna try?

Later we're marching into the dining room for supper and I'm shocked to see a whole ward of little boys sitting at a table. Some of them are as little as my brother Huck who is only seven, and just as angelic looking. I wonder what in the name of Christ they could have done to wind up in this place. At another section of tables is a group of girls. As we march by them I find the prettiest one and wink at her. With the exception of one or two, they are a rough and ugly-looking lot.

After supper, a boy with acne all over his face asks me to be his partner in a game of Spades. I don't want to be his partner because he's very obnoxious. He has a foul mouth and his shirt is covered with food and juice stains. He looks like the kind of boy who picks his nose and eats what he digs out. But I agree to play because I want to meet some of the other boys at the table.

Our first opponents are two black boys from Baltimore. We get into a three-way conversation two minutes into the game and I learn that they are two smooth, fast-talking fellows. I like them from the start. They're well-groomed boys and are as gregarious as any of the black boys I grew up with. I would never have guessed that they are two hardened criminals. They are only thirteen and have already committed a string of burglaries and robberies, they tell me. The judge sent them to the Children's Center to find out what's wrong with them.

There ain't nothing wrong with us, one of them says, laughing and slapping the other's palm.

Yeah, says the other. We're just two good boys from Greenmont Avenue.

We sit around talking and playing cards until the ward supervisor announces that it's bedtime. He says, All new boys remain in the dayroom. As they get up to leave, the Greenmont Avenue boys slap my hand and tell me we'll play tomorrow. After they're gone, I feel good about meeting them and confident I'm going to be all right.

When the supervisor returns, he escorts us new boys past the dormitories and down a long corridor with rooms every ten feet or so on either side. We reach the middle of the corridor and the man stops, unlocks the door to one of the rooms and tells me to step inside. He says, This will be your room for the first week. Then we'll move you into one of the dorms if there're no problems. See you tomorrow, son.

He closes the door and I can hear the metallic click of the lock find its way home. I do a three-hundred-sixty-degree turn around the room and the revelation hits me like a bullet. This isn't any ordinary room. It's a goddamn prison cell. The same kind I saw in a prison movie. It has a stainless steel toilet and sink, a bed bolted to the wall, and a desk and chair.

For a long while I sit there frozen on the edge of the bed, thinking very heavy thoughts. While trying to make sense of everything, I begin to fantasize:

Just this morning I was sitting in a classroom solving quadratic equations and passing notes to the girl sitting next to me. And tonight I'm a goddamn prisoner in the big house. What was my crime? I robbed a bank in broad daylight and shot it out with the cops when they tried to stop me. Rocky, my partner, had gone down in the cross fire. He took a single bullet to the side of his head and died in my arms right there on the bloody sidewalk. Now I'm gonna die. But, no, the judge had spared my life. Don't you remember, Patrick? Moma was crying hysterically. Don't kill my son, she said. Don't kill my boy. He's only fifteen, your Honor. He didn't know what he was doing. He's a good boy, your

Honor… Moma! Moma! Moma! Moma to the rescue.
Where are you now, Moma!

Later I get up and look out the window, pressing my
nose against the thick black screen. From a distance I can see
and hear the night life in the city. Sirens screaming down the
neon-lighted streets. Car horns honking. Red brake lights
twinkling. A train rattling along the tracks.

The sounds and sight make me homesick and all I
can do is lie on the bed and shut my eyes. I think about all
the times Moma took me shopping at night. I remember the
Christmas lights draped above Charles Street and around the
department store windows. Once, while sitting in the car
waiting for Moma, I saw a father and son exiting the
Western Auto Store with a new bike and I imagined it was
my father and me. Remembering these sights makes me
sadder than I've ever been and more homesick than I already
am.

I've never been locked inside a room before, let alone
a prison cell. I tell myself to be strong. Be strong. Moma
always told me to be strong. You're going to be all right.
Then the lights go out and all the feelings I've been holding
back all day come pouring out like a rainstorm. For the first
time in my life I realize I'm truly alone. And I'm afraid.

What's wrong, with me, God? Something's wrong, I
know that much. I want to go home. I want to see
Moma. I want to see Michael and Huck and Suzie. I
want to be normal. I want things to be the way they
used to be. And how was that? Oh, Christ, I don't
know. I'll think about it tomorrow.

Before I fall asleep, I spit in my hand and masturbate
while thinking of Toni and Colleen and other pretty girls I've
known.

The next morning, a boy snaps out after breakfast and
throws a chair at the Plexiglas window of the dormitory. The
chair bounces off. The boy picks it up and throws it again.

After the third time, orderlies come and restrain him with leather handcuffs. Then they lock him in a cell down the hall.

On the third day, two boys get into an argument over a pool game. We all duck for cover when they start hurling balls at each other. One of the Greenmont Avenue boys yells, If either of you ma'fuckers hits me with one of them balls, I'm gonna split your honky-ass head open.

After the orderlies restrain the two boys, the Greenmont Avenue boys go back to their loan-sharking business. Several boys come up to them wanting cigarettes.

Here's how it's going down, the Avenue boys say. We'll give you a half a pack now for a whole pack back on Sunday. Or you can get a pack now for two back on Sunday. And anybody's got Twinkies or candy bars, we'll trade you smokes for something to eat.

The Greenmont Avenue boys talk fast and drive a hard bargain. They give a boy five cigarettes for three Snickers bars and the boy complains. Hey, that's fuckin' highway robbery, he says.

Well, there ain't no other store on this block, so take it or leave it, chump. Now which is it? You smoking or you joking?

The boy snatches up the cigarettes and walks away.

On Sunday my aunts and uncles and grandfather visit. Dressed in their Sunday clothes and smiles, they stand and hug me one by one when I walk through the visiting room door. On the table are four large grocery bags filled with snacks. We sit and talk for two hours. Michael and Suzie and Huck are fine. I don't ask about my mother because to my aunts and uncles, my mother's an outcast. After the visit I'm exhausted but elated. The hugs and kisses and affirmations of love lift my spirits.

When I get back on the ward, the Greenmont Avenue boys are sitting in the dayroom with several packs of cigarettes in front of them. Every Sunday they buy snacks from other boys as they come off their visits. Their brown eyes are the size of silver dollars when they see the four large grocery hags I'm carrying. Hey, man. What you selling us?

I ain't selling nothing, I say. But you're welcome to something to eat.

Cool, bro. We dig that.

There's a boy named Robert who sits alone in the dayroom and never utters a word. I sit beside him and he fidgets in the chair and turns the other way. I hate to see a little kid look so petrified. Besides, he has the same lanky frame and straight brown hair and lazy brown eyes as my brother Huck. He stares out the window and after a few minutes of sitting there watching him out of the corner of my eye, I walk over to the acne-faced boy and ask him if this boy's a deaf-mute or something. He says, No, he's just crazy. Then he tells me his name is Robert and he hasn't spoken to anyone since the night he burned down his family's house while he was playing with matches. His little sister died in the fire.

Knowing how it feels to be sad and lonely, I want to make friends with Robert. I wait until the next day and sit beside him again on the floor, not saying a word, but merely nodding my head to acknowledge his presence. I take a few pieces of Tootsie Roll candy for myself from the bag I'm carrying and then drop the bag on the floor between us. Robert alternates staring at the table tennis game in front of us, and then out the window.

Without looking at him, I say, This place ain't shit. Nothing to do all day. Doctors talking to you all the time. My mother and father don't care shit about me. They're both drunks. I got a little brother at home. His name is Johnny Bair, but we call him Huck. I'd kill anybody who messed with him. He's my partner and we've gone through a lot of shit together. Once we got into trouble for setting the woods on fire, man. We were playing army behind our house. Huck told our mother it was my idea so he wouldn't get in trouble, but he did anyway.

I stop talking and look around the room. I notice that Robert has turned away from the window and the expression on his face has changed. No longer is he wearing a veil of sadness. He seems to be listening to me.

I say, You know what? We're all alike in here. We're all in trouble. If you need anything, you let me know and I'll help you. Then I get up and walk away, leaving the bag of Tootsie Rolls on the floor beside him.

Later that evening we're marching to the dining hall when Robert falls in beside me. I don't say a word to him, but I'm so glad he's acknowledged me that I smile and raise my head high.

We sit down at the table and I say, What's up, Robert? The obnoxious acne-faced boy who's sitting at the same table says, What's the matter, runt? Don't you talk, or the cat got your tongue?

I look at the boy and say, Why don't you shut your mouth, man?

The boy shuts up.

A few nights later we're watching a Clint Eastwood cowboy movie when Robert comes and sits beside the Greenmont Avenue boys and me. I offer him some of my potato chips and he takes a handful. I ask him if he likes cowboy movies and then turn away, not expecting him to answer. Then he speaks the first words anyone's heard from him.

I saw this movie with my dad, he says.

I say, Yeah? It looks like it's going to be a good movie.

It is. He gets shot, Robert says.

The next day I'm called into Dr. Melton's office to describe what I see in the inkblots on the white cardboard squares. Afterward, I tell her that the little boy who burned his house down spoke to me and was eating all his meals with me. She thinks that's wonderful and praises me for my efforts. Then she tells me that Robert has been communicating with her for the past week and isn't it wonderful that he's joining the world again.

Yes, ma'am, I say.

But privately, I'm disappointed. I wanted to be the first person Robert spoke to.

Dr. Melton tells me to keep up the good work and to come out and see the nurses from time to time. She says I am adjusting well and can leave Ward B every morning after breakfast.

For the rest of my stay at the Children's Center, I roam the halls and hang out in the administrative center every day after breakfast, talking to the nurses and doctors and the girls who sit on the bench waiting for their turn with the staff. The nurses buy me sodas and sit and talk with me about music and school and being a nice boy.

After thirty days, Mr. Buffington arrives and tells me how happy he is to hear that I've been getting along so well.

And then he hits me with a bombshell. I can't go home. The environment is not stable, he tells me. Instead, he's found a foster family back in the community of Bowling Brook who've agreed to take me in so I can finish the ninth grade.

I'm not going to no fucking foster home, Mr. Buffington! I yell. That's bullshit! Fucking foster homes are for boys who don't have families, and I have a goddamn family.

Pat, calm down. These people are a very loving family. They own a nice dairy farm right up the road from Bowling Brook. You'll have your own room and you'll be treated just like one of their own children. It's only temporary, until you finish the school year.

That's four goddamn months, Mr. Buffington! And what then? What if you come back again and tell me things haven't changed at home yet? What are you gonna do with me then?

I start to cry and I'm angrier than hell at him. He had no intentions of letting me go home. I'm mad at my mother, too, because she promised me I could come home after the doctors did their evaluation. I ask Mr. Buffington if my grandfather knows about the foster home and he says yes.

How could he let them do this to me? I say. Everyone I love has betrayed me.

After a long pause, Mr. Buffington says, Pat, there's nothing else we can do right now. Things will work out. You just have to have faith.

I don't wanna go to a goddamn foster home, Mr. Buffington.

Pat, it's either the foster home or you can stay here.

Why, Mr. Buffington? Why do I have to stay here? I could go live with my grandfather, for Christ's sake. I don't see why.

Look, son. You have about a minute to make up your mind, and then I've got to get going with or without you.

Then it comes to me that I can run away from the foster home if I want to. That's what I'll do. I'll run away.

I say, What the hell. I want to get the hell out of this place. Let me go get my goddamn property.

Chapter 14

On the way to the foster home we pass Bowling Brook Home for Boys, and I start thinking about Mark Franks and Pop and what they did to me. Butterflies rise in my stomach and I feel nauseous and clammy all over.

I still can't get over how Pop, who was responsible for my safety and well-being, stood there and watched Mark Franks beat the living crap out of me. I picture Pop standing against the attic door the way he did with his arms folded and his face twisted in a wry grin, and all I feel is rage and hatred and the plaintive wish that the two of them would somehow die violent deaths.

I put them out of my mind when we turn onto a narrow dirt road that slices through thick, dark woods. We drive for almost a mile before we pass a pale green cottage and the road opens up to a large farm.

Surrounding the farmhouse are spacious green pastures bordered by tightly strung barbed wire fences. One pasture is covered with bright yellow dandelions and fat black-and-white cows that are chomping away at the grass. In another pasture three horses and a colt stand like statues far off on a high slope. Near the farmhouse are a leaning toolshed, a chicken house, a horse stable and corral, a flower garden, and a colossal white barn.

Before we get out of the car, I tell Mr. Buffington, These people have another thing coming if they think I'm gonna shovel shit or milk any goddamn cows.

He says, You're going to have to do some chores, Pat, I can assure you of that.

Yeah? Well, if they try to make me work like a goddamn slave, I'll run away, Mr. Buffington.

And what's that going to get you, Pat? They'll only find you and then you're headed right to Boys' Village.

We get out of the car and I stay by the passenger door while Mr. Buffington greets the man and woman who are headed toward us. They circle around the car toward me and Mr. Buffington says, Pat, this is Mr. and Mrs. Shoop.

I shake their hand and smile because I don't want to start off on the wrong foot. Mr. Shoop is a big burly man who looks like he could pick up a full-grown ox all by himself. He has curly black hair and rosy red cheeks, and a thick German accent. Mrs. Shoop is a pretty lady with large bones. She's not wearing makeup and she's naturally beautiful. When she introduces me to her two children, her sweet voice reminds me of my old kindergarten teacher.

She says, This is Bruce, who's five, and this is Elena, who's eight. The children smile and shake my hand. They offer to help carry my belongings up to the porch while Mr. Buffington talks with the Shoops in private.

After Mr. Buffington says good-bye, Mrs. Shoop and the children show me to my room on the second floor of the farmhouse. It's a small room with a single bed, dresser, and chair. A corner room, it has two windows, one that overlooks the pastures and the other the front yard and dairy barn. Before they leave the room, Mrs. Shoop tells me she's had lots of children come and stay with them over the years, but never a fifteen-year-old boy. The children are excited to have me staying with them, she says, and so is she.

When she leaves the room, I put my clothes away, unpack my record player, and listen to my Sgt. Peppers album while I dig out my schoolbooks from another box. I lie across the bed and open my algebra book, but I can't concentrate because I'm so overwhelmed by the changes in my surroundings. Only a few hours ago I woke up in a dormitory filled with angry, screaming boys, then dressed and marched into a dining hall filled with more screaming boys. And now I'm free, in a room of my own in a nice warm house filled with friendly people. These thoughts give me hope. I say a prayer and ask God to help me get along with these people so I can go home.

In the middle of my second Hail Mary, the little girl Elena knocks on the door and tells me it's time for dinner.

Everyone is seated when I arrive at the table. Mr. Shoop begins a prayer and thanks God for their new guest and hopes my stay will be a pleasant one. Then we eat a quiet, delicious meal of thick T-bone steaks, mashed potatoes, corn, and homemade biscuits.

After supper, the children take me on a tour along a stone path that ends in front of the big white dairy barn. A tangerine-colored sun is fading slowly over the trees and the air is cool and scented with honeysuckle. The sweet scent reminds me of my grandfather's farm and my relatives there, and I instantly long for home.

A parade of black-and-white cows, called Holsteins, Elena tells me, is making its way through the wide entrance to the barn. Elena says it's time for them to earn their keep. As we walk inside the barn and down the walkway, a banjo and fiddle tune vibrates through the speaker of an old cathedral-shaped radio that stands in a puddle of hay in one of the corners of the barn. The tune mingles with the sweet cries of a hungry calf. A row of glass pipes that run along both sides of the barn suddenly clang and rattle as a stream of blue water gurgles through them at a fast speed. Elena explains that the pipes are being sanitized before the milk runs through them.

I say, You mean you don't milk the cows by hand?

Elena and Bruce laugh. No, silly, Elena says. We use automatic milkers. Just watch Popa.

We sit on a bale of hay and wait for their father to come in. A scrawny red calf trots over to Bruce and Elena and licks Elena's outstretched hand before it wedges its body between Elena and me and nibbles at the bale of hay.

He's a bull calf, Elena says. You can touch him if you'd like.

I rub my hand over its shiny red coat. His ribs are as distinct as the bars on a grill. The calf licks my hand and then trots toward Mr. Shoop, who's walking through the side door with an assortment of rubber hoses over his shoulders.

The children and I follow Mr. Shoop to the first stall where he takes one of the sets of hoses and connects one end to a valve on the glass pipe that runs overhead. Immediately, the four cups on the other end begin to jerk gently and make a sound much like sucking on a straw at the bottom of a milk shake. Mr. Shoop attaches the cups to the cow's teats and within seconds, creamy white milk spurts into the glass pipe. I'm fascinated by it all. I tell Mr. Shoop that my grandfather always milked his cows by hand.

He says, Your grandfather has a dairy farm?

No, sir. He has a tobacco farm, but he's retired now. He used to have a few cows he milked out in the pasture every day.

Well, son, I have thirty cows to milk twice a day and I could never do it if I had to milk them all by hand.

I wouldn't mind helping you if you need me, sir.

I can always use a helping hand. I'll show you tomorrow what I'd like you to do each day, OK?

Yes, sir.

Do you like horses, son?

Oh, yes sir. I love them.

How about I make that part of your daily chores to feed and water the horses?

That's fine with me.

I watch as Mr. Shoop milks all thirty of his cows, four at a time. When he finishes, I follow him and the children into the milk room where the glass pipes come through the wall and connect to a huge stainless steel tank that sits in the middle of the room. Mr. Shoop opens the tank lid and dips a ladle into the creamy pool of milk. He pours some into a cup and invites me to taste it.

When I swallow a mouthful, I almost gag. Yuck! The children laugh and Mr. Shoop is standing there grinning and waiting for me to say something.

It doesn't taste like milk at all. What is that stuff? It tastes like onions.

Son, that's the way milk tastes before it's been homogenized. The onions grow wild in the meadow and the cows eat them. Would you like to try some more?

Uh, no, sir. I'll pass, thank you.

The children laugh again before they drink from their own cups and then lick their lips.

Later that evening, I'm in my room studying when Mrs. Shoop knocks on the door and tells me I have a visitor.

My heart pounds like a drum and I'm flabbergasted; who could possibly know I'm here? What if it's someone from the boys' home? My voice is filled with anxiety when I ask, Who is it, ma'am?

You'll have to come down to the parlor and see. Hurry along and don't keep her waiting!

Her? It's a girl visitor!

I walk into the parlor and the homeliest girl in the entire ninth-grade class at Francis Scott Key High School is sitting there with a pile of textbooks in her lap. She's smiling and looking at me the way I've seen her look at me a hundred times before—like she's Guinevere and I'm Lancelot.

Hello, Pat.

Margaret, it's nice to see you. I'm shocked. How did you know I was here?

I live with my grandmother in the cottage at the end of the lane. Mrs. Shoop told me last week when I came to babysit that they were getting a boy from Bowling Brook and I knew right away it was you even before I asked her your name. Where have you been for the last month?

They put me in a goddamn mental institution, Margaret. The people at the boys' home said I was disturbed, but they just wanted to get rid of me. The doctors said there's nothing wrong with me, I'm just hyperactive. Can you imagine, Margaret? I got beat half to death and they put me away in a goddamn institution. That's crazy, isn't it?

Yeah. But who beat you?

Mark Franks and Pop Carson, our housefather. They beat me till I was knocked out all because I pulled a boy's pants down in front of a girl while we were playing football. It was just a joke.

Is that why you wore those sunglasses to school all week and wouldn't talk to anyone?

Yeah. I had two black eyes and I couldn't see at all out of my right eye. It was swollen shut.

I'm so sorry, Pat. I didn't know and you wouldn't talk to me, or anybody.

I know. I was gonna kill Mark Franks but I changed my mind at the last minute.

All of a sudden this perfect idea comes to me. There are only four months of school left and then I can go home. I can do that time standing on my head if I have a girl to spend time with every day.

I'm staring at her and thinking that she doesn't look so bad sitting there on the couch all dressed up. She's wearing a starched white blouse and plaid skirt that falls below her knees, with brown penny loafers and white socks that are folded over at her ankles. Her knees and ankles are pressed tightly together the way girls do when they have to pee or when they have a lot of class. Margaret has class. Her long brown hair is perfectly coiffed and curled around her slender shoulders, and she has makeup on to hide the blemishes and pock marks on her face. I know she got all dolled up just to come and see me, and I'm thinking how nice it would be right now to walk over to her and kiss her on the lips.

My mind is reeling with desire as I think about all the time I can spend with her if I play my cards right and the endless possibilities—taking her on walks in the woods, through the pastures and meadows, and up in that giant hayloft above the dairy barn.

I look at her with the utmost sincerity and say, You sure look nice, Margaret.

She smiles briefly and then out of habit she closes her mouth to hide her braces. Then she says, Thank you. I just got back from church.

You go to church on a weeknight?

Yes, our youth group meets every Wednesday night.

I'm Catholic. We don't have youth groups in our church.

I know. I used to be Catholic until I came to live with my grandmother. Now I'm a Pentecostal.

A what?

A Pentecostal. Haven't you ever heard of it?

No way, Marg. I've heard of Methodists and Baptists and Protestants, but I've never heard of Pentecostals. What do they believe in?

Well, you know, we believe in Jesus and all that, but we're much more expressive in our worship, especially when we get filled with the Holy Spirit.

I've never heard of such a thing, Margaret. I'm just a regular old Catholic boy. I still know all my Latin.

You were an altar boy?

Yeah, but that was a few years ago. So we're neighbors, huh, Marg?

Yes, isn't that neat? My grandmother says you can come over anytime and we can study together if you'd like. I've brought my books along to show you what chapters we're on.

Thanks, Marg. I've always liked you, you know? You're one of the nicest girls in our class.

She blushes and says, You're not just saying that to be nice, are you?

Hell no, Margaret. You've got more class than all of those other country girls put together.

What about Debbie Morant? I've seen you two passing notes back and forth in homeroom.

Ah, hell, we're just friends, Marg. She has a boyfriend.

Well, what about that black girl? Everyone saw you kissing her at the Sadie Hawkins dance.

We broke up because we couldn't ever be together. I don't have a girlfriend at all now, Margaret.

I walk over and sit beside her.

Would you show me what chapters I need to catch up on?

I give her all my attention and write down the chapters and pages as she calls them out. When she finishes with American History, my knee is resting against hers and she either doesn't notice or doesn't mind. But I don't go any further. I'm a perfect goddamn gentleman.

Marg, I'm way behind. Do you think you can tutor me after school?

I'd be happy to.

I have to start doing chores tomorrow, but I'll come over after I finish them. Do you have a record player, Marg?

We have one in our basement.

Then maybe I'll bring along one of my albums for us to listen to.

That would be neat.

I'm looking at her all serious and about to give her a quick kiss when she says, I'd better be getting home now.

As I'm walking her to the front door, Mrs. Shoop passes us in the hallway. I ask her if I can walk Margaret home and she says it's OK.

Margaret says, You don't have to do that, Pat.

But I want to, Marg.

I want Mrs. Shoop and Margaret to see how much class I have, so I take her books and put them under my arm and then hold the door for her. We walk down the stone path side by side.

As we pass the dairy barn and start down the lane, Margaret says, Isn't it a beautiful night, Pat? Look up in the heavens. God made all of those glorious stars just for us to admire.

Yeah, it sure is beautiful, Marg. It's very romantic too, isn't it? I reach for her hand and hold it all the way to her front porch. It's the perfect gesture to say that I'm excited to be with her and that I want more than just a math lesson from her. Just when I'm again about to kiss her, she opens the door, grabs her books and says, Good night, Pat. See you in school.

Good night, Margaret.

My first day back at school I'm a big celebrity. The kids in my class treat me nice and all my teachers tell me I'll catch up in no time. I discover that it's true what they say about Catholic schools, that you get a better education and learn more. Most of what they teach in the ninth grade in this public school I learned in the eighth grade at Archbishop Neale.

At lunchtime, I find Lonnie and sit with him. I tell him all about my experiences at the children's center and what happened at Bowling Brook and how I came close to murdering Mark Franks. He's glad to see me and offers me a ride back to the foster home after school, but I decline because I didn't get permission and I don't want to tick anybody off.

After school, Mr. Shoop saddles up two of his finest horses and takes me riding all over his farm. After he sees how well I can handle a horse, he tells me I can go riding anytime I want. Then he shows me how he wants the horses fed and how much to feed them.

Afterward, we go up into the hayloft and Mr. Shoop opens a trap door. We toss bales of hay down into the barn and once we have enough, he takes me downstairs and shows me how much hay to place inside each bin where the cows' heads remain while they're being milked. Then he shows me where the broom is and asks me to sweep the entire center aisle of the barn. These are my daily chores.

From the start, I like Mr. Shoop. He's a quiet man and he reminds me of my grandfather the way he pauses before he speaks. At first I think he hesitates to speak because of his thick German accent, but then I think it's because he doesn't waste words or beat around any bushes.

When I ask him if he minds if I smoke, he says, We'd prefer that you didn't smoke, but since it's your choice, our only rules are that you don't smoke in the house or in the barn, son.

I won't, sir.

Then he adds, You'll have to buy your own cigarettes, too.

I know, sir.

Have you ever heard the saying that smoking stunts a boy's growth?

Yes, sir.

I guess that's not true in your case, is it, son?

No sir. I'm six feet two, and still growing.

Before supper, the veterinarian comes and I watch him artificially breed one of Mr. Shoop's best Holsteins. The man puts on a plastic glove that extends all the way up his arm. Then he inserts his gloved hand up the cow's ass and a long plastic rod containing bull semen inside the cow's vagina. When he's ready, he pulls a trigger at the end of the rod, and that releases the semen into the cow, Mr. Shoop tells me. The cow never moves during the entire process. The man pulls his arm out of the cow's ass, and the glove is covered with slimy crap.

After supper I take my schoolbooks over to Margaret's. Her grandmother answers the door. A petite old woman with perfect posture, she smiles and shakes my hand and then leads me to the basement stairs. She says, Margaret's down there waiting for you. If you get hungry, you let her know and we'll fix you something, you hear?

Thank you, ma'am, but I just had dinner.

Well, maybe you'll want a piece of Margaret's cherry pie later on.

I could never say no to cherry pie. That sounds good to me, ma'am. Thank you.

Margaret's sitting at the table doing math.

Hi, Marg. I heard you bake pies.

I love to bake. Did my grandmother offer you something to eat?

Yeah. A piece of your cherry pie. I told her maybe later.

Well, what would you like to study first?

I have that debate I gotta prepare for. Are you for or against the war, Marg?

I'm naturally against war, but it's not quite that simple, you know? The South Vietnamese people want democracy and the North wants them to be under oppressive rule. I should think that the principle of defending their freedom and democracy is one worth fighting for. After all, if America doesn't help them fight off Communism, who will?

Yeah, but what about all of our soldiers getting killed every day? It doesn't make any sense.

I know. That's what makes the whole thing a moral dilemma for me.

I've already made up my mind what I'm going to do if the draft and war are still going on when I turn eighteen, Marg. I'm going to Canada. I'm not losing my goddamn leg or arm or my whole freaking head fighting in a war.

Pat, would you please not use God's name in vain?

I'm sorry, Margaret. It's a habit I have. You want to listen to some music?

Sure. The record player is over there on the table.

I put on my Sam and Dave album. While we're sitting there listening to I'm a Soul Man, Marg asks what my family's like and why I came to the boys' home in the first place. I give her the short version of all the crazy stuff that happened to me, about how Max used to beat me, and how all he and Moma do is drink and stay out half the night. But I also tell her about how great my grandfather and aunts and uncles are on Maple Knoll, and that's when I get real homesick.

Margaret looks like she's going to cry. She says, I'm really sorry, Pat. That's so sad. Can't you go and live with your grandfather?

I don't want to talk about it, Margaret. Just then a slow song, When Something Is Wrong with My Baby, comes on and I ask her to dance with me.

We get up and I wrap my arms around her waist, leaning my head down on her shoulder. We move in perfect step to the music and I pull her even closer to me. It makes me excited, holding her in my arms and smelling her hair and neck. I can tell she's slow-danced before by the way she sways and keeps her right foot inside my lead foot.

I press even closer to her because I want her to feel my excitement. At the same time, I ask her if she likes the song and she says, Yeah. That's all she says.

When the song ends, I cup her face in my hands and kiss her on the lips. She kisses back and even though my tongue rakes against her braces, she's still a good kisser. After a minute we stop and sit on the half-sofa. She grabs a book, opens it and reads, Blessed are the pure in heart, for they will see God. Then she touches my hand and says, Do you know about Jesus?

After that I'm at her house every day. Sometimes we go horseback riding and she helps me do my chores. We toss the bales of hay through the trap door and then we wrestle around in the loose hay until she feels my excitement and wants to tell me more about Jesus. I say, You can tell me later, and then I shove my hand down her pants. She struggles to stop me, but I'm stronger and I get what I want. She starts to cry and says, Pat, don't! Please don't!

Aw, for Christ's sake, Margaret, you know you want it.

Pat, it's wrong. I'm saving myself for when I get married.

Well, goddamn, you sure know how to tease a guy, Margaret. The least you can do is make me feel good.

I grab her hand and place it over my excitement and rub it back and forth until she does it on her own. I say, Don't stop, Margaret. Then we kiss passionately until I've had my fun.

The weeks turn into months and the time I spend with Margaret and the Shoop family is fun and exciting. Elena and Bruce call me their big brother and go out of their way to shower me with affection.

Every Sunday, the Shoops drop me off at St. Joseph's Catholic Church on their way to their own church. On my last Sunday, they invite me to attend church with them. I accept their invitation because I like being with them. It's the first time I've ever stepped foot inside a church that isn't Catholic.

On our way there, I think about everything Sister Thomas Mary every told us about other religions. The Catholic Church is the one true church, she said over and over. And if that's true, it means that all other churches are phonies. Only Catholics truly know God the Father, His son Jesus Christ, and the Holy Spirit. I'm wondering, too, what my grandfather would say if he knew I was about to enter the Pentecostal Church of God.

As soon as we step inside, I'm bug-eyed, amazed at what I see and hear. I'm extremely nervous. We sit in the third pew from the front and the preacher begins shouting from the top of his lungs that we are all SINNERS IN THE HANDS OF AN ANGRY GOD. In the same breath he lowers his voice to a whisper, assuring everyone that despite our sinful nature, there is hope to be found in the body and blood of Jesus Christ.

Repent. Repent. Repent. That is the key to your salvation.

The way the people respond to his sermon is equally frightening. From the mouths of even the children come the strangest remarks and cries.

Amen.

Yes, Lord.

Oh, Jesus! Jesus! Yes, Jesus!

A-a-a-men.

Preach it, Brother.

Cleanse us, Lord!

Then, right in the middle of the sermon, a woman hurls herself in the aisle as if she'd been snatched from her seat by an invisible man and writhes and jerks like an epileptic having a seizure.

Praise the Lord, shouts the preacher. There's at least one among us who's filled with the Holy Ghost.

So that's what it is, I say to myself. She isn't having a seizure at all. But this realization does little to soothe my fears. For no sooner does she start these spasms then several other members of the congregation stand and begin to dance and throw their arms toward heaven, singing and crying like little children.

Thank you, Jesus. Thank you, Jesus.

Praise God. Praise Jesus.

I turn my head slowly toward Mrs. Shoop, who's sitting to my right. I'm hoping she'll give me a simple nod of comfort, an acknowledgment that everything's going to be all right, but she doesn't, for her eyes are closed. Then I turn to Elena who's sitting on my left. She smiles impishly and whispers in my ear, Don't worry. We don't all act like that.

Thank God for that, I whisper back. We both grin.

After the congregation sings Onward Christian Soldiers, the service comes to an end and I walk out of the church, relieved that it's over and ever grateful that I'm just a regular Catholic. On the way home, Mrs. Shoop asks what I thought of the service.

I say, It was a little different from what we Catholics are used to, and everyone laughs.

The day that Mr. Buffington shows up to take me home, everyone's crying. Margaret and I said our good-bye on a morning walk down the lane. I gave her my St. Christopher's medal and even though she's not a Catholic, she told me she'd always keep it with her. Then she handed me a new dictionary and reminded me to use it. Now she's standing beside me smiling and crying at the same time along with Mrs. Shoop and Elena.

Mrs. Shoop gives me a cream-colored wool sweater she knitted herself and I put it on. It fits perfectly. I tell her it's the most handsome sweater I've ever owned, and it truly is.

Elena and Bruce give me a small silver cross and chain. Tears well up in my eyes when I thank them all for treating me so nice and making me feel so welcome. I hug everyone and then get in the car clutching the cross and chain and the beautiful sweater. I can smell the honeysuckle and wild onions and cow shit and hot banana bread we had for breakfast as we drive away, and I hear the laughter of Elena and Bruce as they call my name.

Good-bye, Pat! Good-bye!

I put my hand out the window and wave. It's a beautiful day and I'm going home.

Chapter 15

Our house looks sadder than a funeral parlor when I arrive home. All the window shades and curtains are peeled shut, and the shrubs along the front of the house are in desperate need of pruning.

Mr. Buffington pulls in the driveway and there's no sign of life anywhere. I had expected to see Huck riding his bike along the street or playing ball in the yard with the neighborhood boys, but he's nowhere around. Our bicycles that were scattered in the carport last winter are gone too, and so are the football and basketball we kept in the basement window box on the windward side of the house.

Moma opens the side door and waves at Mr. Buffington as he says good-bye and that he'll be in touch. I walk inside the house and the rooms are all dark and silent.

Where's everyone, Moma?

She doesn't answer. Instead, she disappears into her bedroom. When she walks into my room a few minutes later, she tells me that Suzanne has gone to live with Aunt Frances and Huck is living with Max's mother and Michael is moving to Maple Knoll with our grandfather.

Pat, I feel so abandoned, she says.

She tries to hold back her tears but she can't; they squeeze out of her eyes and dribble down her cheeks.

Just then all my longings to console her and be consoled by her burst out of me and I hug her tightly. I want to cry too because it makes me sad to see her sad and because what she just told me makes me realize that what little family we had is now gone. But I don't cry because I want to show her that I've become a man and men don't cry.

I suddenly remember all the letters she sent me while I was away that are now tied in neat little bundles at the bottom of my suitcase. Each one had been like a salve to soothe my own loneliness. I feel a deep debt of gratitude to her for each one of those letters. I remember, too, every crumb of affection she's ever given me and I'm thankful for every one of them.

It's all right, Moma, I say. You're not *all* alone. You still have me.

I know, Pat, she says, regaining her composure. Everything's going to be all right. Then she hugs me like she never wants to let go.

Over the next two weeks I get my driver's license; visit Huck at his grandmother's; meet Father Whorten, our new assistant parish priest, and his dog Jackie; and catch up with Michael one afternoon when he stops by to get the rest of his belongings. He has his own car, a '64 baby blue Renault that once belonged to Aunt Winn and Uncle Sanford. He's with his friend and classmate Pat Langley, and they invite me to come along with them for the day.

We stop at Maple Knoll and while Michael carries his things up to his room, I walk into the parlor to see my grandfather. He's resting in his big recliner.

Hello, DaDa, I say. He opens his eyes and smiles.

Son, how are you?

I'm fine, sir. I'm glad to be home.

We're all glad you're home too, son. You know you're more than welcome to live here with us.

Thanks, DaDa. I'll let you know. I really appreciate it.

I'm thrilled to no end that he invited me to move in because living with my grandfather would be a dream come true. The reason I don't make a commitment one way or the other is that I don't want to leave my mother completely alone.

But it only takes a month for me to change my mind. Moma's hardly ever home, and I don't see any point in staying there by myself. Still, I'm careful not to remove all my things out of my bedroom.

Michael and I share a handsome bedroom on the second floor of the house. Every day he takes me to school with him in his Renault. Uncle Leo puts up a regulation basketball hoop over the garage and pours a wide concrete court. Michael and I play one-on-one, and on weekends half the varsity basketball team comes over to play. Michael is the captain of the team. Even though I'm not good enough to be on the team, Pat Langley tells me they'll talk to the coach and get me on the squad so I can travel with them to their away games. Pat is Michael's best friend and the nicest guy. Sometimes he and Michael double-date and when they do, Michael lets me drive his car around.

When August rolls around, I have an appointment with the new Mother Superior at Archbishop Neale. I break out with goose bumps when I pull around the circular driveway in front of the Sacred Heart Convent in my brother's car. It feels so good being on the hallowed grounds of my old school, a place that was a sanctuary to me for so many years.

Inside the circle of the driveway stands the familiar colossal statue of the Blessed Virgin Mary surrounded by beds of bright-colored petunias and daffodils and irises. Mrs. Brown, the convent maid and cook, greets me at the door and escorts me to a room right off the main hall. While I'm waiting, I gaze at the gold crucifix of Jesus on the wall and say a prayer that the new Mother Superior will like me and accept me back in school. I promise God not to mess things up if He'll just intervene for me one more time.

I'm opening my eyes and making the sign of the cross when this elderly nun walks into the room, smiles warmly, and sticks out her hand.

Hello, Patrick, I'm Sister Charles.

I stand and shake her hand and she's smiling at me like she's known me all my life.

Hi, Sister. I'm glad to meet you. My brother Michael told me you're pretty cool.

He did? Well, I'll try not to let you down.

Sister gets right to the point.

We're going to let you enroll back in A.N.S. for your tenth-grade year, she says. But the first time you pose any problem, Patrick, you'll be thrown out by your ears.

She says this with a smile, but I can tell she means what she says.

She pauses and I know she's waiting for me to say something. I can't remember the beginning of my speech, so I just start babbling. I tell her how all the time I was away, I prayed constantly to the Blessed Mother and asked her to intervene for me.

I prayed every day, Sister, for a chance to come home and get back to Archbishop Neale and the boys and girls I grew up with and love so much. Thank you for giving me another chance. I've turned over a new leaf, Sister, and I promise I won't let you down.

I don't believe you will, Patrick.

Two weeks later, the school year begins and I'm excited to be starting over. I have three major goals: To do well in school. To find a girlfriend I can devote myself to. And to be looked up to by my classmates for all the right reasons.

Several of my old classmates have left A.N.S. and there are lots of new faces. My best friend, Danny Miller, transferred to Gonzaga in Washington, D.C., one of the top Catholic prep schools in the country. Francis Flynn was expelled sometime last year and is now attending public school, as are my first cousins Andy and Mitch Mills, and Charles Rison, another old pal of mine.

In the year I was away, the girls have ripened and multiplied. There are several new girls who transferred from Our Lady Star of the Sea and they along with all of my old classmates make me feel welcomed and loved.

On Halloween night, the Wilson sisters who live across the highway from our grandfather throw a big party. I am thrilled and excited when I receive an invitation to come, even though I know I was invited mainly because of

Michael's popularity and because I'm friends with most of the junior class who were my fellow classmates until Sister Isidora made me repeat the eighth grade. Bonnie Wilson's a senior and Debbie, who's my age, is in the eleventh grade.

I get to the party and just about every boy there has a girlfriend but me. I dance with Michael's girlfriend, Betty Lou, and I whisper in her ear how I hope she marries my brother one day because she's the classiest girl I've ever known. She asks me if I think Debbie Wilson is cute and I say, What boy wouldn't? She says I should ask her to dance and she's smiling like she knows something I don't.

Three dances later, I ask Debbie where's her boyfriend, and she tells me they broke up right before he left for basic training last summer. Then she says the music's too loud, and do I want to go outside and walk around.

Heck yeah, I answer.

We walk up and down the long gravel road and I tell her all about my adventures of the last year and how happy I am now to be living with my grandfather. She tells me about her family and how wonderful her father has been since they lost their mother to cancer two years ago.

The whole time she's talking I listen like a gentleman, but deep down inside all I'm thinking about is how complete and perfect my life would be if she were my girlfriend. She's a drop-dead pretty girl and very popular at school and among the adults in our community. Ever since I moved in with my grandfather, my aunts have marveled at how sweet and wonderful those Wilson girls are.

Before we go back to the party, I hold her hand and ask if I can call her tomorrow and she says yes. With a single kiss, we trade devotions. When we walk into the party holding hands, all of Debbie's girlfriends start clapping. While we're taking off our jackets, Betty Lou whispers in my ear, Aren't you glad you asked her to dance?

I sure as hell am. Thanks, Bett.

On Saturday, December 7, 1968, I go deer hunting for the first time in my life. I eat a big breakfast with my grandfather and then load Uncle Leo's double-barrel twelve-gauge shotgun with two pumpkin balls. I've never been hunting before and I don't know much about shooting guns. I'm not even that excited about the idea of shooting a goddamn deer in the head with a pumpkin ball either. I'm going mainly because I heard one of my uncles on my mother's side say that killing a deer is a boy's rite of passage into manhood.

I climb up in an old deer stand that's in the fork of a huge oak tree at the edge of the swamp. After two hours of sitting there freezing my ass off and not hearing or seeing any sign of a deer, I get down out of the stand and start for home. Suddenly, I hear movement in the brush. I click the safety off the shotgun and crouch down as I walk toward the field.

When I stand up, I see my cousins Gregory and Wayne Middleton who live on the farm next to my grandfather's. They're two of the nicest boys I've ever known, and they're my second cousins. We're standing there talking about God knows what when Wayne squats down to inspect Uncle Leo's new shotgun.

I'm leaning over the barrel like it's a crutch under my left arm. When the gun goes off, the blast blows me several feet into the air. I fall back to the earth and it feels like my whole body has been inflated with air. The smell of gunpowder sears my nostrils and throat and the blood gurgles in my chest.

I open my eyes and Wayne is leaning over me in a state of shock. He yells to Gregory to go get help and then he asks me to pray with him. But I've already started praying. I pray the Act of Contrition faster than I've ever prayed it. It's a guaranteed ticket to heaven if you're Catholic and say the prayer right before you die. Wayne and I race through the prayer a second time and when we reach the end, I ask him to let me say it again by myself. He holds my hand.

OhmyGodIamheartlysorryforhavingoffendedtheeAnd IdetestallmysinsbecauseIdreadthelossofheavenandthepainsof hellbutmostofallbecausetheyhaveoffendedtheemyGodwhoart allgoodanddeservingofallmyloveIfirmlyresolvewiththehelpof thygracetoconfessmysinstodopenanceandtoamendmylifeAme n.

Now I'm no longer afraid. My destiny is sealed.

I know I'm going to die, for the blood is flowing out of me like a stream. Wayne is crying and telling me over and over how sorry he is. I tell him it's OK and I want to go to sleep now. But he won't let me. I ask him where my left arm is because I don't feel it. I taste blood and I hear it gurgling and I smell gunpowder.

Pat, your arm, it's down by your side, Wayne says. Don't move, man.

I want to go to sleep but Wayne keeps rubbing my face and making me answer questions. You can't go to sleep, he says. You just can't.

When the rescue squad arrives, I know one of the boys. He tells me to hang in there. They lift me onto a canvas stretcher and I can feel branches slapping me in the face as they move me out of the field.

I want water. My mouth and throat feel like a cavity of cotton. We can't give you water, the other boy says. The siren screams and I hear one of the boys telling the other one, He ain't gonna make it.

The next thing I know the ambulance screeches to a halt. I hear a dog barking. A large dog. *Whoofwhoofwhoof.* It's Jackie. Father Whorten's German shepherd. The back door of the ambulance swings open and Father Whorten's standing there with Jackie. Beautiful Jackie.

Inside the emergency room, minutes before I go under the water, the delicious cold water, Father Whorten anoints me with oil and drops of water. A drop lands on my lips and dries right up. The last rites. Extreme unction. An anointment of the dying.

People get ready, there's a train a comin', pickin' up passengers from coast to coast. I have my ticket and I'm on board the train. Bless me, Father, for I have sinned...Glory be to the Father, to the Son, and to the Holy Spirit, as it was in the beginning, is now, and ever shall be, world without end, Amen.

Two days later, I wake up inside a plastic tent. Someone unzips the front of the tent and kisses my cheek. I squint my eyes and try to focus on the face. It's an angel, a crying angel. It's Sister Patricia, Michael's twelfth-grade teacher. Then Aunt Vera leans in and kisses me. I can smell her perfume as her tears splash on my face and run down my neck.

I squint again and look around the room. There are angels at the door. Angels dressed like penguins. Sister Paulette. Sister Gerald Marie. Sister Patricia. They're all saying the rosary. And there's my cousin Wayne, who's crying like a baby. Standing beside them all is Aunt Alice, who's a private registered nurse. Aunt Alice walks to the window and pulls the drapes back.

I lay my head deep into the pillow and close my eyes. I've never felt so loved as I do now. All these goddamn people are here for me. I take a deep breath and then work to ease my head up off the pillow.

I see a bouquet of classmates standing outside the window waving to me, and there's my brother Michael with the entire varsity basketball team. Debbie is waving and crying and blowing kisses, and some of the other girls are crying, too. Then the doctor comes in the room and makes everyone leave except Aunt Alice.

I close my eyes and the next time I wake up, Aunt Alice has my wrist between her fingers, taking my pulse. When she sees I'm awake she smiles and asks me if I'd like to see my father. The question hits me like another bullet. *Do I want to see my father? Do I want to see my father? Mr. Ernest A. Middleton Jr.? I thought the man was dead. Wasn't he killed in a car accident? Daddy, where are you? I've been looking for you. I don't like this new man here. When are you coming home?*

I'm too weak to speak. I nod my head up and down and then Aunt Alice tells me to rest.

Two days later, all the years of longing for my father come to an end when he walks into the room.

Hello, son, he says. I'm your father. There's not the slightest hint of shame on his face.

Hi, Daddy. It's good to see you. He's much heavier than I remembered. There are deep lines pressed in his forehead and red veins all over the whites of his eyes. He shakes my hand, and his hands are just as big as my grandfather's hands.

How're you feeling, son?

I shake my head up and down. My three aunts are in the room, but they're not saying a word. There's a silent contract among them to treat their brother like a stranger. He shamed them and blemished the sacred integrity of the Middleton name, and can never be forgiven. He abandoned three little children, his own flesh and blood, and the penalty is eternal ostracism. Why, then, did they let him come to see me at all? They did it for me because it's the least they can do, since everyone's whispering that I might not make it through another night.

My father comes back to see me the next day after the doctor announces that a blood clot has formed and the bleeding has stopped and I'm going to live after all. My father asks to spend time alone with me and after he and Aunt Vera argue about it, everyone leaves. Daddy takes out a milk shake from the paper sack he's carrying and sticks a straw through the hole in the lid.

Vera says, Strawberry's still your favorite flavor, son, and the doctor said it was OK to bring you one. He helps me lean forward and I taste the milk shake like it's the first one I've had since I was five. At first he doesn't have much to say and the only sound in the room is the metronomic beep of the heart monitor. But then he starts talking as if he's on his own deathbed and wants to come clean. He has a new family and lives in Ohio, he tells me. He has a daughter named Anne who's eight and a son Jimmy who's seven.

They know all about my brother and sister and me and can't wait to meet us in person some day. They're real smart kids. Anne's a dancer. Jimmy's just like me, full of adventure and mischief. He's only seven and already has five merit badges.

He says, Did you know that the boy saved a litter of newborn kittens from drowning when he was only six years old?

He's so caught up in his own goddamn story that I don't have the guts to tell him there's no way I could have possibly known about his son in light of the fact that, as far as I knew, he himself had been killed in a car accident the year I turned six.

As he goes on, I lay my head back on the pillow and listen the way I imagine Father Kelly Reese listened to me in the confessional box last Saturday afternoon when I told him I'd masturbated three times on Aunt Vera's new sheets. At the end of his speech, he tells me he's wanted to see Michael and me for the longest time, but it hadn't worked out until now. Then he gives me his old school ring and says it's time for him to head back to Ohio. He promises to return in a couple of weeks to see us. I sit up and extend my hand, but instead he puts his arms around my head and attempts to hug me. It's an awkward hug and I'm glad when he turns and walks out of the room in a hurry.

Seeing my father after all these years isn't the big deal I thought it would be. I feel as if I've just met some action adventure hero like Batman or the Lone Ranger, someone who plays a role but underneath is just another man. No sooner is he gone then I push him deep down to the bottom of my mind.

Chapter 16

Two weeks after Christmas, the doctor says I can go home. Instead of returning to Maple Knoll, my grandfather tells me I'm going to stay with Aunt Alice until I get my strength back.

I wake up the first morning and I'm depressed and feeling sorry for myself because I can't use my arm. Aunt Alice changes the bandages and dressings on my shoulder and under my arm, and encourages me to get out of bed and start exercising. But I can hardly move my arm and all I can think about is that I'm going to wind up being like a goddamn one-armed bandit.

Aunt Alice says there was very little nerve damage and that the muscles in my left arm and hand need to be used immediately. Then she boots me out of the house and tells me to take a long walk.

Her house is in the city and I don't know the neighborhood. For all I know there may be thugs lingering around every corner. I start up the street and get two blocks before I have to sit down and rest because I'm so goddamn weak. I look around and see kids playing up and down the streets and boys riding bikes everywhere.

I get up and start walking and I try to raise my arm over my head, but it won't go. Lord Jesus Christ, help me! My arm won't work! I start to cry and head home.

The next day, Aunt Alice drives me to a hospital near her house and I start a physical therapy program. The nurses are all very nice, but they don't baby me. Each day they push me a little harder and never let me do less than I did the day before. I see progress immediately, although I go home every night exhausted and in pain.

In just two weeks I can stretch my arm over my head and my fingers start working again. At night, Aunt Alice takes me through more exercises. Thanks to her love and encouragement, my depression quickly dissolves into obdurate determination.

In a month, I'm back at Maple Knoll and into the swing of things at school. The boys and girls in my class treat me like a prince and I've never felt so much love. All the girls want to carry my books from one class to the next. My girlfriend, Debbie, waits for me every day at lunch. She wears the new white sweater Aunt Vera bought me for Christmas.

After school, Michael drives me up to D.C. for my physical therapy sessions. He's the best brother a fellow could ask for. He never complains when he has to make sacrifices and goes out of his way to get me to my appointments. He even invites Debbie and me to double-date with him and Betty Lou sometimes.

But then my grandfather, who's the most generous and loving grandfather in the world, buys me a '64 baby blue Renault that's identical to Michael's except for the automatic transmission. The car's in mint condition and I'm so happy and thankful to own it. Aunt Vera tells me we can't drive both cars to school and I have to pay for my gas, so I continue to ride to school with Michael until I get a part-time job at the Amoco gas station and need my own transportation after school.

Our tenth-grade class is just beginning to make plans for the biggest dance of the school year. Every year, the sophomore class holds a dance to raise money for the junior-senior prom. Everyone in our class is excited and we all pledge to outdo our predecessors. To do that, we'll need to raise a lot of money.

At our class meeting, Julie Posey presents us with a brief history of the dance and its traditions. Then there's a call for volunteers to head the various committees. Julie writes the names of the committees on the board. Decorations. Entertainment. Ticket and Coat Check. Refreshments. Advertisement.

Hands go up for every committee but one, the entertainment. Judy Hayden, our class president says, We're going to need a good band if we expect to draw a big crowd. Who wants to head the entertainment committee?

Before Judy gets her last words out, she and several other boys and girls turn to me, grinning conspiratorially. My reputation for knowing music, for once having my own garage band, and for following the local band scene is well known.

Judy says, Who's better suited to head this committee than Patrick Middleton? The whole class voices their agreement.

I want the job more than anything, and I accept. Then Judy asks the class if there are any preferences or favorite bands they want me to contact. The names of the same old bands that have been playing at every firehouse dance and private party for the past three or four years come up. Almost half the class wants me to contact the Suburbans and the other half wants the Executioners. A few hands go up for the Warringtons. Though I haven't been in contact with my old friend Jimmy Tree, who heads the Executioners, I know I could book them easily. All three of these bands are decent, and they're within our two hundred and fifty-dollar budget.

But I already know the band I'm going to go after, the one band that will pack our Sacred Heart Church hall beyond capacity. I stand up and very boldly announce that none of the bands mentioned will draw anymore than a decent crowd, and it's my intention to hire a band that will fill the church hall to the rafters and raise more money than we ever imagined.

Judy says, Getting the right band is important, but we have to stay within our budget. We'll leave the decision in your good hands, Patrick.

In my mind, my classmates have just entrusted me with the task of creating an enchanted evening for everyone who attends our dance, and the band—the music!—is the key to it all. There's only one thing I need to do to create the most spectacular and memorable dance any of us will ever attend. I'm going to hire Paul Wills and the Fabulous Corvettes, an all-black band that will bring its own crowd.

The next day after school I walk into the garage of Barnes Chevrolet where Bernard Briscoe's father, Charlie, works and ask him where I can find Bernard these days. Mr. Briscoe has worked at Barnes ever since I was a little boy, and he's the only mechanic who's ever worked on our family's cars. He's a nice man and a devout Catholic. He tells me I can find Bernard flipping hamburgers at the La Plata Diner.

I walk across the street and into the back door of the diner. I haven't seen Bernard since the day he and Melvin came to my house to tell me they were quitting my band to join Paul Wills and the Corvettes, and that was almost two years ago. Bernard's standing over the hot grill frying onions and hamburgers. He's surprised and glad to see me. When I tell him I want the Corvettes to play at our sophomore dance, he laughs incredulously.

I say, What's so goddamn funny, Bernard?

He says, You've gotta be joking, Pat! Those nuns would have a fit if we showed up. They ain't going for that.

Then I go into this long spill about how I'm in charge of hiring the band and that our tenth-grade class agreed unanimously that I should get the Corvettes.

He says, You're bullshitting, Pat. None of those kids have ever heard us play.

No, they haven't, but they've all heard about how great you guys sound and how you pack every goddamn establishment you play at.

Ya'll got four hundred dollars? Cuz that's what it's gonna cost you.

Bernard's a sucker for nostalgia, so I try to appeal to him there.

Look, Bernard, we're trying to raise enough money to put on the best junior-senior prom our school's ever had. The only way we can do that is to fill up the church hall, and the only way we can ever hope to do that is to have the best goddamn band in the metropolitan D.C. area playing, and that's the fricking Corvettes. Man, look, you'll be performing in front of all your old classmates, they'll be dancing to your music, man, and this is for a worthy cause. And I didn't tell you that Melvin's mother will be working at the dance that night, did I? Don't you know how proud she'll be to get to hear Melvin perform for an entire evening?

Of course, I'm lying through my teeth, but Bernard knows that Mrs. Brown works at the convent, so he doesn't question me on this.

OK, he says. What about the money? You telling me they're gonna cough up four hundred dollars for us to play?

Well, not exactly, Bernard. Here's the thing. I was hoping that you, Melvin, and Paul would play for free and that that would bring the price down close to our budget of two hundred and fifty dollars.

Two hundred and fifty dollars! Are you crazy, dude? We get four hundred a night, man. That's fifty bucks for each member. We don't do no charity work unless it's for the NAACP, and that's a fact.

What if I can get Melvin and Paul to play for nothing? Will you agree too? Come on, Bernard, this is for a good cause, man.

Well, seeing how that tight ass Melvin will never play a gig for free, I'll say yeah. If they both agree, I'll play too.

Before I leave the diner, he tells me where I can find Paul and Melvin, and then I thank him and assure him he won't regret it.

It's been years since I've seen little Paul Wills. Growing up, we played cowboys and Indians together, picked blackberries on old man Schwab's private property, and ate peanut butter sandwiches while we sang our favorite R&B songs on the back porch of his family's shack. We also wore the same clothes. Paul's mother had eight children to take care of and so there wasn't any room for being proud. At least once a year, Moma would clean our closets and dresser drawers out, gathering all the clothes we'd outgrown or simply didn't wear any longer and give them to Midget, Paul's mother. Michael and I always included one or two of our favorite toys..

Paul is still living on Washington Avenue, but in a better house. When I pull into his driveway in my little Renault, Paul and another fellow are in the front yard working under the hood of a car. Paul looks at me as I'm getting out of the car and at first he doesn't recognize me. But the other fellow does.

Pat Middleton, how in the hell are you, boy?

Hey, Melvin. You're looking good, man. You sure have gotten tall.

Paul says, Pat, my, my, my! I didn't even recognize you, man!

We shake hands and then hug each other like long lost brothers would.

Paul says, My mother's not home, but she sure would like to see you.

I'd like to see her, too, Paul. How's she doing?

She's fine, you know. Working every day as usual.

I get right down to business. I start out by telling them I need their help. I run the same rap on them that I ran on Bernard, how we're trying to raise money for our junior-senior prom and everyone wants a great band but our budget's only two hundred and fifty bucks. I tell them that I've already talked to Bernard and he agreed to play for free if the two of them will. When I finish, Paul's smiling and looking at Melvin as if to say, What do you wanna do?

But Melvin's frowning and shaking his head. I go right on talking before he has a chance to say no.

Look, man, we've never had a dance in the history of our school where the Corvettes played. Melvin, everyone in our high school knows how famous the Corvettes are, including all your old classmates, and they wanna hear you guys play bad. This is for a worthy cause, man. Your mom's even gonna be at the dance, Melvin.

Melvin says, Now how do you know that?

We've asked her to be one of the chaperones, Melvin, I say, lying through my teeth.

Dig, man, two-fifty's just enough to pay the other fellows in the band, Melvin says. That means me, Paul, and Bernard would have to play for free. We ain't never done no kind of charity playing like that. And even the NACCP gave us a couple of amps when we played for them. Hell, man, you're asking a lot.

Paul, smiling from ear to ear, says, What the hell, Mel. I'll do it if you'll do it.

After complaining about how bad he needs a couple of dollars and a pint of wine, Melvin gives in and I can't thank him enough. I knew he was a sucker for nostalgia.

Before I leave, Paul puts the place, time, and date of the dance in his calendar book and then I give him a list of personal song requests for that night. He says the band knows all the songs on my list and all I need to do is ask him that night. I thank them about ten more times before I leave.

On the Saturday afternoon of the dance, I go through every potentially disastrous scenario I can think of. I dismiss each one as something that God just won't allow to happen. What if all these kids don't show up? What if I let everyone down? What if Paul and the Corvettes don't make it? What if the crowd I'm counting on does show up and there's a fight?

All afternoon I pace around the Sacred Heart Church hall, telling Judy and Julie and the other girls who are hard at work with decorating the hall that the streamers on one side of the hall aren't symmetric with the ones on the other side. Julie tells me to go fly a kite and Judy says I can put them up myself if I don't like it. I wind up throwing a fit when I see the bandstand decorations because the girls have it all wrong. I want the streamers twisting all the way down to the floor every five feet, and they have simply made a box design around the stage. Julie tells me to calm down and explain what's wrong and then she rearranges the streamers the way I want them. She even adds a beautiful touch to it when she overlaps the green and gold streamers as she twists them down to the floor. By five o'clock, everything that can be done is done, and we all go home to shower and get dressed.

Aunt Vera tells me I've never looked more handsome. She runs her fingers through my hair and tells me to go comb it better. I tell her I don't have time because it's getting late and I have to pick up Debbie and then go meet the band.

Debbie and I get to Sacred Heart just as the band is unloading their equipment. Sister Mary Pio and Sister Gerald Marie are at the door setting up a reception table. On the table is a box of ties for boys who show up not wearing one. Paul and Bernard are fast at work setting up the band's equipment while Melvin and the other musicians gripe about having to bring in everything without them. After they do a sound check, the band members disappear into the kitchen. Fifteen minutes later they march out in single file and onto the bandstand, and my heart pounds with excitement. They're wearing matching blue satin jackets trimmed in gold and white shirts with black pants and black bow ties, and they're all smiling proudly.

The kids from Archbishop Neale arrive almost at the same time and start dancing up a storm. Those who aren't dancing are sitting along the side walls getting comfortable with their dates or standing around the bandstand, clapping to the beat of the music and fascinated by the choreography and showmanship of the band. When they break into James Brown's Papa's Got a Brand New Bag, Debbie and I hit the dance floor and I start showing off. A little later I see my brother Michael come through the door with Betty Lou and I'm so happy that he and all his friends are sharing this night with us.

An hour goes by and I start to get nervous and fidgety because we only have an average crowd, mostly kids from our school and a few from the local high schools. I keep looking at the door hoping to see more kids coming in, but they don't.

But Holy Mother of God, all of that changes a little before ten o'clock. Several of my friends are complaining that the lights are too bright, so I walk toward the kitchen to dim them some. When I pass the Sisters at the door, I look out and see droves of black kids coming up the walkways. One of the first boys through the door is Bernard Savoy, a longtime friend of my brother's and mine. Bernard says his school had a basketball game and won. He says just about everyone at the game is on their way to the dance. I tell him that I sure am glad to see him and everyone else behind him.

Black kids are pouring into the hall like rain. They quickly shed their coats and start dancing. While most of the white kids are doing a version of the jerk or the shimmy or the hitchhike, the black kids are doing what looks like a new dance. They're free-styling and fast-dancing closer to their partners than we've ever seen. Debbie and I get right back on the dance floor as soon as the band starts playing I Just Can't Stop Dancin', by Archie Bell and the Drells. Paul sings the song with such soul and grace that I get goose bumps.

> *There's a place, I eat lunch every day*
> *As soon as I get there, the jukebox starts to play*
> *I can't even eat my lunch in peace*
> *Music makes me get off my feet, Cuz*
> *I just can't stop dancin', Ooh*
> *I just can't stop dancin'*
> *I just can't stop dancin'*
> *I just can't stop dancin'*

That's followed by an instrumental called The Horse, by Cliff Noble and the Knights. And after that, Paul sings my favorite song by Otis Redding called, I've Been Lovin' You a Little Too Long to Stop Now.

It's that very song that the black kids introduce us white kids to a new dance. It's called the slow grind and it's easy to do and out of sight. All you do is pull your girl real close to you and press your thigh between her legs so that each time your inside leg moves forward it rubs against her groin.

Bernard had once demonstrated the slow grind to my cousin Mitch Mills and me at an eighth-grade sock hop and the girl he was dancing with slapped him upside his head, even though she kept right on dancing with him. After he walked off the dance floor, Bernard said the slow grind is the one dance where a fellow can usually find out just how far he can expect to go with his girl. And to that Mitch told Bernard, If that's true, it doesn't look like you're gonna get very far with yours..

Sister Gerald Marie catches on to us after about two more slow songs. We're dancing to Going in Circles by the Friends of Distinction when Sister Gerald Marie and Sister Mary Pio start weaving through the crowded dance floor, their eyes like eagles, admonishing us not to dance so close.

You're too close, kids. Separate a little, please.

Yes, Sister.

OK, Sister.

But it's too late. The craze has caught on and it's much too fun to quit. We simply wait until the Sisters pass by and then we pull our partners closely against us and move our thighs back and forth the way the black boys are doing.

When the band plays the last slow song of the night, Debbie and I walk up to the bandstand and dance right in front of where Paul is playing his organ and singing. I watch the sweat glistening and sparkling from Paul's and Bernard's and Melvin's faces while the flashing colored lights shine on them. I look around and see Michael and Betty Lou, Pat Langley and Patti Abel, Dennis Phelps and Kathy Robb, Ricky Dyer and Mary Jo Dodson, and I'm burning up with pride and joy over the role I've played in creating this enchanted evening for all the couples who are going steady. It's a night none of us will ever forget.

When the lights come up, the only thing people are talking about is how great the band sounded and how this was the best dance they've ever been to. Not only did we raise far more money than we'd hoped to raise, but this is the first time in any of our lives, and in the history of our school, when so many black and white kids have shared an evening together.

Going out the door, my brother Michael turns to me and says, Pat, that was the funkiest dance this school's ever had. Way to go, man!

It's the proudest moment of my life.

Chapter 17

I'm returning from Indian Head, Maryland, with Ikie Wills and James Swann, two black boys I've known since I was small. It's raining like it does in one of those horror movies. Suddenly, my baby blue Renault slides across the road, flips over three times and lands next to a tree. We're all thrown from the car.

When we come together, no one is hurt. You'd never know it from the looks of the car. It's smashed together like an accordion. The cops show up and, after taking some measurements and talking to me for five minutes, they decide that the accident wasn't my fault. They help me get the car towed to Charlie Swann's gas station and then they drop all three of us off in La Plata.

I know I'm going to hear Aunt Vera's wrath like I've never heard it before. So, instead of going home, I stay with my mother for two whole weeks. When I return to Maple Knoll, my grandfather says very little about the accident. I know he's just glad I'm alive. Aunt Vera chews me up one side and down the other when she walks through the door from work. She makes it clear that I won't own another car unless I buy it myself.

And that's just what I end up doing. My Uncle Jimmy Mills has a green '59 Chevy Impala convertible for sale that's in mint condition. Though it's worth a lot more, he only charges me two hundred and fifty dollars. I have another job as a short-order cook at the Pirate's Inn Restaurant in La Plata and I'm making decent money. After I pay off Uncle Jimmy, I buy a new white convertible top, install a three-speed floor shift, an eight-track tape player, a pair of air shocks to jack the rear end up, and a set of Corvette rally wheels. I also buy a small racing air filter to go over the carburetor so that when you floor the gas, it makes the car sound tough.

On the last day of tenth grade, Father Whorten comes into our classroom with his German shepherd, Jackie, and wants to know who owns the fine-looking '59 Impala parked in his parking space.

I raise my hand and say, Sorry, Father, it was the only vacant spot.

Jackie starts humping Keith Dyer's leg and Father waves me off. Keith's embarrassed and tries to be cool by saying that the dog smells his collie, Fred. Father gives Jackie a command and the dog barks and then lets go of Keith.

All the boys and girls stifle laughter, and Father grins as Jackie lies down at Father's feet. Sister Gerald Marie is red in the face and tells the class to be still while she and Father finish their conversation out in the hall.

That same day I stop by to see my mother and she's all curled up in bed and crying like a baby. She's as pale as a cadaver and I'm terrified. I've never seen her look so sad and sickly. The flesh on her face droops like dough and her jet-black hair, which has always been meticulously styled, is streaked with gray and hangs in greasy strands. It looks like she tried to put on lipstick and lost her concentration and now her face resembles a sad clown. I also notice that her nightgown is on inside out.

Moma, we gotta get you some help, I plead, holding her hand as I sit on the side of her bed.

She's crying and hiding her head. After a minute or two, she turns over and asks me to call her sister Anna Lee and ask her if she can come over.

I rush out of the room to make the call and the whole time I'm terrified that Moma's going to die. I tell Aunt Anna Lee it's an emergency, that I think Moma's dying and to come over right away. After I hang up the phone, I pray to St. Jude, Moma's favorite saint.

Please, St. Jude, intervene for my mother and ask God to watch over her. She has a picture of you in her room and she prays to you all the time. Then I pray right to God to please let Moma be all right.

The ambulance pulls in the driveway and Aunt Anna Lee's right behind them. The rescue squad man bundles Moma up and lifts her onto the stretcher and off they go. The whole time Moma's crying and curled up in a ball, and she's so embarrassed that she keeps her face hidden.

They take her to Physicians Memorial Hospital, and they won't let me see her there, so I go on to work. The next morning, I call the hospital and the lady tells me they've moved Moma somewhere else but the lady's not at liberty to tell me where. I say, But I'm her goddamn son, and I have a right to know where my mother is! She apologizes and asks if I want to talk to a chaplain.

I say, Screw you and the fucking chaplain, lady.

I drive back to our old house and the place is sealed shut like a tomb. When I call Aunt Anna Lee, she says Moma's been admitted to the Crownsville State Hospital up near Baltimore. When I call the place, the receptionist tells me no visitors for two weeks.

I call Aunt Anna Lee back. She tells me to continue to pray. She says Moma's going to be all right after she gets some rest.

All the way down the highway I tell myself Moma's stopped crying by now and she's fixed her hair and cleaned herself up. When I see her again, she'll be like brand new. She'll look like Maggie again. The Maggie in *Cat on a Hot Tin Roof.*

At first I think I shouldn't drive up to Baltimore to see her because maybe her dignity's at stake. But when I weigh the humiliation and embarrassment she might suffer over my seeing her in an asylum for alcoholics against my own need to see her, my need wins out.

When I arrive at the Crownsville State Hospital, a black lady with no neck directs me to the building Moma's in. I walk through two sets of doors and another lady asks me whom I'm here to see. I say, My mother, ma'am. Mrs. Mary Evelyn Bair.

The lady directs me to another set of doors. I walk through them and see Moma sitting on the side of her bed fixing her hair. When she looks up and sees me entering the ward, she rises quickly and heads toward me in an obvious attempt to shield me from the view in the room.

Hello, Miss Mary, I say.

Hi, Pat. She hugs me until I say, Moma, you look great! Just like Maggie.

Thanks, Pat. I feel great, too. Let's go for a walk.

As Moma leads me off the ward, tears are rolling down her cheeks like miniature waterfalls. There's a black woman sitting on the steps outside Moma's building talking to herself. Moma says, Miss Elsie, I want you to meet my son Pat.

The mammoth woman stands and she's almost six feet tall. She's wearing a lime green dress that hangs over her huge frame like a tent. On her feet are work boots without shoestrings. The tongues are curled back toward her toes. Covering her black and silver wooly hair is an orange scarf that's tied in six knots under her chin.

Yeah, yeah, Miz Mary.

Elsie, this is Pat.

The woman looks at me and then down to the ground and then back at me. She's doesn't have a tooth in her mouth. Her smile is all pink gums.

Pat. Yeah, yeah, Pat. Hi, ya, Pat.

Nice to meet you, Miss Elsie.

All of a sudden Miss Elsie Polk starts laughing like a school on fire. Moma says, Elsie, behave yourself, girl, and Elsie stops laughing. She stares up into the sky.

You want to go to the commissary with us, Elsie?

Commissary. Goodies. Yeah, yeah. Let's go.

You can come along, but you have to behave, honey.

Yeah. All right.

We start down the sidewalk while Miss Elsie talks to herself and smacks her lips together as if she were chewing a wad of gum. *Smack, smack, smack. Yeah, yeah, yeah. Smack, smack, smack.* These sounds are followed by an explosion of laughter.

Inside the commissary I ask Miss Elsie what she'd like to have and she starts pointing to the barbecue potato chips, cheese crackers, chocolate chip cookies, and every candy bar on the rack.

I pick up several items as she's pointing to them and she says, Yeah, yeah. Um-um-um. Goodies.

Moma admonishes me to stop. She says Miss Elsie doesn't need all those sweets. But I don't dare. I know what it's like to have a sweet tooth, and to be lonely and longing for something sweet to make you feel better.

I'm standing in front of the cashier with an armful of candy bars, cakes, and bags of chips when Miss Elsie points to the chewing gum rack. I buy her the largest pack of Juicy Fruit they sell and watch her put four pieces in her mouth at once.

Smack, smack, smack. Um-um. Yeah, yeah, yeah. Goodies. Thank ya. Sho' is good. Smack, smack, smack.

We sit at the table and Moma orders ice cream sundaes for us and an ice cream soda for Miss Elsie. I tell Moma all about my job as a short-order cook at the Pirate's Inn and how the owner, Mr. McConnell, has just offered me a full-time job as evening manager at his other business, McConnell's Drive-In, a hamburger and ice cream joint that's a multiracial hangout for all the local kids.

She asks about Michael and Huck and Suzie and I tell her Mike's fine and I stop by to see Huck every other day and he's fine too. I haven't seen Suzanne, so I don't know how she's doing.

Pat, you're my first visitor and I knew you would be. Anna Lee is supposed to come tomorrow, but it's OK if she doesn't. You're who I wanted to see. Thanks for coming, son.

When we get back to Moma's building, she tells me she'll be home in another month. I tell her I want to come back next week to see her but she says no, she'll be home soon. There's so much I want to say to her, but leave without saying anything, and that's the way it always is. I want to tell her how sorry I am she had to come here and that I want more than anything for her to be happy.

I kiss her good-bye and start out the door, fighting back my tears. I'm thankful that she's found the will to get better, and I'm also proud as hell that she made friends with someone like Miss Elsie

Something's happening to me that I don't understand. I took the new job as night manager at McConnell's Drive-In and I love it. The jukebox is filled with my favorite songs by James Brown, Wilson Pickett, Junior Walker, Marvin Gaye, Sam and Dave, the Supremes, Otis Redding, and Archie Bell and the Drells. All the black kids I grew up with are in the place every day, along with my cousins Bobby and Mitch Mills and other white kids I know. I have a mint-conditioned car and a new girlfriend named Cindy and Moma's home and back to work at the La Plata Florist. I'm sure I should be happy and content, but I'm not.

Lots of nights, I cruise around looking for excitement and a new thrill. One night, Mitch and I pick up an older woman who buys us beer and a pint of bourbon for herself. We take her to a motel room and she strips for us. Then we take turns doing it with her and afterward I feel bad because the woman's real nice and she tells us how she lost her husband and daughter in a car accident and all she does now is drink and sleep with strangers.

Inside myself, I'm confused and lonely most of the time. I know there's something wrong with me, but I can't tell what it is. I can't even talk about what I'm feeling inside either because I don't know how.

Father Whorten asks me to serve Mass at a funeral he's doing and I agree to do it because I think it will bring me closer to God. But right in the middle of Mass, I feel like a hypocrite because I don't feel God's presence and I don't feel I belong on the altar. I vow right then and there never to step foot inside a church again.

One night I go to a dance without my new girlfriend Cindy and run into my old girlfriend Debbie. She's nice as she can be to me and it makes me sick because I broke up with her for selfish reasons. Seeing her brings back all the swell memories we had and now I think I'm still in love with her. And that's my biggest problem. I'll see a girl and fall in love with her right on the spot if she's my type. Then I'll do all the right things to make her fall in love with me. I'll fall in love with her until a new girl I want to be with comes along and then I dump the old girl as quick as that. It's the same with my mother and my aunts and uncles and every damn body else who's ever loved me. I can stand being around them for a while, and then I get sick and tired of their love and have to get away for a while.

But I know I'm not all bad because I do have some principles that I think I'd die for. I've just turned seventeen and I know that what distinguishes one seventeen-year-old boy from another is not so much the style of clothes he wears or the kind of car he drives or even the number of friends he has or the success or lack of success of his parents. It's what he stands for.

A couple of boys I know call me a nigger lover one afternoon in the White Room pool hall. I'm with a black boy named James Harvey and we're having a soda and playing a game of pool. A public school boy named Jerry Getty calls me to the side and says he wants to have a talk with me. I've never met Jerry Getty before, but I've heard about how he likes to fight and start trouble. He says, What're you doing, bringing that nigger in here?

I say, Man, everybody in the county knows and likes Harvey and the schools have been integrated, so what's your problem?

He says, Don't you know if you let one in, you gotta let another one in and then another and then the place turns to shit? They got their joints to shoot pool, and this is ours.

Well, guess what, asshole? I say. We're not leaving till we're finished.

Five minutes later, Jerry Getty and some of his idiot friends get up in our faces and tell us we have to leave. One of the boys says, This ain't nothing personal, Harvey, but y'all gotta leave.

Harvey runs the last two balls on the table then tosses the cue stick on top of the table. He says, Yeah, OK, motherfuckas, I'm leaving! You motherfuckas got some nerve!

We get outside and I say, Harvey, we gotta go back, man. We can't let them get away with this.

Harvey says, I drank wine with that punk motherfucka in the boys' room at school, man. Hell no, they ain't getting away with shit. They just took away our own black school and made us go to theirs and now I can't shoot pool in a public place?

The irony of the whole thing is not just the name of the place, the White Room, but it's also that two black night clubs called Pat and Gee Gee's and the Moonlight Inn are right up the street. These joints are still segregated, but only because most white people don't care to patronize them. I've always wanted to see the inside of the Moonlight Inn because groups like Junior Walker and the All Stars and Sam and Dave play there every summer.

Harvey pulls into Pat and Gee Gee's and goes inside by himself. When he comes back, he's got six other black fellows with him. We all get into the back of a pickup truck and burn rubber all the way to the White Room's parking lot. Harvey has a knife on him and I take it and stick it under my belt.

Jerry Getty and six or seven other white boys are standing in the lot. One of them is my cousin Bobby Mills who's just pulled up in his '64 Corvette. Jerry Getty steps forward and points his finger at me. My adrenaline is flowing and I'm ready for a fight because I know I'm in the right.

You got a smart mouth on you, punk! he says. You still think I'm an asshole?

He starts moving closer and puffing out his chest and arms like he's some kind of goddamn gorilla.

In one quick, motion I take the knife from my waist, step forward and pull the knife hard against his side. He throws his hands up in a boxing stance and then someone behind him tells him he's bleeding. Just as I'm about to stab him in the stomach, he backs off, puts his hand to his side and comes up with a wet red palm. Bobby Mills knocks the knife out of my hand and sucker-punches me. When I go down, he jumps on top of me and starts punching me. Harvey and another boy pull him off and Harvey says, Bobby, I know you ain't in this shit.

Bobby accuses me of starting the trouble.

One of the black fellows who came to help says, If you punk motherfuckas don't wanna get seriously fucked up, you'd better get your asses inside right now.

I'm still excited and wanting to fight. Jerry Getty's standing there with his t-shirt off, wiping the blood from the superficial cut. I stare holes through him until he and the others decide to go back inside. Then Harvey tells Bobby what happened. Bobby says, Harvey you know damn well you're welcome inside anytime I'm around.

Then he tells me I'd better watch my back because Jerry Getty's gonna be looking for me.

It doesn't take long before word spreads around that I cut Jerry Getty's side open with a knife. Some of the boys in my eleventh-grade class treat me like a hero when we're together at a party down on Chapel Point Road. But some of the same girls I've gone to school with and socialized with all my life won't even look at me now. My old classmate Francis Flynn is at the party, and he tells me that Jerry Getty's there too.

I say, Good for him, Francis. Maybe I'll go say hello to him. Where's he at?

Francis says, He's down on the shoreline with his girl and a bunch of other people. You want me to go with you?

Hell, no, Francis. If you went along, it wouldn't be a fair fight. Maybe we'll just sit here and hang out with you for a while.

At first I'm ready to leave the party because I have my girlfriend Cindy with me and I don't want her to see the bad side of me if Jerry Getty and I lock horns. But then I think, How's that gonna look if I leave just because a boy who wants to kick my ass is around? There's no way I'm backing down. I want Jerry Getty to know I'm here and not hiding.

Francis brings us sodas and then asks me twenty questions about how I've been doing since I got out of the boys' home. I'm telling him about Mark Franks and how I almost murdered him when Jerry Getty comes walking up the hill with his girlfriend. He tries to stare me down as he walks by, but I learned in the children's center that all you have to do when another boy's trying to intimidate you is fill your mind and eyes with rage and you'll never get stared down.

In the morning Aunt Vera comes in my room and asks me how my new white convertible top got torn. I get out of bed and run out to my car. There are two long slashes on the side of the car roof and I know right then and there that Jerry Getty and I are even.

My mind is everywhere but in my classroom. Sister Geneva tells me I'm wasting my mind and talents. I hardly do enough work to get by, and sometimes I turn in my homework too late. The only thing is, I'm not a behavioral problem or anything like that. What's different now is that I've lost sight of my goals and I just can't seem to concentrate for very long.

Two weeks before Christmas, I'm joyriding all over the county with Ikie Wills, Charlie Brown, and Bobby Mills. It's snowing like mad and it's a school night. We pull into my stepfather Maxie's old bar and grill that now has two gasoline pumps out front. The four of us are arguing over who's going to pay for the gas because the gauge is sitting on empty. It's my goddamn car we're riding in, and it's only fair that they chip in. But all three of them say they're broke.

I order two dollars of gas and when the attendant taps on the window to collect, I stick a .22 starter's pistol out the window and jokingly tell the guy to give me all the money.

He takes off running and I'm yelling to him to come back, that I was only joking. Instead of waiting around, I try to pull out of the place in a hurry and the car hits ice and goes sideways. We're stuck in a snowbank. Bobby, Ikie, and Charlie Brown get out to push and we're just about out onto the main road when a mob of drunks pours out of the bar and hurls beer bottles at us. When the first bottle hits the car, I fire the pistol into the air.

I yell, You motherfuckers better get back!

And they do. They don't know that the pistol's a blank.

Bobby, Ikie, and Charlie jump back inside and we speed off. We don't get ten miles down the road before we're swarmed by Maryland State Police cars. We pull over and we're immediately surrounded.

Freeze! Exit the car one by one! Drop to the ground!

Four angels in the snow.

When we get to the sheriff's department, a detective tells us we're all being charged with attempted armed robbery and conspiracy. Bobby, Ikie, and Charlie look at me accusingly.

Goddammit, say something, Pat! Ikie says.

I tell the detective I'm responsible for the prank, that the others didn't even know I had a blank pistol, let alone that I was gonna pull it out. Hell, even I didn't know I was gonna pull it out till I did. I was only fooling around, sir. This is all a mistake. The gun's not even real. So how can you charge me with armed robbery?

The detective says, You'll have to tell it to the judge, son.

Bobby and Ikie are released to their parents in a couple of hours, but no one comes for Charlie Brown and me. I don't have the courage to call my grandfather, so I try calling my mother. But she's not at home.

After sitting handcuffed to a chair for three hours, the deputy sheriff takes Charlie Brown and me to the juvenile section of the county jail, the same county jail I passed by on my bike when I was a small boy, cursing and teasing the prisoners as I went along.

A couple of days later, Mr. Buffington, my probation officer, comes to see me. This time, he tells me, I'm in serious trouble. The only hope I have of not being sent to the Maryland Training School for Boys is if I join the army. He says that Moma will have to sign for me because I'm only seventeen. He can arrange everything, he tells me, but I need to be sure that this is what I really want to do. He gives me the rest of the day to think about it.

I think about it all night. The last place I want to be is locked up in an institution with a bunch of crazy, violent boys. But every night when I watch the news, my skin crawls when I see American soldiers lying in rice paddies in Vietnam with their arms and legs blown off. All night I'm awake, thinking about this awful dilemma.

Army. Navy. Air Force. Marines. Choose one and you'll be freefreefree. It's not just a job, it's an adventure. Look, stupid, if you make it through, they'll look up to you. If you don't, they'll look down 'cause you'll be in the ground. And it's one, two, three, what are we fightin' for? Don't ask me, I don't give a damn, Next stop is Vietnam. And it's five, six, seven, open up the pearly gates. Well, there ain't no time to wonder why, Whoopee! We're all gonna die.

A section of last week's newspaper is sprawled out on the top bunk of the cell and it reads: World News. This month's body count rose to 2,494 American soldiers.

Holy shit!

A platoon of marines was overrun this morning by ARVN forces along the Ho Chi Minh Trail. There were no survivors.

No survivors. Oh, hell no! No, sirree, Bob! I will not join the goddamn army!

The next day I tell Mr. Buffington I'll take my chances before Judge Diggs.

Two weeks later I'm standing beside Mr. Pete Bowling, the lawyer Moma hired for me, and I try to explain to Judge Diggs that it was just a prank.

I wasn't serious, Your Honor, I say.

Well, by God, I am, young man, he says. I am committing you to the Maryland Training School for Boys for an indefinite period of time. I hope it does you some good, son. Sheriff, take him away.

The sheriff lets me talk to my mother for a minute before I leave the courtroom. She's crying and I tell her not to worry because they have to release me in five months when I turn eighteen.

Earlier in the morning I had rehearsed in my mind how I would respond if the judge sent me away, and one thing I knew I couldn't do is cry. There are three other boys in the juvenile section of the jail who are training school bound, and I can't let them see me cry. Still, I'm terrified as I hug and kiss my mother good-bye. I smile to let her know that I'm all right, and then they take me away.

On the drive to the training school, all I can think about is getting my act together so I can deal with whatever situations come my way. This isn't the Maryland Children's Center I'm headed to or some boys' home or foster home. This is a bona fide prison for boys. All the stories I've heard about the Maryland Training School for Boys and all the images I have in my mind now grip me with terror.

The sheriff seems to drive at a frantic speed. The cars and buildings and scenery we pass are one big blur. After a while, the terror settles into anxiety and sheer loneliness. In my mind it's like an Indy car race. At first Johnny Fear, the number one car is in the lead, with Mario Anxiety only a few car lengths behind. Cal Loneliness is coming out of the pits. On the last lap, Mario Anxiety gives Johnny Fear a run for his money but loses out.

When we pull up in front of the brownstone administration building of the Maryland Training School for Boys, Johnny Fear has taken over the race.

Chapter 18

I'm standing inside the receiving room of the Maryland Training School for Boys, waiting for the deputy sheriff to remove the handcuffs. Three boys with freshly shaved heads are seated on a bench, staring and sizing me up as the deputy hands my commitment papers to the female clerk.

I say to myself, A picture's worth a thousand words. The handcuffs are more than just a picture; they're notice to these boys that I'm mean and dangerous. When the cuffs come off, I shake the stiffness out of my wrists and take a seat next to the other new arrivals. I no longer feel dangerous. I'm terrified.

After the deputy leaves, I start pushing buttons inside my head until I find the one marked countenance.

All right, motherfuckas! I ain't scared of none of you punks. Leave me the fuck alone. Don't start no shit, there won't be none.

All the while I'm thinking these things, I'm about to throw up.

During the next two hours, other new arrivals join me on the bench. One by one we're escorted in and out of the receiving room; the photo ID room; the barber's chair; the medical examiner's room; and the psychologist's office. In every room, the goddamn people are unwilling or unable to shake off rudeness and indifference. *Don't they know this shit's traumatic enough!*

Somewhere between the psychologist's interview and the doctor's stoic examination, I push another button. It's the one that opens the door to the place where all my determination is stored. I make a promise to myself right then and there that I won't be intimidated or terrified by any of this. I won't go out of my way to pick a fight, but I won't run from one either. *I'll eat a little crow, fellows, but that's as far as I'm gonna go.*

After the last boy sees the doctor, all thirteen of us march in single file out the back door of the administration building and onto the main grounds of the training school. The January wind stings our freshly shaved heads like a whip while we march around a field that's flanked by a row of white cottages on either side. The parade stops in front of the last cottage on the left. A plaque over the doorway reads Howard Cottage.

We are escorted to the basement where our last names are already written on a piece of masking tape that's stuck to a metal locker. We walk to one end of the room where a boy is standing behind a counter chewing on the handle of a plastic spoon. Over the counter is a sign that reads, Basic Issues. The boy hands us a set of bed linen, two towels and a washcloth, underwear, socks, three pairs of khaki trousers and three shirts, a cap, a pair each of dress shoes and work boots, a navy pea coat, a toothbrush, a bar of soap, five postage stamps, four cigarettes, and a plastic comb.

After we shove our things in the locker, the cottage mom, Mrs. Jon John, introduces herself and tells us what we have coming during our four-week stay in the orientation cottage, how to behave, and what will happen if we don't. When Mrs. Jon John pauses, a chubby white kid belts out he wants a phone call.

Mrs. Jon John tells him he'll get one in two weeks if he behaves himself. Then she tells us we can watch television or play table games in the dayroom until it's time for bed.

I sit on the bench away from the others and try to determine which boys are the toughest. Sometimes you can tell by looking into a boy's eyes how tough he is. Sometimes you can tell by his voice and the things he says. But not always. Sometimes a quiet, soft-spoken and soft-looking boy will take your head off if you provoke him just a little. My experience in the Maryland Children's Center reminds me to be ever vigilant. I pretend I'm in some kind of survival school and there are lessons to be learned.

Lesson one: Don't stare. Learn to look into the eyes of another boy long enough to acknowledge his presence and register in his mind's eye the countenance of anger and confidence you wear on your own face. If you don't, you must be prepared for retaliation: *Hey, what you lookin' at, white boy? Somethin' in your eye, motherfucka? You lookin' at me, punk?*

Lesson two: Exude a tough guy, I-don't-give-a-fuck attitude as naturally and as often as the opportunity arises. Use other boys as your role models. *Now, class, here's how you pull this lesson off. While reading your mail, let your cigarette hang from the corner of your mouth like James Cagney and turn your head sideways to keep the smoke from burning your eyes. Every now and then, let your eyes glaze over with rage like Stanley Kowalski. Oh, yeah, and put a hitch in your giddyup; in other words, when you walk, walk with a gait, a dip, a stride, that says I'm a bad and dangerous boy. And when you enter a crowded bathroom, don't hesitate to make your way through the crowd and to the urinal and hold your hang-down proud.*

At nine o'clock, they put us to bed in a dormitory where all thirty boys sleep three feet apart. They make us get on our knees and pray some stupid prayer that's not even a Catholic prayer. Then the night watchman tells us we have to sit up in bed and raise our hand anytime we want to use the latrine in the middle of the night.

The next morning after breakfast, Mrs. Jon John walks us through the cottage, assigning duties in groups of three. The dayroom, bathroom, shower, and locker room are in the basement, and this is where she assigns me and three boys named P-Rat, Elmo, and Funky Melvin.

All day we paste-wax and shine the burnt red cement floors on our hands and knees. Mrs. Jon John walks behind us, checking our work one by one as we rub and wax, push and pull the gray wool shine rags and wooden brushes over every inch. None of us speaks while we work. At least not in words. Our body language says it all: *Missed a spot, I got it. I need a break. Can you help me? Heads up. Here she comes.* On the second day, our knees open up like tomatoes. I kneel on two wool rags, hoping it will ease the pain, but it doesn't help. It only stops the blood from getting on the floor.

After five days, I get my first three letters from home. One from my mother, one from my grandfather and Aunt Vera, and one from Sister Patricia Navard. My grandfather and mother send love and money orders. I'm reading the letter from Sister Patricia Navard when P-Rat and his friend Funky Melvin sit down beside me.

What you in for, Middleton? P-Rat says, rubbing the scabs on his knees.

I say, Armed robbery.

How long you here for?

Till I'm eighteen.

Me too. Say, me and Funky Melvin's been checking you out, and you're all right for a white boy.

Gee, thanks.

So listen, man. We're going over the hill. You wanna come with us?

Naw, man. I'll be eighteen in four months and they can't keep me any longer than that.

You sure?

Yep. Thanks anyway.

OK. See you later, white boy.

Two hours later a whistle blows and word is two boys went over the hill. We're all told to stand against the wall to be counted. Two boys are missing. P-Rat and Funky Melvin. I hope they get away.

The next day I'm called to the counselor's office and told I have to take a high school grade level placement test. I tell the man I'm in the eleventh grade at Archbishop Neale

School in La Plata, Maryland, so why do I have to take a placement test. He says it's routine and mandatory.

My test scores put me in the twelfth grade and they move me to another cottage a week later.

On my first night in Charles Cottage, a fight breaks out in the basement lavatory. I'm standing at the urinal conjuring up images of running water, which is the only way I can get the flow started when there are other boys around. I hear someone say, You ain't tough, nigger. Another boy says, Lemme show you.

I'm peeing when the fight goes down. *Niagara Falls. April showers. Hey, fellows, I don't mean to rain on your parade, but I have to go.*

I shake the last drops of rain and turn around just in time to see blood splatter against the wall. The boy standing over the black boy looks ten years older than any of us. He's tall and broad shouldered with thick, hairy arms and wiry eyebrows accented by a perpetual scowl on his face.

No one saw the pool ball until it rolled across the floor, smeared with the blood of the black boy who said, Lemme show you.

The next morning, the cottage counselor interrogates us one at a time. When it's my turn, I tell him I just got here and I don't know anything. He says, Get out and send in the next boy.

Ms. Viola Plenty, the cottage mom, says, OK! Since none of you saw anything last night, you can all see the inside of this cottage for the next month. That means no movies, no canteen, and no playing ball. And during your free time you can all clean every damn inch of this place. Do you hear me? Are there any questions? Anybody want to hit *me* in the head with a pool ball?

They call Ms. Viola Plenty the crazy bitch with the cock-teasing hug. One minute they say she's consoling a boy so closely that their groins kiss, and the next she's beating him into submission.

During my second week in Charles Cottage, I'm washing dishes when I personally witness that Ms. Viola

Plenty is all they say she is—stone crazy. A boy named Boy-Boy smacks Little Andy in the ass with a dish towel and Ms. Viola Plenty, who isn't anywhere to be seen, sees it all. She shoots out of the pantry and hits Boy-Boy upside the head with a plastic whiffle ball bat.

Ms. Plenty screams, Do you want to be incorrigible forever? If you do, you'd better find somewhere else to practice, boy!

She hits Boy-Boy three more times before she grabs Little Andy by the scruff of the neck and beats him across his ass until he says ten times what she tells him to say: *I will not horseplay when I'm supposed to be drying dishes.*

After witnessing the wrath of Ms. Viola Plenty, I save all my scrutiny for the grease and grime on the pots and pans. I take my time and get every black mark and every speck of food off every pot that's put in front of me.

Any boy here who says he's not afraid is a goddamn liar. Sometimes I get so afraid that my hands sweat profusely. My mouth gets as dry as a cotton ball, and my heart pounds like a war drum. Sometimes my thoughts zig and zag like a game of connect-the-dots, all because I can't concentrate because I'm so worried about showing others how afraid I am.

Some boys get so afraid they crack like an egg and spill tears on the floor the first time another boy bullies them out of something. Once they expose themselves this way, their options are forever limited. They're forced to submit, they succumb to any pressure they encounter, and they're used and abused. Some of them see it as a trade-off. In exchange for being someone else's doormat or pansy, they're given protection and security. In reality, they rid themselves of anguishing fear and terror and replace it with a fear that's more bearable.

Most of the boys take the other extreme. They fight. They say to themselves, *I'm not gonna take shit from anyone. Fuck being afraid. I'll fight the biggest, baddest motherfucker who comes along, and I'll use whatever it takes—a baseball bat, a hammer, or a chair—to protect myself. Nobody's gonna fuck with me.* These boys turn fear into a very dangerous weapon.

Then there are those who may have started out carrying a knife and possessing the guts to use it, but they discover another way to proceed, a way that's more palatable to their temperament and disposition. Mr. Charles Dickens, the author of *Oliver Twist*, calls these boys the artful dodgers. Manipulation and the con are the tools of their trade, panache their calling card. The artful dodger makes an art out of getting what he wants. Like one of those cardsharks, he always keeps a trick up his sleeve, a hole card. He's acutely aware of his environment, of the strongest and weakest forces present, and he usually has the savvy to win the graces of those who present a potential threat to him. As soon as I met Oliver Twist in the pages of that book, I knew we had everything in common.

At the Maryland Children's Center, every older boy had a story about how some boys get banged in the ass here. The stories are enough to multiply one's fears.

Although I'm afraid and I squeeze my anus tighter than a vise grip the first time I witness a boy getting reamed in the ass, I keep my composure. In my second week in Charles Cottage, I walk into the shower room and see a black boy lying on his goddamn stomach with his underwear crumbled down around his ankles. I watch from the corner of my eye as I pass by the boy and two other larger boys standing over him staring at me as I pass. I stare straight ahead at the wall as if they're not even there. My heart's pounding and I'm afraid as hell, but I don't show it. I take the shower all the way on the end and say a prayer while I'm washing myself. I pray, God, please keep me safe from sexual perverts and other bullies.

I don't even bother to dry off when I finish showering. I slip on my underwear and walk away as the two boys take turns lying on the smaller boy's back. I swear to God I'll never let this happen to me. *But what if you're overpowered? Well, they'll still have to unlock that vise grip.*

And what if they succeed in doing that? Then, goddammit, they'd better make me like it!

It doesn't take long to discover it's a privilege to be in Charles Cottage. There's no waxing floors on my hands and knees here. Three times a day I wash and put away the dishes. Between meals I study geometry and social studies and in the evenings I beat every boy in the cottage in table tennis. One evening, two boys get in a simple fistfight over what television show they want to watch. Ms. Viola Plenty separates them and tells them to clear out their lockers. Ten minutes later, the boys are transferred to Baltimore Cottage. Ms. Viola Plenty tells them they can fight all day once they get there. Then she tells the rest of us she will not tolerate fighting, bullying, or back talking.

I learn too that the black boy I saw lying on his back in the shower isn't a victim at all. Every night, he turns tricks for candy bars and cigarettes in the shower or one of the bathroom stalls. They call him Candy and he walks and talks just like Hilda Brown, a pretty black girl who attends Archbishop Neale.

Moma's getting married for the third time. She sends me another money order and says she won't be able to visit because she's going on her honeymoon. I'm hurt that she's not coming, but I get over it when Sister Patricia Navard comes to see me. She's looking out the window when I enter the dining room where we receive our visitors.

I say, Hello, Sister, and the second she turns around and sees me, she starts bawling. She stands and hugs me. At first I feel awkward as hell, but then I forget she's a nun and hug her like she's Aunt Vera.

We sit down and Sister's still crying. I almost belt out, goddamn, Sister, it's not that bad here, but I catch myself and leave off the goddamn. I say hell instead and Sister grimaces.

She says, Patrick, we've missed you. The sisters send their love. How have you been getting along?

I tell her about the whole goddamn ordeal and how I shouldn't be here because I wasn't really robbing the place.

When it's her turn, she wants to talk about my hunting accident. Something she says hits me like a kick in the groin. She says, Has it ever occurred to you that maybe you knew the safety wasn't on?

I say, Sister, what are you talking about?

I think you knew, Patrick. I think you were crying out for help.

You think I let my cousin Wayne pull the trigger just so I could get some attention, Sister?

Not attention, Patrick, but love.

Come on, Sister, that's crazy. I don't want to kill myself.

I'm not saying you do. I don't think you were consciously aware of what you were doing either. But didn't you tell Wayne it was OK for him to pull the trigger because the safety was on?

Yes, Sister, I think so.

Why would you tell someone they can pull the trigger if the safety is on? Can you explain that to me, Mister?

I don't know, Sister. I never really thought about it before.

Well, I want you to think about it for me. Will you do that?

Yes, Sister.

She puts her hands inside her robe and produces a small white box, opens it and removes a multicolored cross on a sterling chain.

This is for you, she says. It's from all of the sisters.

Thank you, Sister. I'll never take it off.

When she's gone, I'm really sad. Seeing her reminds me of all my classmates and the other sisters and how much I miss them all. I'm confused, too, because Sister Patricia-Navard thinks I tried to kill myself, and she's a goddamn psychologist.

Two days later, my childhood companion Billy White walks through the front door of Charles Cottage and we're happy as hell to see each other. He's two feet taller than he was the last time he and I went stealing Coca-Cola bottles from behind the Foodland store, but he's just as skinny and he's still wearing double-thick eye glasses that are two sizes too big for his face. Now his face is blotched with acne.

I say, Look what the goddamn cat drug in. Billy White, man, it sure is good to see you!

He says, Hey, dude. Far out. The last time I saw you, you were serving the ten o'clock Mass at Sacred Heart.

Yeah, and still faking my Latin. Now we're both goddamn criminals. So what'd you do to get here?

Dude, I was dealing the best acid in Charles County. My chick brought this cat around who seemed hip, you know? He got high with us a couple of times, man, and I thought he was cool so I sold him a hundred hits of orange sunshine. The next day I got arrested. The creep was an undercover cop, man. It freaked me out. What about you?

I'm standing there practically amazed because after listening to him, I realize that Billy's turned into a bona fide hippie. He talks just like the hippies I met the times I went to Georgetown with Jimmy Tree and he sort of tiptoes when he walks, which gives the appearance that he's floating. Billy's always been weird, but now he seems a little weirder. Now he wears a perpetual smile on his face, probably the result of taking too many acid trips. Still, it's the coolest thing to know that someone you've known all your life turns out to be a goddamn hippie.

I say, They got me for a stupid armed robbery that I didn't even commit. It was all a misunderstanding. They said I tried to rob a gas station attendant, but I didn't. I was just fooling around.

Billy says, Won't you be eighteen this year?

Yeah. In three months. They have to let me out of here in three months.

Yeah, me too. Hey, I heard you got shot a couple of years ago, man.

It was a deer hunting accident, that's all. So you want to study together for the high school equivalency exam?

Yeah, man, that'll be cool.

I'm about to take Billy down to the basement and show him around when Ms. Viola Plenty walks in the room and says to him, Are you Mr. White?

Billy says, That's me, ma'am.

Ms. Plenty says, Go downstairs and put your things in your locker. Find the one with your name on it. Then report to Mr. Donovan's office. Milliton, you come with me.

I follow Ms. Plenty into the dining room where we're alone. She adjusts her eyeglasses and says, I need someone to clean my apartment, Milliton. Someone I can depend on and trust not to steal from me. Can I depend on you?

Yes, ma'am, I say. I'm very dependable, Ms. Plenty.

That's good. You can get started right now. Come with me.

I follow her to the third floor and into her apartment. The second I lay eyes on the room, I wonder why she hasn't hired two more boys to help me. There are cups and saucers and bowls and dirty clothes scattered all over the living room. We walk into the kitchen and the dirty dishes are stacked two feet high in the sink. Knowing that Ms. Plenty has a headful of moods, I'm careful not to show my amazement.

You can start in here, Milliton. Take your time and do a good job. You don't have to clean the entire place in one day. Save some work for tomorrow. Now here's a pack of cigarettes and a book of matches. You'll have to give them back to me before you go back downstairs. I don't want anybody accusing me of playing favorites. You understand that, don't you, Milliton?

Yes, ma'am.

I'm about to tell her my name's Middleton, not Milliton, when she opens the refrigerator and invites me to have a soda.

Don't drink them all, Milliton. I'll be around to check on you later. Do you have any questions?

No, ma'am. I'll just get started.

When she's gone, I open the pack of cigarettes and take out five. I light one and stash the others down in my sock. Then I open the refrigerator and take out a grape Nehi. It takes me five minutes to find a bottle opener in the bottom of the sink. After I gulp down the soda, I wash every last dish in the sink and put them away in the cabinets. Before I scrub the kitchen floor, I light another cigarette and drink another grape Nehi.

The next day, I clean the living room and help Ms. Viola Plenty change the sheets on her queen-size bed. I stand on one side and pull the sheet down while Ms. Plenty does the same on her side. When she leans over, I see the curves of her chocolate brown breasts and when I stand up straight I have to turn away to hide my stiffness.

Ms. Plenty leans against the dresser, shifts her weight, and stands on one foot, scratching the back of her calf with her toe. Watching her painted red toe nail scratching her velvet leg is such a sensuous gesture that it fills me with excitement and gratitude.

Ms. Plenty says, Thank you, Milliton, I can manage from here.

I say, Yes, ma'am, Ms. Plenty. I'll go clean the bathroom now if that's all right.

That's fine, Milliton. Just be careful with my ceramic geegaws over the toilet. My late husband won them for me in Atlantic City. Have you ever been to Atlantic City, Milliton?

I say, No, ma'am, but I've been to Ocean City, Maryland, lots of times.

Have you? Then you must have eaten salt water taffy before.

Oh, yes, ma'am.

You like?

I sure do.

Well, I have three different flavors. Maybe I'll give you some after you clean the bathroom.

That'd be nice, Ms. Plenty.

In her bathroom, the door closed, I squeeze my groin and look around the room for things that are familiar to me. A bottle of Chanel. A jar of skin cream. Feminine hygiene deodorant. A lavender bra and matching panties hanging in the shower.

I run the bathwater so Ms. Plenty can't hear me and then I take the lavender panties off the line and place them against my cheek. I close my eyes and picture what I just saw of Ms. Plenty's pretty brown breasts and it's over the minute I touch myself. I lean against the door, excited to giddiness, and muffle a grateful sigh.

Spending my days in Ms. Plenty's apartment is almost like being free. She lets me play her record player and turn the television on when I'm cleaning her living room. She has every Sam Cooke record out and all the old rhythm and blues 45s I grew up listening to. Sometimes we sit on her couch eating taffy and she talks to me about her family. She tells me about her twin sister who died at birth so that Ms. Plenty could live. I come to know her dead husband, whose picture is in every room of her apartment. She teaches me how to sew buttons on my shirt and how to iron a stiff crease in a pair of pants. She shows me pictures of her when she was a child with pigtails. She was the cutest thing.

In the evenings, Billy and I study math and sentence structure rules. I give him extra cigarettes and candy bars that I smuggle out of Ms. Plenty's apartment. Sometimes we talk about our hometown and the fun we had together and what we're going to do when we go home. We stay to ourselves and watch each other's back and the other boys know without having to be told that Billy and I will go down fighting for each other even if it means getting kicked out of Charles Cottage.

Every night when I go into the basement lavatory to relieve or wash myself, I'm introduced to a new lesson on the ways of criminality. Soap and water will remove the ink marks from used postage stamps so you can use them again. A double-edge razor will mold perfectly into the end of a heated toothbrush to make an awesome weapon. Placing masking tape over glass will prevent the glass from shattering and mute the noise during a midnight burglary. Boxcars are a pair of fours in craps and snake eyes are a pair of ones.

One Saturday, our cottage goes on a field trip that's intended to discourage us from our criminal ways. They take us to 954 Forest Street in downtown Baltimore, the address of the hundred-year-old Maryland State Penitentiary. Some of the boys are giggling and joking that we're going to tour the University of Maryland. Before we get off the bus, Mr. Donovan, our cottage counselor, makes a speech.

Mr. Donovan says, Fellows, what you're about to witness is no laughing matter. We're going inside the toughest prison in the state, and one of the toughest joints in the country. This is the Maryland State Penitentiary. We want you all to see firsthand what prison looks like on the inside. If you have any questions during the tour, save them until we get back outside and the guard or I will try to answer them.

Every one of us is cocky and arrogant until we pass through the administration entrance and the iron gates slam shut behind us. They take us to a room where a huge prison guard shouts at us to take our clothes off. He makes us bend over and spread our ass cheeks while another guard shines a flashlight on us and barks orders as if we're real prisoners.

After we're dressed again, we follow the guide to a huge cellblock that looks just like ones I've seen in the movies. It's five stories high and as long as a football field. It reminds me of a human beehive made of cement and steel bars. Heavy mesh screens separate one section of the colossal hive from another. Everywhere we turn there are bees staring at us with desperation and lust in their bulging dark eyes, and their mocking reproaches.

Hey, you pretty white thing...Sweet boy, sweet boy. Come up to my room, won't you? I've got all kinds of cakes and pies and cookies for you...One-potato-two-potato-three-potato-four, my name's Daddy Pimpin' and you gonna by my whore...Swing low, sweet cherry ass...

The fat, greasy-haired sergeant who's escorting us shouts, You men get off the tier and back inside your cells. He's smoking a raggedy black cigar that looks like a turd on fire.

We reach the middle of the cellblock and the sergeant turns around. Welcome to the big house, boys. He speaks like a tough guy and I think he probably is.

Before we leave the block, I take one last look up at the massive beehive and into the eyes of the tattoo-covered killer bees who are still leaning over the rails and raining cat-calls down on us. At that instant, something deep inside tells me, as sure as a trump card, that I'll be back here to stay one day.

When we get outside, no one asks a single question.

On the last Saturday in April, thirteen of us board the training school bus for one last field trip. Our destination is a local high school auditorium. We're going to take our high school equivalency exam. Billy and I try to sit near each other in case we need help, but the examiners seat us alphabetically and we're spaced several tables apart, so we can't possibly cheat. Just about every topic or subtopic we studied is on the test. After five hours, we're finished and glad of it.

The day the test results are posted, we're called into Mr. Donovan's office one by one and given the news. Billy comes out wearing that perpetual smile of his.

I got it, Dude, he says. I'm out of here, man.

I congratulate him and then it's my turn to go in.

Mr. Donovan says, Congratulations, Middleton. You're now a high school graduate. And by the way, you're going home on May 15.

I'm going home on my goddamn eighteenth birthday.

Chapter 19

The day I register for the draft, I hear Edwin Starr's new song on the radio: *War/What is it good for?/Absolutely nothing.*

I already have my mind made up that I'll go to Canada before I let them send me to Vietnam. I'll be a goddamn conscientious objector. It's not that I don't love my country or that I'm not patriotic or anything like that. During my childhood, I had my share of plastic soldiers and toy tanks and model warships and fighter planes. I played G.I. Joe with the neighborhood boys and killed my share of Japs and Krauts. *Combat* was one of my favorite television shows and I often dreamed of being a real soldier one day.

But that was before I saw all those caskets being unloaded from the rear end of cargo planes every night on the evening news. One of those caskets contained the body of Bobby Shegog, a boy Michael and I knew from Little League. Bobby hadn't been in Vietnam long before he had his limbs blown off and died.

I watch the protesters too. We have no business being over there, they say. Those Vietnamese people haven't done anything to us. When I visit my grandfather one Sunday, he tells me the war's about stopping Communism from spreading. I ask him if we're winning and he says it doesn't seem that way, and it could go on for a long time. I tell him I'm worried about getting drafted and he says I shouldn't worry. He gives me a letter to take to the draft board when I go to register. It's a certified letter from Dr. Arturo Montero, the doctor who saved my life when I was shot, and it details the extent of my injuries.

When I hand the letter over to the draft board doctor, he tells me to get undressed for a physical. I give an Academy Award performance when it comes to removing my shirt. I fake like my left arm is as dead as a goddamn broken tree limb. The doctor takes a good, long look at my scars and tells me to get dressed. He gives me a 4-F status, which means I'm completely exempt from the draft.

While I was away, Moma moved to Forestville, Maryland, with her new husband, Bill, who's a life insurance salesman. He's almost twenty years older than Moma, and he treats her like a queen. I've never seen her so happy.

When I move in with them, Bill does everything to make me feel welcome. He and Moma take me shopping and buy me new clothes, and Bill helps me wire my new stereo system in my bedroom. He's a decent man and I really like him.

I don't waste any time getting a job. The man who owns the Shell service station across the street from our apartment hires me on the spot. The place has four bays and it does a thriving business. It's located right up the street from the main entrance to Andrews Air Force Base, where the president of the United States keeps his airplanes.

My new boss, Mr. Hill, lets me take on jobs I've never done before all because I show confidence. One day I change the water pump on a big Chrysler Imperial. When I finish and start the engine, water leaks all over the place. I take everything apart and discover that I forgot to include the gasket. I learn two valuable lessons—that time is money and I have to be more careful the next time.

During the first three months I'm home, I save just about every dime I earn for a decent car. The only money I spend is on personal tools so that I can repair cars off the job. For three months I don't go anywhere except to work and back and to the swimming pool in the apartment complex once or twice a week.

The worst thing about these first few months home is that I'm lonelier than I've ever been. Sometimes I get depressed, I'm so lonely. Many nights I go to bed thinking about my old girlfriends and classmates and how much I miss them. I'm living in another county now where I don't know a soul, and there's no way I can see any of my old friends until I have my own car. Wanting to see them keeps me focused on working double shifts and fixing cars for people who live in our apartment complex so I can earn additional money.

By the end of the summer, I have enough money saved to buy a sharp-looking metallic blue '64 Chevy Impala. The first weekend with my new car I drive down to Charles County looking for some of my old friends. My cousins Mitch and Bobby Mills and big James Gant, a black boy I grew up with, are sitting at the counter inside McConnell's Drive-In. They're all nice to me but what strikes me hard is that they seem indifferent, as though I was never away and their seeing me again is anything but a big deal.

I drive up to Waldorf intending to stop in to see my grandfather, but at the last minute I turn in my old girlfriend Debbie Wilson's driveway. She's nice to me too, but the first thing out of her mouth after hello is that she's going steady with someone. I'm just about sick to my stomach, hearing her say it.

On my way out of the county, I swear I'll never come back except when I come to visit my brother Huck. I'll find new friends and to hell with all of my old ones.

The next weekend I discover a real popular singles club called the Quenset Hut that's only a couple of miles from our apartment. The place is on the Maryland-D.C. line and it draws a lot of girls from all over the metropolitan area. I meet this girl named Joanne who's twenty-two years old. She's tall and beautiful with platinum blond hair and blue eyes. I fall in love with her instantly.

For the next eight months I'm at Joanne's house almost every night. She's divorced and has two little boys. On welfare, she receives little money from her ex-husband, so I offer to help her pay her bills. Sometimes I take her little boys to the park and buy them toys and candy.

One night, Joanne's bawling like a baby when I walk into her apartment. At first she won't tell me what's wrong. She keeps saying over and over that it's not my problem. That's a fucking game girls play. I get angry as hell and threaten to leave and that's when she drops a bomb on me. She tells me she's pregnant and needs money for an abortion. Having the baby is out of the question, she says, because she's doing all she can to take care of two boys. She just can't handle another child.

Not to mention the fact that the last thing I want is to have this kind of responsibility hanging over me. Moma reminds me every time I go out the door to be careful and make sure I don't get any girls pregnant. Now I've done it, and I'll be goddamned if I'm going to let this happen when I can do something about it. I really care about Joanne, and I want to do the right thing, so I go to my boss and borrow the three hundred dollars she needs to get the abortion.

I'm on my way to her apartment to give her the money when this fat girl named Teresa who lives in the apartment below Joanne's stops me in front of the building and says she has something to tell me. Teresa is Joanne's babysitter and she's real nice. There's urgency in her voice and I'm thinking that something awful has happened to Joanne.

I follow her into her apartment and when we get inside she invites me to sit down.

Pat, I've got something to tell you, she says, but you've gotta swear you won't say anything to Joanne.

I say, Yeah, OK. I'll keep it to myself. What is it, Teresa?

Joanne's not pregnant, Pat. She's moving back to Texas and she's trying to play you for whatever she can get.

Goddamn, I say. Are you sure? Is that what she said?

Yes. She even bragged that she hasn't let you have sex with her for four or five days because she's been on her period and you think she has a yeast infection.

My stomach knots up and I feel sick all over.

So the bitch is on her period. Well, ya can't be on the rag and pregnant at the same time, now can ya? Liar! Liar! Cunt on fire! But it's OK. It's OK. Turnabout's fair play. Turn the game around like a goddamn tennis match. Advantage MIDDLETON!

In the few seconds it takes me to think these things, I already know what I'm going to do.

Teresa, why in the hell are you telling me about this?

She looks at me shyly and says, Because you're a nice guy and you've been really good to her and her little boys.

I reach out for her hand and she gives it to me. I'm so thankful to her and tickled pink that she tipped me off and saved me from being *had* that I kiss her.

Right before I leave she asks me again to swear not to tell Joanne. Then she invites me to come back and see her sometime. I assure her I won't say a goddamn word and I promise to visit her one night real soon.

Walking up to Joanne's apartment, I realize she's been using me all along. I think about all the times right before we'd have sex when she broke down about how she needed money to pay this bill or that bill, and every goddamn time, I left the money on the table for her. I feel like a sucker that's been licked a few times and then thrown in the dirt. And to think I was crazy about this *bitch. Yeah. And she was just about to play your stupid ass like a slot machine.*

The more I think about it, the more I want to punch her in the face. But, hell no. I'm going to turn the beat around. I'm going to get even.

I walk into her apartment and she's all smiles after I tell her I have the money she needs for the abortion. She throws her arms around me and says real seductively, My yeast infection's all cleared up, and the boys are in bed. She's wearing a black nightie and smelling sexy sweet.

Here's the money, Joanne. I pull three one-hundred-dollar bills from my wallet and drop them on her coffee table. Then I turn out the lights, take her hand firmly in mine, and lead her to her bedroom.

In the middle of the night when she's sleeping soundly, I gather my clothes and walk into the living room. I snatch the bills from the coffee table and then I empty out her purse. A packet of airline tickets falls to the table and I'm excited to no end to see them. Three one-way tickets from Washington National to Dallas. She's leaving tomorrow.

Well, turnabout's fair play, wouldn't you say, Jo?

I rummage through her change purse and snatch her diamond ring. Then I count her money and take two one-hundred-dollar bills and leave the small bills for her. *I'm outta here.*

Getting even with Joanne makes getting over her a hell of a lot easier.

In September, I land a great new job as a mechanic at the Potomac Cab Company in Washington, D.C. It's a decent forty-hour-a-week job with the opportunity for pay raises every six months. I'm hired as a tune-up and brake job mechanic. After two weeks on the job, the owner Mr. Kellogg has me doing other jobs that involve troubleshooting electrical shorts, changing water and fuel pumps and head gaskets, and pulling blown engines and replacing them with rebuilt ones. The business is located right off South Capitol Street and there are usually a dozen or more cabs sitting around waiting to be serviced. I work right alongside the head mechanic, a fellow named Charlie who's eager to teach me whenever I ask him for help. Charlie tells me I'm a natural at turning wrenches and I can make a decent living for myself.

I like my work so much that I enroll in a yearlong night course at Lincoln Technical Institute. The school is only a few blocks from the cab company, so on the evenings I have classes, I usually stay and do extra work until I get hungry. I get my supper at a soul food takeout joint that's second to none. I get to know a fine-looking black girl who works there and we flirt back and forth. I want to ask her out, but I never do because there's always a brother around and I don't want any trouble.

The classes at Lincoln Tech are fascinating to me. Most of the other fellows in my class are already decent mechanics and are enrolled because they want to learn the finer skills of rebuilding engines, diagnosing and rebuilding automatic transmissions, and using engine analysis machines. The course is expensive, but well worth the money.

On Saturdays I drive down to Charles County to see Huck. I always give him a few dollars. He's only eleven and I know what it feels like to be eleven and have dollars in your pocket. Sometimes I take him back to Moma's for the day and evening. He loves being with me just as much as I love having him around.

When I just about blow the clutch out of my car, I drive into La Plata to see if I can find Duck Willis, a top-notch high-performance mechanic. I want a four-speed transmission for my car and a new clutch. Duck has worked at the Texaco station in La Plata since I started high school. He and his brothers Nathan and Edward were daily patrons of McConnell's Drive-In when I worked there. They're all good fellows. Duck owns a '64 Pontiac GTO with a 427 Corvette engine in it. It's the fastest car in the D.C. area. There's only one other car around that might be faster, and that's my cousin Bobby Mills' '64 Corvette. They'll probably never race because Bobby and Duck are good friends.

Whenever some fellow comes along to challenge Duck to a race, people come from all over to watch and bet. My cousin Mitch Mills and I once watched Duck smoke a '69 Camaro. Duck took home a wad of money.

I find Duck wiping his car down on the side of the service station. We talk for a half hour before he says, Yeah, Slick. I can get you what you need, but can you get me what I need?

I say, What the hell's that, Duck? I got the money to pay you.

He says, I need some white girls, man. And as smooth as you are, I know you got plenty of them.

That's all you want, Duck? Hell, that ain't nothing. I can get you all the white girls you want.

Wait a minute, Jim, he says. I'll put your car together for nothing, but you've got to pay for the parts. The only thing's free's the labor.

True to his word, Duck has a rebuilt four-speed transmission wrapped in a plastic sheet in the back room of the service station. He gives me a decent price on the trans and tells me he'll order the clutch, pressure plate, and throw-out bearing on Monday and sell it all to me for what it costs him. Then he offers to throw in a Holley dual-feed high-performance carburetor that will increase my horsepower.

The weekend after Duck transforms my car, I take him into Georgetown. Duck looks a little like Marvin Gaye and he dances real smooth. By the end of the night, he has a real cute-looking girl on his arm. He teases me because the girl I hook up with is drunk and her girlfriend won't let her leave with me. Duck's a real goddamn sport, though. He says, Don't worry, Slick. I'll share mine with you.

We drive up Wisconsin Avenue until we find a dark side street. I pull into an alley and Duck asks me to take a walk around the block. When I return ten minutes later, he's standing outside the driver's door smoking a cigarette. He says, Go ahead, motherfucka, but don't take all night.

I have to wake the girl up and then she wants to argue with me until I tell her I'll take her to get something to eat after we're through.

For the rest of the summer, Duck and I hang out together just about every weekend.

One night Duck takes me into the Moonlight Inn where my friends Paul Wills and the Corvettes are performing. Duck fixes me up with a pretty yellow-skinned girl named Beverly who's a good friend of the girl he picks up. After the dance is over, we ride around half the night listening to Aretha Franklin and Booker T & the MGs.

At five in the morning, Duck gets a room at Swan's Motel. He tells me to wait in the car until he's finished and then the girl and I can use the room. Three hours later,

Duck's still in the room. I knock on the door a dozen times and Duck finally appears. He says, Motherfucka, what time is it?

I say, Christ, Duck, you've been in there three hours. It's eight thirty.

Oh, shit. We gotta go. Look, man. I need you to do me a favor.

What kind of favor?

Take these girls home for me. I have to be somewhere in a half hour. I'll drop you off at your car and you take them home for me. All right?

Shit, Duck. You're trying to stiff me, man. Where in the hell do you have to be on a Sunday morning? Tell me that.

I ain't trying to stiff you, motherfucka. I'd do it for you. Look, here's the key to the room. All you got to do is take the one girl down to Bel Alton and then you and Beverly can drive back here and stay till noon if you want.

I don't want the damn key, Duck. We couldn't wait any longer. We already did it in the backseat.

No, you didn't! Not in my car, you didn't!

Yeah, we did.

I know there better not be no goddamn stains on my seat.

There aren't, Duck, for Christ's sake.

There better not be.

Back at the Texaco station where my car sat all night, the girls say good-bye to Duck. Before I get out of the car, I look at him curiously.

Duck, I was wondering about something.

Come on, I gotta go. What?

Where do you have to be on a Sunday morning?

Church, man. I gotta take my mother and sisters to church.

Well, I'll be damned, I say. You are one hell of a fellow. I'll call you next week, all right?

Yeah, OK.

Duck lays rubber and waves back at us before he turns on to Charles Street and disappears.

Two weeks later, Moma wakes me up on Saturday morning and says there's two detectives at the door who want to speak with me. She says, You haven't done anything wrong, have you?

I say, Hell, no, Moma, not that I know of.

I get dressed quickly and walk to the door where these flattop-wearing state police detectives eye me up and down like I've done something wrong.

Are you William Patrick Middleton?

Yes, sir?

Is that your '64 Chevy parked out front?

Yes, sir.

Were you driving that car last night?

Yes, sir.

Would you mind riding down to the state police barracks with us, Mr. Middleton? We want to talk to you about your activities last night.

Am I under arrest, sir? What's this about?

You're not under arrest, Mr. Middleton. We just want to ask you some questions.

I can refuse to go, but I don't because I don't want them to start asking me questions in front of my mother, even though I haven't done anything wrong. It's one thing to be questioned by the police; it's an entirely different matter to be questioned by the police in front of your mother.

When we get inside the interrogation room, both detectives let loose with a barrage of questions.

Where did I go last night? Who was I with? What's his name? Where does he live? Do I know the girl in this photo? Did I have sex with her? Did my friend?

I answer their questions and then ask one of my own.

So what's the problem?

The problem, the cop says, is that the girl says you and your buddy raped her.

Holy Mother of God! No! No! No! Say it ain't so, goddammit! I didn't rape nobody.

A valve opens up inside my head and my whole body's flooded with fear and anxiety.

I say, I don't have anything else to say until I talk to a lawyer.

They charge me with rape and assault and battery and take me to the Charles County jail, as the so-called rape took place on a back road in Charles County. Later that night, they bring Duck in, and he sends a note up to my cell. It says, *Don't say nothing!*

Duck doesn't need to tell me a thing. I've been around criminals long enough to know better than to offer the cops any help. I'm already angry at myself for letting them dupe me into telling them that Duck was with me. I won't give them the time of day.

The next morning the detective who arrested me comes to my cell with a medical doctor. He says that the girl I had sex with has a venereal disease and the doctor is going to give me a shot of penicillin to protect me. I refuse to take the shot. I don't believe him for a second.

We go before the judge on Monday morning for a bail hearing. I'm absolutely sure I'm going to get out on bail, because Moma has hired Maurice Flynn, the best criminal trial lawyer in Charles County, to represent me.

But, goddamn, I'm wrong. Duck gets bail after his NAACP lawyer who comes all the way from Baltimore points out to Judge Diggs that Duck has never been in trouble a day in his life. The judge refuses to set bail for me. Instead, he has me committed to a fucking mental institution for a thirty-day evaluation.

Alone in my cell that night, I break down and cry for the first time in a long time. I'm thoroughly disgusted with myself. I always have to show off, to be the big shot, and now it's backfired again.

Kind of hazardous to your own health, aren't you, buddy? You're all by yourself again, aren't you? You don't have any friends, do you? With friends like you, Patty boy, who needs enemies?

I stare into the metal mirror on the wall and I'm ashamed at what I see. I was doing so good. I had a great job. A nice car. I was saving money for my own place. And now look.

For a lack of anything better to do, I open the Bible on the table and start reading. I get all the way to the story about Judas Iscariot and how he betrayed Christ before I toss the Bible back on the table and bury my head in the pillow.

You sorry motherfucker you. You knew damn well that girl didn't want Duck screwing her. Remember? She said she didn't want to do it with him. And you told her to just go along with it. Remember! And then you watched Duck mount her and part her like the Red Sea. You remember?

Yeah, I remember, all right, but it wasn't exactly *rape*.

The next day the sheriff's deputy drives me to the Clifton T. Perkins State Hospital. I'm so filled with anger and self-contempt that I don't pay much attention to old Johnny Fear. The place is a maximum-security institution for the criminally and mentally insane and all that, and I suppose I should be good and scared, and maybe I am, but I don't let myself acknowledge it. I can hide my fears and worries just like I imagine a prisoner of war hides his contempt for his captors. No sooner do I get on the ward than I force Johnny Fear way down on the apron of a sharp curve and put him right out of the race. In the time it takes to blink my eyes, I take on the countenance of a *you'd-better-not-fuck-with-me-'cause-I'm-a-little-bit-crazy-too-fellow.*

After two days, I find out who the crazies are on the ward. Every time the opportunity arises, I position myself near them and talk their talk—a babbling, incoherent gibberish. I talk to myself and respond. I hold conversations with imaginary foes. *Oh, say can you see? Why you lookin' at me? By the dawn's whorly light, oh so bright. How you been? Why you ask? What so proudly we wail. You writin' a book, motherfucker?*

But it's all overkill. There are only one or two really dangerous and scary men on our ward, and they're kept drugged and in leather restraints. Most of them are as innocuous as a fucking scarecrow.

During my thirty-day stay, I sometimes lose myself in the lives of these men. I wonder what kind of life they had, what happened to make them so pathetic, if they'll ever be normal again, and if they ever were in the first place. I sit and play cards with some of them and I can't help but think how much better off I am. Though I'm very much aware that I'm living in my own house of agony and turmoil, I can't help but think that God has dealt these guys a crueler blow. Acknowledging this makes living with myself a little easier.

The interviews start coming during my second week. A train of social workers, psychologists, psychiatrists, and counselors. One tests my IQ; another, my eye-hand coordination and dexterity; another, my ability to draw a house, a tree, and a female. Another shows me the same cardboard squares with blots of ink spilled on them that they showed me at the Maryland Children's Center.

The doctor says, Tell me what you see on each card.

Well, let's see, I say to myself. *In this one I see my mother lying across the bed naked with her legs spread open. And in this one I see her voluptuous breasts. See right there is the outline of her nipples so hard they look like little bullets, don't you think, Doc?*

These are the sorts of images you would want to report seeing if you want to be declared seriously disturbed, I was told. That not being the case, I say what I actually imagine I see—a butterfly, a spider, a volcano, a bat with a cut on its ear, and things like that.

Another doctor shows me a series of pictures and tells me to put my own story to each picture. My imagination reels. I go into so much detail, conjuring all sorts of plots and circumstances, that the poor old doctor gets frustrated and tells me to try and complete the story in a sentence or two.

This other doctor who has hair growing out of his ears keeps his eyes closed practically the whole time I'm in his office. He wants to know about my childhood and my siblings and mother and my rotten stepfather. After I tell him about them, I tell him about my grandfather and aunts and uncles and how they love my siblings and me so much. Then he asks about my dear old dad. He says, What does your father do for a living?

I can't tell him because I don't know the answer. I think I remember being told he's some kind of traveling salesman or something like that, but I'm not sure. Besides, I really don't want to go into personal details with some stranger who's about as warm as a fucking ice cube.

The doctor goes, Wait a minute, son. Go back a minute. What do you mean by this or that? How did that make you feel?

I'm glad as hell when it's all over.

Thirty days pass and I'm back at the county jail. Two detectives bring in a black fellow who is charged with raping and killing two fourteen-year-old white boys he picked up hitchhiking on Route 488, a back road that leads from outside the city limits of La Plata all the way to Waldorf where my grandfather lives. His name is Lamont Robinson and he's twenty-two years old, but Homer, the jailer, puts him on the juvenile side of the jail, to protect him from adult prisoners who might kill him for what he did.

This idiot's cell has a perfect view of the shower room, and his second day there, he sees me drying off when I step out of the shower. As I'm walking back to my cell, I pass by his door and he has his face pressed into the square opening in the door; he's licking his lips like a goddamn dog. His eyes are rounder than half dollars as he stands there moaning and saying something about my milky white skin.

That night the pervert sends me a note with a piece of cellophane from the outside of a pack of cigarettes attached to it. The note reads:

> You got the prettiest skin I ever seen. If I could get out of this cell tonite I would come into yours and make love to your pretty white ass but I can't so I want you to do something for me. I want you to jerk off into this

*piece of plastic and send it over to me later tonite. Keep
this to yourself white boy or you'll be sorry!*

After reading the note I call over to my friend Charlie
Brown and tell him about this freak. Charlie says to read the
note out loud so everyone can hear it. When I don't because
it's so embarrassing, Charlie calls himself having fun by
taunting the maniac.

*Hey, you ugly-ass niggah! You black piece of shit!
Everybody knows you sucked them white boys' dicks before
you killed them, you dick-eating faggot! They gonna fry your
dumb ass! You want some cum, niggah? I'll give you some
cum!*

And on and on he goes until the whole cellblock is up
on their doors screaming and laughing and just having fun.

The next morning I call my lawyer to let him know
I'm back from the nut house and would he please get me out
on bail. It will take at least a week for the hearing to be
scheduled, he tells me. *And what if the judge won't give you
bail? What if those loony tune doctors wrote in their report
that you're socially maladjusted? What then, boy? What if
they want to commit you? Fuck 'em. If they commit me, at
least I know the place ain't as bad as all that.*

It's Thursday night and Reverend Duley is preaching
on the cellblock. Homer says he's been coming here every
Thursday evening for twenty years. A farmer by day and a
preacher by night, he's a giant of a man with thick hands,
dirty fingernails, and a mat of black hair held together by
some cheap hair grease. His black suit and tie are so wrinkled
and worn out that they've lost their sheen.

What amazes me about Reverend Duley is that he has
a loving smile on his face even when the prisoners ridicule
him, shake their hang-downs at him when he passes by, and
shower him and God with the worst cusswords one can
imagine. Sometimes they spit on him, and once a prisoner
hurled a cup of piss in his face. Reverend Duley is immune to
these attacks. He reminds me of Christ the way he walks
about the tiers totally oblivious to the hatred and madness.

The first time he stopped in front of my cell, I told him what I thought of his religion.

As a Catholic, I've been taught that there's only one true religion—ours. Reverend Duley says, It doesn't matter what team you're on, son. You must mend your ways, for the wages of sin are death. Jesus loves you, but you need to repent and turn your life over to Him.

I tell him about the experience I had at the Holy Roller church the time I was living with the foster family and how that sort of environment freaked me out. He says, That sort of worship has nothing to do with whether you believe in Jesus Christ as your personal savior.

He reads to me from the Bible. I drop my head and close my eyes in an earnest effort to concentrate. He asks me if I honestly believe that God would allow only Catholics into the kingdom of heaven.

He says, Do you truly believe that all the good Christian brothers and sisters in the world are going to be denied a seat in heaven just because they aren't Catholics?

Reverend Duley is a smart man. I'm thinking of the foster family I stayed with and how close they were to God. And if God won't let them into the kingdom of heaven, then I don't want to go either. It just doesn't make sense to me that people like the Shoop family and this meek and humble Reverend Duley are going to be kept out of heaven just because they aren't Catholics.

I look at the Reverend and say, I believe that anyone can get to heaven if they believe in Christ.

He asks me to pray with him. I bow my head nervously, for I'm not used to praying the way Reverend Duley prays. He ad-libs and speaks to God as if God is right there in the room.

When he finishes, I tell him I'm getting out on bail in a couple of days and I probably won't see him again. He gives me a card with the name and address of a church on it. He says, Go there one Sunday, and you'll find people who will love and care for you like you've never known before.

Thank you, Reverend Duley. Maybe I will.

I lay on my bed and read the words on the card he left me. The Pentecostal Assembly of God Church, located on Morningside Road in Camp Springs, Maryland. Services on Sunday mornings at 9 and Sunday evenings at 7:30. Youth services held on Friday evenings at 7:30. I fold the card and turn it over in my hand. Then I start the prayer every Catholic says when he enters the confessional. Bless me, Father, for I have sinned.

Chapter 20

The city streets, sidewalks, and houses in the neighborhood where Moma and Bill have bought their new house greet me like a friend the day I get released from the county jail. The new three-bedroom house in District Heights, Maryland, is only a few blocks from the Washington, D.C. line. It has a finished basement and a chain link fence that runs all the way around the house and beautiful flowers and shrubs along the border. A sidewalk runs down the length of our street and curves around the corner, where it continues on for miles and miles in both directions along the business district.

I taste my freedom with a high strut and stroll past the florist shop, the Giant food store, the shopping center, the Kentucky Fried Chicken joint, the funeral parlor, the movie theater, and the Catholic high school and cathedral. I pass several fine-looking girls along the way and it feels good just saying hello to them as they walk by. Though Christmas is still a month away, I feel as if it's already arrived for me. I'm living right in the pulse of the big city, and I love the hustle and bustle.

Within a couple of weeks, my life comes together like a five-card straight. While I was locked up, I had to sell my car to help Moma pay for the attorney, and now I'm in dire need of transportation again. Only a week after I'm home, my brother Michael signs over his -'66 Plymouth Valiant to me, as he has just bought a brand-new car.

My old boss at the cab company won't hire me back, so I have to look for another job. Michael helps me get hired on at the Potomac and Electric Power Company (PEPCO) where he works. I get hired as a steam operator at the Buzzard Point plant in Southeast D.C. I hate the job from the get-go, but I'm glad to be working right away. It's one of those union jobs where you have ten men doing the work that two men could easily do.

I work the midnight shift and the only busy hour or two of work occurs early in the morning before sunup when we have to fire up all the boilers to produce enough electricity for when the city wakes up. Most of the night we play cards or sleep or sit around talking. The fellows I work with are a decent bunch, mostly married guys who are committed to their families. It feels good to be around these kind of fellows after being in jail for sixty-odd days with a bunch of goddamn criminals.

Having a decent job and my own transportation relieves a lot of my anxiety and worries. Every day I pause and think: *You're doing fine, kiddo. You've got a good job, a way to get around. Now just maintain a steady course and things will work out like a charm.*

But no sooner do I think these things than that doubting rat comes gnawing through my harvest of optimism. *Yeah, but something's wrong, damn it. You've been happy before, you know. Don't fake it, buddy. It's only a matter of time before you fall flat on your pretty face again. Something's missing and you know it. Can you find what it is? Come on, make the connection... Ah, who played that song?: "Someone to care/Someone to share/To be loved/ To be loved."*

The second Sunday I'm free, I drive down old Morningside Road until I see a new church up ahead. The sign on the front lawn reads: Pentecostal Assembly of God Church. I pull into the new parking lot in the rear and it's almost filled. Families with children and teens my age are making their way inside the back entrance. A little girl skipping across the parking lot in a pink dress sees me pressed down behind the wheel of my car and waves at me.

I get inside a few minutes before the service begins and slip into one of the pews near the back. Every pew is filled with men, women, and children of all ages, just like Reverend Duley said it would be. Two children in front of me turn around and smile, their faces beaming with joy and beauty. The young couple sitting beside me turns and smiles, too, extending warm handshakes to me. After I get through these initial greetings, I'm relieved and a little calmer.

I look around the room and the first thing I notice is there's no holy water bowls anywhere, no statues or stations of the cross. No scent of incense in the air. But the place is beautiful. A teal carpet covers the floor all the way up to the altar, where it changes to plum red. There are long narrow stained-glass windows on both sides of the room and a huge frosted-glass window in the shape of a cross behind the altar. The light from the sun illuminates the cross.

During the sermon I can't concentrate on what the preacher is saying. I'm too busy observing the rituals and habits of the congregation. Aside from the fact that no one genuflects or makes the sign of the cross or answers tired old phrases from a tired old priest with one foot in the grave, not a single person is rolling in the aisles. Several people seem to be encouraging the preacher.

What impresses me the most is how normal and happy all the people seem to be. When you grow up Catholic, you're encouraged to believe that non-Catholics are hopeless people. But these faces that shine and beam with love tell me something different. These people are praying alongside their family members and truly worshipping God, not showing up for church out of habit and obligation.

When the service is over, I get up quickly to leave with the full intention of returning next Sunday. I turn around and I'm surrounded by a reception of men and women who introduce themselves and welcome me to their church.

A whole entourage of teens walks up to me and introduces themselves one by one. A boy who's about my

age asks me to come back for the evening service. I'm so overwhelmed by everyone's hospitality that I accept, even though I've never been to church twice in the same day in my entire life.

He says, My name's Mark. What's yours?

Pat. I'm Pat Middleton, and it's nice meeting all of you.

For the rest of the day all I can think about is that a whole new world may have just opened up to me.

The evening service lasts about an hour. After this gospel quartet sings a beautiful song called "He Touched Me," the minister invites anyone who wishes to be *saved* to come to the altar. It's a very stirring moment for me. For one thing, the song is unlike any song I've ever heard sung in church and it's so awesome it makes me cry. As I watch the young people around me praying with their eyes closed and their faces shining so radiantly, I know they have something that's special, something I've never seen before. These kids have a living relationship with Jesus.

I look around and see husbands and wives holding hands and praying together. Grown men are crying tears of salvation as the quartet sings. *He touched me/Oh-oh, He touched me/And all my sorrows turned to joy/Something happened, and now I know/He touched me and made me whole.*

Hearing those words sung in perfect harmony and the soft cries of the church organ and watching people holding hands and weeping joyous tears while the minister beckons softly from the microphone causes me to collapse right there in the pew and cry uncontrollably. I start talking to Jesus like I've never done before.

Can you really, Jesus? Can you really take away all of my worries and fears? I have so many, you know. And can you save me too? Can you save me from doing these stupid things I do over and over?

I feel hands pressing against my shoulders and I hear the minister whispering, Come to Jesus. He'll take away all of your worries and fears. He will love you like you've never

been loved before. All you have to do is ask Him. Won't you come now? Anyone. We invite you to come. Jesus wants you now.

The boy who invited me to come tonight and his girlfriend have their arms around me.

Jesus loves you, Pat, Mark says.

And so do we, the girl says.

Once again the minister extends an invitation to anyone who wants to be saved.

I stand and walk down the aisle to the altar. I kneel and the minister kneels in front of me. The boy Mark and his girlfriend kneel on either side of me.

The minister says, I'm Pastor Morris. What's your name?

Through a veil of tears I say, Pat, Reverend.

Welcome to our church, Pat. Are you a born-again Christian?

I'm Catholic, Reverend, but I want to be *saved*.

Do you believe that Jesus died on the cross for you?

Yes, I do.

Do you accept Him as your personal savior?

Yes, I do.

Lord, this young man Pat is coming to you humbly and asking you, Lord, to open his heart and come inside. Fill him with your spirit, Lord, and let him know your love and grace.

The pastor continues to pray over me for several minutes. Before he moves on, he welcomes me again to his church and invites me to return on Friday evening for the youth service. I assure him I'll come.

After the service, I meet several more boys and girls who are in their early and late teens. There's Brian and Cindy, who are both seventeen; Mark and Karen; David and Lynn; Sue and Linda Pervis; and Becky Morris, the pastor's daughter. They invite me to come along with them to the International House of Pancakes, which I learn is a Sunday evening ritual for them.

It's enough that I leave the church filled with the spiritual experience I had at the altar, for I was moved in a way I've never experienced before. But at the IHOP the kids make me feel like I'm the most special person in the world. They ask me to be a part of their group, and they press me to say I'll come back.

Without any trace of doubt, I know I'm being invited to be a part of something that's very special; for these are the most polite and loving kids I've ever been around.

As the weeks pass, I come to know all the boys and girls in the congregation and their families. Just about every Sunday I'm invited to dinner at a different house. I can't get over how awesome these people make me feel. But then I start to wonder if they'll feel the same about me when they learn about my past. One thing I know for sure, I'm not about to spoil the roll I'm on by telling anyone now.

Moma says I sure have turned over a new leaf. That's because I'm starting to act like the boys and girls in the church. I start praying and reading the Bible every day. Almost overnight, my disposition changes. I'm more cheerful and considerate than I've ever been and my fits of withdrawing and giving others the silent treatment are a thing of the past. I've even stopped riding around looking for girls and masturbating. Even while driving in my car I pray and sing the new gospel songs I've been learning. For the first time in my life, I feel clean inside.

One thing that really sells me on these kids and their faith is that I haven't once heard one of them swear or call one another names or stay angry for very long. I watch like a hawk for the first sign of hypocrisy among them, but there is none. They love Jesus morning, noon, and night, and complacency is nowhere to be found among them. Not one of them has the slightest inhibition when it comes to witnessing to strangers about the love of Jesus Christ.

Their weekend activities are straight out of a manual on ways to have wholesome fun and live a clean Christian life. These activities are a real culture shock to me, but I welcome them the way I imagine Lazarus welcomed his new life.

On Friday nights, we go roller skating or to the movies or out to eat. Sometimes, we go to one of their houses and play charades. One Saturday afternoon a bunch of us go to the mall in front of the Washington Monument. We boys play flag football, while the girls throw Frisbees around.

What really scares me is that I'll come out of the trance I'm in. I'm already aware that my greatest temptations are subtly calling out to me. There are three or four teen couples going steady, and I wonder if any of them are going all the way. I'm hoping with all my heart they are because physical intimacy is one need I know Jesus can never help me with. If these boys and girls are so good and dandy that they don't need physical love and passion, I reason, then they're too good for me.

One night my question is answered when Brian asks me to pray with him because his girlfriend Cindy is late with her period and might be pregnant. I pray alongside him and at the end of my prayer, I thank Jesus that at least one of these Christian couples shares my need for physical intimacy.

The more I see young couples together and sharing affections on our youth outings, the more I begin to long again for a girl of my own. I keep a close vigil on all the girls in the congregation who seem available. Every time I look her way, this girl named Linda who sings in the church's quartet is staring at me. I ask Brian about her and he says she's twenty-two years old and married. When I ask where her husband is, he says, Vietnam.

I'm nervous as hell when Linda asks if I want to go and get something to eat after a youth service gathering. I end up telling her my whole life story and about the criminal charges that are hanging over me. I start crying. We're sitting at the edge of the McDonald's parking lot and she reaches out to hug me. She tells me everything's going to be all right because I have Jesus in my life now. Then she prays to Jesus out loud while she runs her fingers through my hair and continues to hold me. Afterward, I feel as though a ball and chain have been lifted from my neck, and I don't want to let go of her.

The next Sunday morning something happens that almost makes me walk out of church and never return. I'm sitting in the pew beside Brian and Cindy and the gospel quartet has just stepped up on the altar to sing. Linda, who's looking finer than a runway model, smiles and winks at me very innocently. It's one of those gestures that says, I'm in your corner, friend.

But Brian nudges me and says, You naughty boy. We saw you two leave together on Friday night.

Being a jerk, I smile like I have a secret. The thought now planted, I look around at all the couples sitting together, and I lose myself in a fantasy about Linda. I remember how I felt two nights ago when Linda hugged me and my head was pressed against her breasts. I had started to get an erection but fought it off by remembering my grandmother on her deathbed. It's a trick I learned as a child whenever I had to wipe a smirk off my face. All I would have to do is picture the day my mother pulled me out of school to see my grandmother one last time while she lay on her deathbed smiling up at me. Picturing myself holding her shriveled old hand and watching the tearful faces of the grownups in the room always waxed me angelic.

But I don't think of my grandmother for long now as I begin to fantasize uncontrollably about Linda. I try with all my heart to think about Jesus.

In the name of Jesus I reject these thoughts. Linda, I want to fuck you so bad!... Come here, Pat. Touch my breasts. It's OK. We're both vulnerable right now... No-No-No! Jesus, help me, please! This isn't fair! Lay down with me, Pat. Kiss me. I'm yours, yours, yours... "He touched me/Oh-oh, He touched me/ (louder) OH-OH, HE TOUCHED ME? AND ALL MY SORROWS TURNED TO JOY."... Lord, Jesus, help me, please! Rid me of these evil thoughts.

The more I cry out inside for Jesus, the dirtier my thoughts get: *Come here, Pat. Lay me down right here on the altar and fuck me, you handsome boy... Jesus fucked Mary Magdalene, you know?*

But Jesus is nowhere to be found. When I can't control my thoughts, I feel so defeated that I want to get up and leave. *You can't even act right in church, goddammit. Who are you trying to fool anyway? You can't hang with these people.*

But I'm hell-bent on making a home in this church. I'm not about to give up the good feelings I get when I'm here, so I stay in the pew.

After the quartet finishes singing and Pastor Morris announces the youth retreat that's taking place the last weekend in January, the closing hymn is sung and I walk to the altar and make a genuinely sorrowful act of contrition.

For the next couple of weeks all Brian and Mark and the other kids talk about is the weekend retreat they're headed for in the mountains of western Maryland. Sixteen of the kids from our church have signed up. At first I don't have any plans on attending because I don't have a girlfriend and I don't want to be alone. But then Mark and Brian assure me that lots of girls from other churches will be making the retreat and it doesn't matter anyway because they want me to go.

On the last Friday in January, we leave in a little caravan early in the morning for the two-hour trip to the retreat lodge. There are five cars in our group and the church bus. I have just bought a '66 Chevy van and Moma made curtains for the side and rear windows and gave me a thick piece of carpet for the rear floor.

The back of the van is filled with blankets, sleeping bags, and small suitcases and duffle bags. Nestled together in the middle of the floor are Brian and Cindy, Mark and Melinda, and the two Ranson girls. We're singing songs and telling jokes and having a great time. Linda Pervis rides up front with me. She's on the U.S. Olympic kayak team and all she does is train and go to church. She's tall and pretty and has a husky voice. She's as sweet as a box of chocolate candy and I like her. The problem is that she doesn't date and when I ask her why, she tells me it's a long story and she'll tell me some day.

Snow is falling like a benediction when we reach the mountaintop and pull into the lodge. We're right in the middle of a magnificent pine forest. All around the lodge are beautiful log cabins. The girls' quarters are on one side and the boys' on the other.

In the center of the grounds is the main building that's made of beautiful white stone and glass. The stone walls go up about four feet and smoke glass windows about eight feet high take over, wrapping around the building like a pair of giant sunglasses.

We go inside to get our cabin assignments and all these pretty girls are standing around in tight jeans and sweaters. They're wearing lipstick and eye shadow and they've done all they needed to look glamorous.

Praise the Lord! I say to myself. *I'm going to have one of these pretty Christian girls!* I make eye contact with one or two of them who are smiling at me, and my countenance is that of a once incorrigible boy.

We get settled into our cabins and there's two hours to kill before dinner. Brian, David and I decide to visit the cottage where the girls from our church are staying.

I open the front door and storm inside.

This is a raid, ladies! I say.

The girls scream and giggle. Some throw pillows and hairbrushes at us, and others cheer. Brian and David find their girlfriends and start making out. As we're leaving I notice this beautiful girl with long blond hair sitting on the top bunk near the front door. She has the bluest eyes and the prettiest smile I've ever seen.

I stop in front of her bunk.

Tonight, I'm coming back to kidnap you, I say.

She says, Promise?

Yes, I do.

We get outside and my heart's pounding. I grab Brian by his jacket and demand to know, *Who's that gorgeous girl, man?*

Brian says, That's Pam Simpson. Her and her mother and little sister go to our church.

Yeah, well, how come I've never seen her before?

They come every Sunday, Pat, but they always leave right after the service. They don't come to evening services and Pam doesn't attend youth services either.

I have to meet her, that's all there is to it. How old is she?

She's a senior at a private Christian academy in Washington, D.C. If you want, I'll introduce you to her tonight.

No, that's OK. I'll introduce myself.

From the time we leave the cottage until I see her again at dinner, I'm obsessed with the image of her face and hair and smile.

In the dining hall I pass by her table and we exchange smiles. Then I say a prayer. *Please, God. I haven't asked you for much. Let this girl be the one for me, Lord.*

I'm so excited and nervous that I can hardly eat a crumb of food.

After dinner we all go outside and there's a thick blanket of snow on the ground. Someone starts throwing snowballs and the next thing we know it's the girls against the boys. A little girl comes up to me and hits me in the face with a delicious snowball. She's giggling and pointing at the blond-haired, blue-eyed girl named Pam.

The little girl says, That's from her.

I pick the little girl up and twirl her around and she laughs hysterically. Before I let her go I give her a big hug and say, Thank you, precious. You just made my night.

Pam is bending over making a snowball when I tackle her. I'm sitting on top of her about to wash her pretty face with a handful of snow. We look into each other's eyes and I know without a hint of wonder that I'm in love with her. She's staring back at me and I say, I'll let you up if you'll go inside and have a cup of hot chocolate with me.

She says, That would be nice.

We sit by the fireplace with our hot chocolate and she tells me about her family and school and how she can't wait for her senior year to be over. We start talking about music and she tells me she listens to Black Sabbath.

I say, That's not very Christian-like, is it?

She says, No. My mom doesn't know I listen to them.

Before we return to our cottages for the evening, I say, Do you have a boyfriend? If you do, I think I'm just gonna die right here and now.

She smiles and shakes her head no.

I say, Thank you, Jesus. I'm so glad. See you tomorrow.

During the night another snow storm moves in and the next morning we're told we have to evacuate the mountain because there isn't enough food and supplies to last if we get snowed in for more than a couple of days. I find Pam and ask her to go with me while I call my mom. The pay phones are all being used, so we have to stand in line and wait. We're disappointed because we have to leave.

But then they make an announcement that everyone's to meet at the National Guard Armory in Frederick, Maryland.

We rush back to our cottages and throw our belongings together as if we're on our way to a bomb shelter. I meet Pam back outside as she's about to board our church bus, and I'm so ecstatic over the way I feel about her that I forget to ask her if she wants to ride with me. It's as if I'm not even sure that this is all real.

She says, I guess I'll see you at the armory.

I say, Sure for.

What'd you say?

For sure.

But her bus never arrives. I spend the entire night in abject misery on the floor watching the other couples snuggled together in their sleeping bags.

Some luck I have, I think. What if something happened to her? What if I never see her again?

My nerves come undone for the two days it takes me to get her unlisted phone number. After calling every Simpson in the phone book, I call Pastor Morris's house and the pastor's daughter, Becky, answers the phone. I tell her I need the Simpson girl's phone number because she left her boots in my van. Becky says, The Simpsons have a private number and I'm not supposed to give it out.

I say, Well, I really do need to return her boots and, besides, I'm not a stranger.

She gives me the number.

Until now I've been as confident as God when it comes to calling girls. But now I'm not so confident. I want Pam more than I've ever wanted anyone in my life, and I'm afraid that she might not feel the same about me. I play one round after another of that old game called what-if. What if my tongue ties in a bow and my words and sentences turn dyslexic when I hear her voice? *Thigh, maP. This is Rat. Go out and chatterbox would you, please, with me on Saturday if the weather's nice on a picnic?* Or what if she says, Hello, who is this? I'm sorry, but I don't know any Pat. Oh, God, I'll die right there on the spot. Or what if she does remember me and says, Pat, you're really a sweet boy, but I'm not interested after all. And what if, oh, man, what if she does like me but then doesn't want to have anything to do with me once I tell her about my past?

These are my neurotic worries.

But then I call her and she says hello as if she's been expecting me to call the whole damn time. We talk for two hours before she tells me her mother needs to use the phone.

I ask her if she'd like to go to a movie this Saturday and she says, I'd love to.

Two Mules for Sister Sara is playing at the RKO Keith Theater, and it's the perfect opportunity for me to tell Pam about my Catholic school upbringing. I tell her that most nuns don't act like Shirley MacLaine, and she reminds me that Shirley MacLaine's only disguised as a nun, that she's really a prostitute in the movie. Then we start talking about the Vietnam War and I learn she's a fervent follower of President Nixon and a dyed-in-the-wool Republican.

But I'm immediately impressed by her knowledge of social and political events and by the way she expresses herself. When I tell her it's high time Nixon gets us out of Vietnam, she reminds me that he didn't get us there in the first place, but says he'll definitely get us out. Not only is she beautiful and glamorous and witty, she's the most intelligent and reflective girl I've ever known.

We end up debating about Nixon's workfare proposal, a program that's designed to do away with one of President Johnson's most important entitlement programs for the underclass. She says there are lots of people on welfare who are capable of working. I say, Yeah, but what kind of jobs are available for them?

Every issue we debate, she wins because all I can think about is that I want to spend the rest of my life with her.

Before I take her home, I take her to meet my mother. While we're there, we go into my bedroom and play one of my favorite records and I sing along. It's Jay and the Americans' version of "Walkin' in the Rain":

> *I want her, I need her,*
> *And some day, some way*
> *Wo-oo, wo-oo-wo, I'll meet her*
> *She'll be kind of shy*
> *And real good looking too,*
> *And I'll know that she'll be my girl*
> *By the things she likes to do...*

When the song's over, I tell her the song's about us, that she's shy and beautiful and I'm crazy about her. Then we kiss until it's time for her to go home.

On the way back from her house, I tell God that I will never ask him for another thing in this world if he'll just let Pam be mine.

I'm at her house almost every night of the week. The rule is I have to leave at nine o'clock on school nights. On Fridays and Saturdays we go roller skating or to the movies or out to eat with some of the kids from church. Sometimes we go to Moma's and play cards. We play a game called Pitch. It's a partners game. Sometimes my sister, Suzanne, and her husband, Jack, come to play against Pam and me and Moma and Bill. Pam and I sometimes cheat to win.

When summer rolls around, I get permission from the owners of the Martha Washington Hotel to go swimming in their pool. They let us use a room to change in, and sometimes we don't even make it to the pool.

Pam's parents accept me as part of their family. One night, after I know she's in love with me, I tell her about my past. I want to tell her parents too, but Pam's afraid. Her parents have always been strict with her, and she says there's no way they would allow us to continue dating if they learn about my delinquent past. As far as her mother knows, I'm just a good Christian boy who attends the same wonderful church they attend and I have the same healthy Christian values that they have.

And that's the way I present myself. I am, by nature, a polite and respectful boy.

More than once during the next eight months I thank God with all the reverence I possess for helping me get my life together. Never in my life have I been so happy or felt so truly loved and blessed. I'm so in love with this wonderful Christian girl and she's just accepted my proposal to marry me.

Except for the charges that are hanging over my head like a guillotine, my life is perfect. I have an awesome new job doing what I love to do. I'm a senior mechanic in a small garage and service station. To make extra money, I clean office buildings for a young fellow who has his own part-time building maintenance business. His name is Bill and he's a real shrewd businessman. He has office buildings all over Prince George's County, and he's making a ton of money.

The whole time I'm working for Bill, I watch every move he makes because I'm a naturally curious person. I ask lots of questions and learn everything I can about his business. Once he lets me use his van to deliver supplies to a building I'm cleaning for him. There's a ledger on the seat and I can't help but look inside. He's grossing close to five thousand dollars a month. He pays the mostly teenagers who work for him the minimum wage of $2.10 an hour. I memorize what he gets paid a month for each building. Then I calculate that after he pays his help and for his janitorial supplies, he probably nets close to three grand a month, and that's in addition to his full-time pay as a fireman at Andrews Air Force Base.

This guy is rolling in the dough.

One day Bill invites me to have lunch at his new three-bedroom split-level house. He says he wants me to see for myself what his part-time business is doing for his family. Only twenty-five years old, he and his wife and two kids have it all. A beautiful new home with furniture in every room, a billiard table in the fully finished basement game room, a swimming pool in the backyard, a new station wagon, and a Chevy van in the driveway.

After he shows me all the fruits of his labor, he tells me he intends to expand his cleaning business and wants me to be his partner. That's when I tell him about the criminal charges that are hanging over me and just what happened. He says that could happen to anybody and if I go up the river, there's a job waiting for me when I come home.

Two weeks before we get married, Pam's father calls me into his den for a private talk. A quiet, easygoing man, he's the senior partner in a very successful electrical company with his two brothers. He speaks slowly and deliberately, as if he's weighing the effect of each word before he speaks. I practically gasp and turn beet red when he tells me he and Mrs. Simpson know about my past. They know I've been to reform school and that I still have criminal charges pending against me.

He says, Now it doesn't matter what you've done before you started dating Pam. All that matters to me is how you treat her. If you ever hurt her in any way, you'll have to answer to me. Do you understand that?

I look at him in shock and then relief. I tell him he'll never have to worry about me hurting Pam because I love her more than I've ever loved anyone.

Pam and I are both relieved that the cat is out of the bag. Pam says my aunts told her mom all about my past the night they attended Pam's bridal shower. I know they told her because it was the right thing to do and they weren't trying to hurt me, but I'm still hurt about it. And I feel betrayed.

The only thing is, they would have found out about it soon enough anyway. Two months after we're married, the guillotine drops. I'm called before the judge and the son of a bitch sentences me to five years in the Maryland State Penitentiary. Duck and I both plead guilty to assault because our lawyers said we'd get hammered if we took a trial and got found guilty. Because he's never been in trouble in his life, Duck gets probation and I'm mad as hell.

The sheriff lets me say good-bye to Pam. She's crying softly as I hold her in my arms. I tell her I love her and I'll be home soon.

She says, I'll be there the first day you're allowed to have visits. And then we hug again until the goddamn sheriff has to pry us apart.

Chapter 21

As I'm climbing the hundred-year-old steps to the entrance of the Maryland state pen—the same steps I walked up with my childhood friend Billy White just a year and a half ago—Johnny Fear revs the engine and floors the accelerator. *Hold on to your bowels, boy, 'cause here he comes.*

I cry inside for Jesus, but the noise from the engine drowns out my pleas. Slow down and get a grip on yourself or you'll crash and look like an amateur. Don't try to fix it, Jim, just turn the engine off. Turn the goddamn engine off. But I'm scared shitless.

After I'm processed, they lead me down the same sorry-ass cellblock I walked down with the boys from the Maryland Training School. I look up and see those black-eyed killer bees staring down at me and I again squeeze and lock my anus tighter than a vise grip.

They don't know you're afraid, do they? Come on, man, everyone's afraid. Yeah, but you can act like you're not afraid, can't you? If it quacks like a duck and walks like a duck, it must be a duck. If ya walk like a tough guy and act like a tough guy, ya must be a tough guy. Yeah, but you sure don't look like a tough guy, Patsy, boy. You're too damn pretty to look tough.

We arrive on the orientation tier and the guard yells, Twelve on three!

That would be the twelfth cell on the third tier, I reason.

The door opens with a clank! I'm relieved when it closes behind me. Safe and relieved, I sit down on a dirty mattress and stare at bright red walls covered with food and dried spit. And to think last night I slept in a warm bed under crisp clean sheets and beside a beautiful wife. Now I have my own red cell in the middle of a colossal concrete hive of killer bees.

The noise is maddening. Radios blasting, sirens screaming, metal clinging and clanging on metal. And angry dogs howling and barking at the moon. *This ain't nothing but a humbug, and you know it. Just stay calm. You got Jesus on your side now. Jesus, keep me safe while I'm here, please. Don't make me have to kill nobody cuz I gotta defend myself and I'm scared as shit.*

Solace comes when I think about Pam and all her love and everything I have waiting for me at home. I have a year and three months to do before I'm eligible for parole. That's one-fourth of five years. Hold on, Pam. I'll be home soon.

I think about all I've been through and about how Moma always says I'm strong. Then I stare at the ceiling until I fall asleep.

On my way to breakfast the next morning, I'm greeted by the rapist murderer named Lamont Robinson. The same Lamont Robinson who wanted to drink my sperm in the county jail. I'm scared like I've never been scared before, but I don't show it. Now I'm trying my goddamnedest to be hard and cool at the same time while this crazy-looking motherfucker is walking beside me looking me up and down.

How you doin', white boy? You remember me?

Yeah, sure. How's it going?

Well, you know? Same old shit. What you in for?

Assault, man.

How much time they give you?

Five years.

I see they got you up on three tier in twelve cell. That's my old cell. You need anything?

No, I don't need anything, but thanks.

We sit at different tables and when I look up halfway through eating a bowl of cereal, I'm relieved to see he's gone. When I look around, killer bees are all over the place and they're staring at me. I get up nonchalantly and start the long walk back to my cell. Just as I turn the corner inside the cellblock, someone grabs me from behind and pulls me behind a set of doors.

You say one word and I'll cut your throat, bitch!

It's Robinson and he has a knife pressed against my neck. His other hand is moving over my chest and stomach and down to my groin.

For a couple of seconds, I let go of my tension and relax and he lets up. That's when I break free and grab the nearest object, a mop bucket filled with water.

With one violent whirl, I fling the bucket at him. It doesn't hurt him, but the crash of the metal bucket against the floor attracts the attention of guards nearby. Within seconds, three of them surround me and place me in handcuffs. Then they grab Robinson and frisk him. He doesn't have the knife on him. They find it behind the door.

All the way to the captain's office I thank God for the bucket of water. You're safe now, fellow, I tell myself. Count your lucky stars.

The captain wants to know if I'm hurt and how did I run into that animal my second day here.

I say, I ain't hurt, sir, and I knew Robinson from the county jail a couple of years back.

He says, You're one lucky son-of-a-bitch, son. Do you know what would have happened to you if my officers hadn't gotten there?

I say, I handled myself pretty good, sir. And maybe he was the one who was lucky! *Did you ever think about that, fat man? Ya think I was just gonna lay down and unlock the goddamn vault for him?*

The captain says, I'm placing you in administrative segregation until your transfer comes through. You're too goddamn young and frail-looking to be in this joint in the first place. Sergeant, escort this young punk to the South Wing.

The South Wing is the filthiest and loudest place on earth. I stay awake half the night listening to the screams and madness and watching mice run in and out of my cell. Men talk about other men's mothers, and some goddamn weirdo keeps calling out my cell number and wanting to know my name. I ignore him by closing my eyes and concentrating on all the things I want to do when I get out of this hellhole.

When I finally fall asleep, I dream about my future. In my dream, I'm the president of my own building maintenance business. I'm dressed in a nice blue suit and sitting in front of the manager of some large office building, asking him all kinds of questions: How many square feet of office space does his building have? How much is carpeted and how much is tiled? Does he want window cleaning included in the contract? If so, how often does he want them cleaned? Bimonthly? Quarterly? What about supplies? Soap, toilet paper, wax, stripper, trash can liners, etc? Does he want my company to furnish these supplies?

When I awaken from the dream, my skin is covered with goose bumps. In my dream I had put to use every piece of information I'd gleaned from Bill while I was working for him, including how to bid on buildings. Now, the vision I had in that dream takes on a life of its own. I know without any hesitation what I'm going to do with my future. I'm going to start my own business.

For the rest of my days in solitary confinement, I plan and figure and make mental notes of buildings and businesses I plan to take over. If Bill Tanner can make it in this business, I know that Pam and I can do even better. We're going to have everything Bill and his wife have and a lot more.

Thirty days and I'm transferred out of the Maryland penitentiary. Instead of going to the penal farm in Hagerstown where most fellows my age are sent, they send me to the Southern Maryland Correctional Camp in Hughesville. I'm baffled and ecstatic because this camp is where fellows with nine months or fewer left on their sentence are sent.

I call Pam first and then Moma to let them know of my good fortune. I tell Moma I'm wearing my own clothes and they gave me my wallet and money back and the authorities must have made a big mistake.

Moma says like hell they did. They didn't want me to get off with just probation, she says, so the judge arranged for me to do thirty days in the pen and another sixty at the camp. She says as long as I don't get into any trouble, I'll be placed on probation in sixty days.

Later that evening I find the camp chapel and go inside to say a prayer. *Thank you, God, for bringing me safely through another storm. Now please help me down this one last road.*

Pam is working as an oral surgeon's assistant. Every night when she gets off work, she comes to visit me. On weekends we take long walks around the grounds and she brings a basket filled with food and drinks. I tell her all about my plans to go into business. She listens with great enthusiasm.

One day she tells me about a scandal that's going on in our church. Part of the congregation wants to oust Pastor Morris and his family. Pam says as far as her mother knows the pastor hasn't done anything wrong. We're both sad that some of our friends are involved in this cruel plot to get rid of a decent man and his family. Pam says maybe we should look for a new church when I come home.

The Isley Brothers have a new song out called "I've Got Work To Do." The lyrics go, *I'm taking care of business/Woman can't you see/I've gotta make it for you/And you've gotta make it for me*…For the first three weeks I'm home these lyrics stay in my head night and day.

Pam is so thorough she already has the Maryland, Virginia, and Washington, D.C., yellow pages laid out on the dining room table when I walk through our apartment door.

All morning and afternoon I'm on the phone calling real estate agents, bank managers, car dealerships, office building managers, and various storefront businesses. In the evenings, Pam and I visit my mother and grandfather and aunts and Pam's family. Then we drive around identifying buildings and businesses we want to go after.

On Sundays, we visit new churches. Pastor Morris was forced out of the Pentecostal Assembly of God Church, and we don't want to go back there after the way the congregation treated him and his family. The pastor holds Sunday services in an elementary school auditorium and we attend a couple of times, but it's not the same. We visit other churches in the area too, but we can't find one we like enough to want to come back.

It's just as well because I have a blazing obsession to build our cleaning business into an empire. My obsession is more intense than any of Monty Hall's deals.

Would the gentleman dressed like a janitor in a drum please stand up? Sir, I'm going to give you fifty dollars. Now I want to know if you'll give me the fifty dollars back for what's behind curtain number one, curtain number two, or curtain number three?

Well, Monty, I'd rather have what's in that box you're holding.

You want the box? That's good. I like a man who's willing to take a chance. Let's open the box. The box contains a card. Sir, would you please read what's on the card?

The card says I win ALL the prizes behind the curtains, Monty! A brand-new three-bedroom brick house with modern appliances and wall-to-wall carpet in every room. A walk-in closet filled with sharkskin suits and silk ties and umpteen pairs of shoes. A sports and luxury car parked in a driveway bordered by rows of red, yellow, and purple flowers.

I envision winning all of these prizes and so much more. And what makes it so easy from the get-go is that that doubting Thomas is nowhere on the road to Jericho. I know without a grain of doubt that I will build my empire as surely as I'm alive. And I will join the junior Chamber of Commerce and be given the Youngest Businessman of the Year award my first year out. I'll rub elbows with bankers and real estate brokers and headmasters of private schools.

For six months, all I do for eighteen hours a day is work and plan and scheme. In the morning, I dress in the double-breasted sharkskin suit Pam bought me and go out to meet in person the people I made appointments with over the phone.

By the end of the first month, I have contracts to clean seven storefront offices, a hair salon, and a travel agency. These contracts are worth close to fifteen hundred dollars a month.

In the evenings after Pam gets home from work and changes clothes, we have dinner in a nice restaurant and then go off to clean our businesses. We develop a routine so that when we enter any given premise, we each know what tasks the other will perform. We never get bored. We take great pride in doing superb work. Sometimes we take along a radio to listen to while we work.

During the second month, we land two huge contracts that establish us as a bona fide business. One is the East-West Lincoln-Mercury dealership and the other is the Marlow Heights Twin Towers apartment complex. The car dealership pays five hundred a month. We clean the place six nights a week and it takes the two of us about an hour. The apartment complex is another cash cow. Most of the tenants are military people from Andrews Air Force Base, so there's a constant turnover. Each time someone vacates an apartment, we're paid forty dollars to go in and clean it. They average five to six turnovers a week.

We hire our first employee, a fourteen-year-old black boy named Daryl who lives in our apartment complex with his mother and four younger brothers and sisters. Pam and I are both fond of Daryl; he's a hard worker and we pay him generously. Every night we buy him dinner, and one

Saturday we make a day out of taking him shopping in the mall and buying him clothes and work boots.

We start off our evenings cleaning the small storefront offices, then the car dealership, which we can't enter until after nine when it closes. By the time we finish the showroom floor, it's time to take Daryl home. Sometimes, I drop Pam off at our apartment and then clean the Marlow apartments all night.

Only four months after we start the business, Pam quits her job as an oral surgeon's assistant and joins me full time in the business. We have just landed another major contract to clean a three story medical center that's located right beside the Marlow Heights shopping center. In the weeks it took to cultivate this contract, we discovered that the current cleaning company was charging $650 a month to clean the place three nights a week. What sold the owner was that I kept pressing the fact that our company is only five minutes away from his building and we'd be on call throughout the day in the event of an emergency. That, and the fact that I had underbid the old company by a hundred dollars a month.

From the start, Pam and I enjoy the fruits of our hard work. We never once think about pinching our money like misers. Pam wants me to look *GQ*-sharp when I go out to meet potential clients, so she takes me shopping almost every week to buy more suits and ties and shoes. We buy a new black-on-black LTD Brougham right off the showroom floor and a new Mazda pickup truck. Then we move into the Marlborough House, a ritzy uptown high-rise building that's located off Branch Avenue and Suitland Parkway. Pam's father turns us on to his accountant and attorney, too, and we form a corporation for tax purposes and get insured and bonded so that I can start going after banks.

The living room of our apartment looks like a warehouse. There are six-gallon cans of wax, floor stripper, and sealer stacked all the way to the ceiling as well as new vacuum cleaners, floor machines, carpet cleaners, mops, buckets, and brooms everywhere. Pam says it's time to get an office.

We drive down St. Barnabas Road and see a five-story office building we never noticed before. It's located right in the heart of the area where we're concentrating most of our business. Dressed like two Madison Avenue executives, we enter the lobby and meet the building manager. After introducing ourselves and stating our business, he escorts us to an office in the rear of the building.

The man says, Unfortunately, we don't have anyone cleaning our building at this time because the top four floors are completely vacant.

He offers to take our business card and call us when new tenants start renting space. But I press the matter further.

I say, We want to make you an offer, sir. We're a young company that's growing fast, and right now we're in need of some office space. If you'll give us five hundred square feet somewhere in the building, we'll keep the lobby, elevators, and entire first floor of the building clean in exchange for the rent.

After some discussion, during which we learn that the Peoples National Bank, which occupies the corner suite on the first floor, hires its own cleaners, we cut a deal with an old-fashioned handshake. The next day, we move into a large suite on the fourth floor. It has two small offices we use for storage, a large office for me, and a reception area for Pam.

We're just about to go out and purchase some secondhand filing cabinets and desks and chairs for the office when I seize on an opportunity to get it all free.

For the last four months that we've cleaned a travel agency's offices, we haven't received a single monthly payment. Every time we stop by to ask for our money, the receptionist apologizes and chucks a lame excuse that the checks are made out in their Honolulu office and that there's obviously something wrong with the accounting department.

She always assures me with a pretty smile that the check will be in the mail soon.

One evening when we go in to clean the place, we discover that the filing cabinets and desk drawers have been emptied out. It's obvious the people left suddenly and quickly. All that's left is a box of brochures in the top of the closet. The telephones are still connected and they're ringing the whole time we're there. I pick up the phone and say, Hello.

Is this the travel agency?

Yes.

This is Martha Lansdowe. My husband and I still haven't received our plane tickets and travel package, and we're supposed to be leaving next week.

Ma'am, I'm the cleaning guy. It looks like these people have moved out of this place in a hurry. You might wanna call the Better Business Bureau.

But that's not possible! We sent them over seven hundred dollars.

I'm sorry, ma'am. That's just about how much money they owe me.

The lady hangs up and I'm standing there thinking, Those sorry sons-of-bitches are probably already back in Hawaii lying on the beach, sipping on some tropical drink and laughing at the scores of gullible people they ripped off, not to mention that stupid-ass fellow who cleaned their offices so meticulously for all those months while he waited, *Hahaha!,* for his goddamn money.

The very next day, I back my van up to the rear door of the travel agency and Daryl and I take every piece of furniture in the place. We have to make several trips to get it all. When we're finished, we have two L-shaped receptionist's desks with beautiful swivel chairs, an executive desk and leather chair, four file cabinets, a conference table and set of chairs, two IBM Selectric typewriters, and a small Xerox machine. We even roll up the wall-to-wall carpet and take that. All of this brand-new furniture is worth a lot more than what they owe me, so we feel good about it. Aloha, you slimy bastards! Now we're even.

In August, we take over the Peoples National Bank on the first floor of our office building. We do such a fine job that we're asked to take over three other branch offices. These are the most impressive contracts we have on our list of references, and we're as excited as we can be to have them.

Every week Pam and I inspect the banks during the day, just to be seen. Sometimes when I walk inside the main vault to vacuum the carpet, I feel like the cat who swallowed the canary. I look around and see all that clean, green money. Look at all of this moola! *Brother, can you spare a dime? A dime? Are you crazy? Take a whole goddamn stack, Jack. Aw, no. You won't trick me, Jim. Hey, I like to sing but I ain't no temptation. No, sirree, Bob, I'm taking care of business and I'm getting my own goddamn money.*

I use the contracts with the four branches of the Peoples National Bank as references to land contracts on two Citizens National Bank branches. Ninety percent of the floors in these banks are carpeted, and that makes cleaning them a cinch. Most nights, one person can be in and out in thirty minutes.

I get to know a young salesman from the janitorial supply company we're dealing with and he starts giving me leads on buildings that are about to change cleaning companies because of poor service. His name's Rudy and he's a top-notch salesman. He arranges for me to take classes his company offers its new employees in training. I learn all about the effects of different cleaning chemicals on different floor surfaces and the proper ways to use and maintain equipment and supplies.

Tile, marble, terrazzo, and wooden floors require different approaches to restoration and maintenance, I learn. I take this knowledge and set up classes for my own employees to ensure they know the proper ways to strip, seal, and wax floors with different surfaces; remove stubborn stains out of carpets; wash windows quickly without leaving streaks; and clean desks and other table surfaces the way we want them cleaned.

Pam buys a large, detailed map of the metropolitan area and hangs it on the wall in my office. Then she pins blue flags on the map to indicate the location of the buildings we have under contract. She uses yellow flags for the location of buildings we've bid on and red flags at the sites of those we intend to go after in the near future. On each flag she places a tag with the name of the building. Every couple of weeks, we sit in the office late at night reviewing the map and planning while sipping on a bottle of wine and savoring our good fortune.

We're still doing a big portion of the cleaning, but we're doing less and less of it as the weeks go by and we acquire good, loyal workers. We pay my cousin Mitch two hundred a week to supervise the larger buildings and to clean a couple of the smaller buildings himself. We also hire two husband-and-wife teams part time and they are excellent, dependable workers who require very little supervision.

All summer, I keep my eye on a rival company called General Maintenance. This multimillion-dollar company is located in downtown Washington, D.C. It has buildings all over Maryland and Virginia, and holds 60 percent of the high-rise federal and private office buildings in D.C. I hear General Maintenance's name over and over as I begin to contact some of the private and parochial schools in D.C. and Maryland. At first, I'm in awe of the size and power of this Goliath of a company. My awe dissolves into guile, though, when I realize I'll have to throw stones at it if I want bigger and better contracts.

And that's just what I do. There's a private school in Northwest that I'd trade for any three of my other accounts. It's called Maret School, and it goes from kindergarten to the twelfth grade. Located in the center of one of the most affluent residential areas in Washington, D.C., the school is home to the children of senators and diplomats and all kinds of other important people.

Pam and I pull into the school parking lot and start walking around the grounds until we run into the engineer. We learn that General Maintenance has been cleaning the school for several years. The engineer says the cleaners aren't doing that good a job, and I should talk to the headmaster, Mr. Peter Sturtevant, who's not in today.

The next day, I call General Maintenance and ask to speak to the general manager. When he gets on the phone, I identify myself as the headmaster of a private school in the Maryland suburbs. I tell him I'm interested in changing cleaning services and that my good friend who's the headmaster of Maret School recommended that I call General Maintenance. I go on to say that my school has just about the same amount of square feet of cleaning space as Maret and would he please give me a ballpark monthly figure. I speak to him like a man who doesn't have time for small talk or beating around the bush.

But the man is reluctant to quote a price. He keeps saying he can stop by my school the next day and quickly look the place over. I tell him I understand, that we're just trying to get a rough estimate before we invite him and other companies out to bid. Before he can say another word, I say, Incidentally, what are you charging my friend Pete Sturtevant to clean Maret?

He blurts out, $2,700 a month.

Having just hit Goliath in the eye with a rock, I lean back in my chair, smile, and tell him that seems like a reasonable fee. I thank him, ask him to repeat his name, and assure him we'll be sending him a formal invitation to bid on our school in a couple of weeks.

Bidding on the relatively smaller buildings we have in our portfolio is one thing. We sometimes underbid these jobs, but we can't afford to look like amateurs now. Without contacting the fellow from General Maintenance and duping him, we wouldn't know how to proceed with a bid on Maret School. Now we do, goddammit!

I dial Mr. Sturtevant, introduce myself, and ask him if Pam and I can drive out and offer a proposal to clean his school. I tell him I met his engineer last week and learned that the place needs better building maintenance. Before he answers, he asks me questions about the cleaning business and then he talks about his golf game. Right in the middle of a sentence, he says someone's on another line and to come next Tuesday at nine in the morning.

Pam and I work the appointment like a pit crew at an Indy car race. Mr. Sturtevant is a tall, slim man in his fifties with salt and pepper hair, a permanent tan, and a *Father Knows Best* smile. He offers us coffee and doughnuts in his office and, after some small talk, he escorts us through the five buildings that make up the school, pointing out the areas where General Maintenance has been neglecting.

Along the way, Pam and I consult quietly and take notes and draw diagrams of the layout of each floor in each building. Once, Pam stops and bends down to feel the texture of a stain on the carpet in the library and makes a passing comment to me about it. It's a keen move on her part, designed for no other reason than to demonstrate that she knows what she's doing.

Back in his office, he asks each of us about our educational backgrounds and experiences and we both shine like new quarters. He asks if I play golf and I tell him no, but I used to caddy for a Catholic priest when I was a kid. Then we get down to the nitty-gritty.

We present him with our formal proposal. We've already decided on a fee, and Pam fills it in before she hands him the proposal.

Pam and I glance at one another hopefully while he sits back in his chair, lowers his glasses, and reads intently.

He says, Do you really think you can clean this place for this amount? He seems both amazed and impressed.

I say, We certainly can, sir.

He says, Well, let me tell you a little secret. We're paying GM four hundred dollars a month more than what you're proposing here.

That doesn't surprise me, sir. General Maintenance is a conglomerate. It has district directors, regional directors, and building supervisors to pay in addition to a fleet of janitors. General Maintenance pays its top workers good money, sir. We're a small company, and we only have a few employees and little overhead. My wife and I supervise our own buildings, so we don't have a bunch of people to pay. If you'll give us the contract on a sixty-day contingency basis, I guarantee you'll stay with us.

Like I know what the hell General Maintenance pays their employees. The thing is, my intuition tells me that winning an argument of this kind is all in the presentation. The facts. You quickly and assertively slide the facts down their throats until they have no choice but to swallow them.

And he does. A week later the contract comes signed in the mail along with a note from Mr. Peter Sturtevant: *Congratulations! You can start moving your equipment in immediately.*

This is our first twenty-three-hundred-dollar a month contract, and we know there ain't no stopping us now.

We take over two other schools that fall—St. Thomas Apostle, a small Catholic school located only a mile up the street from Maret School, and St. Anne's in Upper Marlboro, Maryland. Combined, these two contracts are worth twenty-eight hundred a month.

Now, we have fifteen part-time employees on our payroll and we keep a running ad in the classified section of the *Washington Post* every Sunday for more help. We start each part-time worker off at the minimum wage of $2.10 an hour. Workers who stay with us and show loyalty and dependability are rewarded with periodic raises and the opportunity to become supervisors in their building.

Every Friday night Pam and I make our rounds together, delivering supplies and payroll and taking inventory. Pam is meticulous when it comes to keeping records. She knows exactly how many rolls of toilet paper are used each day at each site and how many gallons of floor stripper and wax are required to service a particular area, and she knows when supplies are missing.

By the end of September, a little over six months into the business, we're grossing close to nine grand a month. Here's what our account sheet looks like:

ACCOUNTS
MONTHLY FEE
Marlow Towers (average)
$500
Camp Springs Beauty Salon
125
Clinton Realty
75
Prince George's Realty
75
Marlow Realty
125
Marlow Heights Medical Center
550
East-West Lincoln Mercury
500
Lowe's Chevrolet
500
St. Barnabas Road Building
(Clean for free in exchange for office space.)
Peoples National Bank (four branches)
650
Citizens National Bank (three branches)
525
Maret School
2500
St. Thomas Apostle School
900
St. Anne's School
1900
Gross Monthly Income
$8725
(as of September 1973)

Naturally, with growth comes additional overhead. There are monthly truck and car payments, a large payroll and new equipment and supplies. But even after these expenses are taken care of, the money is still piling up. We take no weekly pay checks for ourselves; instead, whenever we need money, we go to the bank and make a withdrawal.

In October, we withdraw a thousand dollars and fly to Disney World. The trip turns out to be a disaster. We're standing in line to buy film for our camera when a small slip of paper trickles out of my wallet as I'm removing some bills. Pam reaches down and picks it up and then curiously opens it and reads the girl's name and phone number. After a brief argument in which I'm appalled that she doesn't believe me, I convince her that I got this girl's name and number to fix her up with my cousin Mitch. I'm lying through my goddamn teeth.

When we return from Disney World I learn that not only has Pam not forgotten about the incident, but she memorized the girl's phone number as well. She calls the girl and then confronts me. I lie again, but this time with more indignance and wrath. I break a lamp and storm around the apartment.

I don't give a goddamn what the girl said, that phone number was for Mitch!

Pam cries and tears at her heart for several days; because she doesn't want to believe I'm fooling around on her, she puts herself in denial, and we go on.

Chapter 22

If you ask me why I cheat on her, I'd say it just comes down to bad character, a lack of morals. Being *saved* at the Pentecostal Assembly of God Church hasn't changed me at all. Deep down inside me there's a stew of discontent and wanting, and I've known about it for a long time.

I'm not home a year from the correctional camp before that old wisp of restlessness rises like an erection. I start wanting and going after every woman who turns my head. During the day, I'm the responsible, hard-working husband and businessman, but at night after I've made my rounds, I hit the clubs and cocktail lounges long enough to find a woman who's looking for the same thing I'm looking for.

Once, after being out with a woman half the night, I cut myself under one eye and rub my knuckle into my other eye until it bruises; then I scrape my elbows along the side of a brick wall until they start to bleed. When I get home at four thirty in the morning, Pam's sitting up crying her eyes out until she sees the condition I'm in. I tell her two guys robbed me and I was knocked out for a couple of hours and it was horrible. She wants to call the police and take me to the emergency room, but I wave her off.

Being unfaithful to Pam is only half of it. Every pathological flaw I have starts running out of me like pus from a sore. Mingling with bankers, doctors, lawyers, monsignors, and all kinds of other important people makes me feel awfully powerful and important. My arrogance and corruption grows in proportion to the growth of the business. A prime example:

I've been focusing much of my energy on acquiring an account that will catapult the business to another level. A millionaire attorney named Gil Giordano, who also happens to be one of the most important figures in Maryland's Democratic party, owns Southway Realty Company. Mr. Giordano owns four large medical buildings and has another one under construction. What makes this account so alluring is that all four buildings are located within a ten-mile radius of our central location. The four buildings combined would be worth about ten grand a month.

For three weeks, I tap dance with Ron Sellers, who manages Southway Realty, about submitting a bid on one or more of his buildings. I finally reel him in like a fish, and he says we should do lunch.

A week later, Pam and I take him to the Pagoda Seven, a plush restaurant in the Iverson Mall. Mr. Sellers orders the biggest steak on the menu. While he's devouring it, he tells us he's really not at all unhappy with his current cleaning company, but we can bid on his new building that's about to open in a couple of months.

I would be just as discouraged as Pam is about our prospects of getting our foot in the door if it weren't for two things. One is the way Mr. Ron Sellers makes it a point to tell me how beautiful Pam is when she's away from the table. The other is the way he licks his lips and stares hungrily at the pretty young waitress. This balding, forty-something, married-with-two-children, businessman likes young meat.

I immediately think about a girl I know named Laurie who's a blond bombshell. At the drop of a hat, she'd set up Mr. Ron Sellers like a bowling pin for me. *I'll have pictures taken of the two of them going in and out of a motel room with Laurie draped on him like a new suit. Then we'll see who squirms like a fish on a hook.*

Before I set him up, though, I go right to the top. For three days straight, I call Mr. Gilbert Giordano's office, but the damn secretary won't put me through. I need an appointment just to talk with this cat on the goddamn phone. On the fourth day, I tell the receptionist I'm calling about a case of vandalism I witnessed inside Mr. Giordano's 4400 Stamp Road building. The lady puts me right through. *How amazing!*

When he comes on the line, I introduce myself and tell him I recently accompanied my wife to her doctor's appointment on the fourth floor of his 4400 Stamp Road building and we ran into some juveniles who were loitering in the stairwell area and jiggling the lock to a storage room. I chased them off, I tell him, and I'm just calling to let him know about it. I go on:

Also, sir, I spoke with a few tenants in the building and they're not at all happy about the quality of cleaning their suites are getting. My wife and I operate a very successful cleaning business and we'd like to make you an offer, sir.

The man's so thankful and impressed that he tells me to come to his office in the morning and see him. Then he hangs up.

Again, I take Pam along and we're both dressed to kill. His 4400 Stamp Road building has a vacant office on the first floor that looks to be about fifteen hundred square feet and just what we need, I tell him. We're presently in the St. Barnabas Road office building, but we're on the fourth floor and carrying supplies and equipment up and down in the elevator is growing old.

Pam gracefully takes out our proposal and a list of our top accounts from her leather briefcase, hands them to him, and encourages him to call any of our accounts. We pause to let him read over the material and when I see his eyes move to the bottom of the last page, I propose that he give us a six-month contract to clean the building and a contract for the vacant office space on the first floor.

I say, Because we always have someone in our office during working hours, we'll be able to keep an eye on the security of the building and handle any daily problems the tenants might have.

He says, I like your idea. And like any good businessman, I like the idea that your contract will save me a hundred dollars a month.

He tells us to give him a couple of weeks to get the current cleaning company out of the building. We're to call his real estate manager, Mr. Ron Sellers, to make arrangements to move into the first floor suite whenever we're ready. The last thing he says is, I want you to deal directly with me in the future.

As we get up to leave, I assure him he'll find our service to be superior. We shake hands and I look him dead in the eye and say, It's our intention, sir, to eventually be the only company cleaning all your buildings.

The day we move into our new office, Ron Sellers meets us to hand over the keys and show us around the suite. He congratulates us on landing the contract and then says if we do a good job, he'll seriously consider giving us a chance to bid on one of his other buildings in the future.

I despise his big-shot attitude and condescending ways, but I'm on a mission and I'm too slick to tip my hand. I really want to say, *That's really noble of you, Mr. Dickhead, sir, but we don't deal with lackeys.* The next time he patronizes me, I decide, I'll pimp Laurie right into his goddamn lap.

Pam and I celebrate the landing of the Southway Realty account by buying a forty-two thousand-dollar, three-bedroom house in a brand-new housing development. It's a corner lot and has a full basement. After we move in, Pam shows me where she wants shrubs and flowers planted. We put up our mailbox with our name on it, and we buy an AKC registered Irish setter puppy we name Red. But for the dirty little lie I'm living, we're living the American dream.

After running a special ad in the *Washington Post* and interviewing a dozen fellows, we hire a young black fellow named Tom Harrison to replace my cousin Mitch, who quits on us and moves back to Charles County. Tom, who has a wife and new baby to support, is a hard worker and proves to be willing to make sacrifices for the good of the business. He works fourteen to sixteen hours a day, seven days a week, and he catches on to the business quickly.

Pam and I watch how he conducts himself during his daily routine. He automatically assumes the supervisory role whenever he's on a job site. He never gets excited or rattled when workers fail to show up and he has to stay longer to do their work. He handles complaints from building managers just as I would, and he conducts himself in a professional manner at all times. Consequently, we reward him with a big salary promotion and monthly bonuses. We give him a new Mazda pickup truck to use on the job and take home with him at night.

We also hire another full-time employee named Don to become our general manager. Don's job is to inspect all the buildings during the day and talk with tenants and building managers. He also fills in whenever we're short of help, and he makes sure that Tom gets whatever supplies he needs on time.

But Don turns out to be a thug, an ex-con who served time in Leavenworth for robbing and beating up a fellow when he was in the army. Before I fire him for running a numbers racket with my employees, he introduces me to a friend of his named Sal. A sharp dresser in his mid-thirties, Sal carries himself like an old-time gentleman gangster. He's soft spoken, short and burly, and always strapped with a thick wad of hundred-dollar bills. When he talks, he has this funny way of rocking back and forth on the ball of his feet. I can't help but like the guy.

During the day, Sal starts hanging around the office and running errands for me. He shows me his portfolio of stocks and I'm impressed and fascinated by this guy. One afternoon he drives me to a nightclub in downtown D.C. and tells me the place is for sale and he wants to buy it. The small club right off Dupont Circle is filled with customers at one in the afternoon. We sit at the end of the bar and Sal tells me he wants me to go in halves with him on the place. He needs ten grand to close the deal. After we meet with the owner and look over the books, I ask Sal why he needs me to go in halves with him.

He says, I don't *need* you or your money, Patty. You see, I like the way you run your cleaning business and I want to be your partner.

I'll have to think about it, Sal. I'll have to think real hard about this.

I know that Pam will never agree to investing in a nightclub. For one thing, she detests Sal and the last place she wants me to be in is a nightclub. So what do I do?

One evening I tell her I'm not sure I want to be married any longer. We should separate for a while, I say.

She cries and then begs me to come to my senses.

Pat, please stop and realize what you're about to throw away.

But I ignore her pleas.

Two days later, she gathers some of her clothes and goes home to her mother. Every morning she comes to the office and takes care of business. We talk about getting back together again. I feel so goddamn guilty and torn over hearing the desperation in her voice. I still love her but I'm stone-sick with power. I don't want to settle down; I don't want to be monogamous.

On a Friday night, I meet a girl in Georgetown and fall in love with her the second I lay eyes on her. Her name's Sally Sullivan and she works for the National Institutes of Health. With red hair, sparkling green eyes, light freckles sprinkled over her nose, and a body that won't quit, she's the most beautiful woman I've ever laid eyes on. She owns a silver Corvette, too.

I start staying at her apartment almost every night. In the morning I drive across town to our office and Pam's sitting behind her desk hard at work, looking elegant and sad at the same time. We talk about getting back together, but I continue to vacillate. I still love her, but I'm caught up in my own world. After meeting Sal and listening to some of his ideas, my demeanor changes just as it had when I started attending the Pentecostal Assembly of God Church. Then, I had become just like those gentle, loving kids who never swore or stayed angry or became so arrogant and cocky that their friends didn't know them anymore. Now, I want to be somebody so important that anyone would know it just by looking at me. I want to be loved and respected and wanted and needed and free of any obligations to anyone.

One morning, Sal walks into my office carrying his briefcase and a newspaper under his arm. He says, You're carrying a cash payroll around every two weeks and you need a piece for your own protection.

He takes out a small pistol from his briefcase and hands it to me. He says, I want you to have this.

It's a nickel-plated .32 with a pearl-white handle. I hold it in my hand and feel the adrenaline rush through me. My fantasies run like a pack of greyhounds chasing a rabbit. *Take this, you dirty rat! PowPowPow! Don't you know I'll bust a cap in your ass if you mess with me!*

That same day, I go out and buy a leather shoulder holster. I stand in front of Pam's floor-length mirror and put it on. *Yeah, boy! Damn, you look so cool and distinguished. Ain't nobody gonna mess with you, son!*

It's the weekend of my twenty-second birthday, and I'm taking Huck and Sally to Ocean City. In case of an emergency, I leave the phone number of our motel with Moma.

Later that night, while Huck's on the Boardwalk playing games in the penny arcade and Sally and I are resting across the bed, someone knocks sharply on the door.

I say, Huck, are you back already?

This isn't Huck! Open the door, you son-of-a-bitch!

Sally's frightened out of her mind and runs into the bathroom to hide. I get dressed and go to the door and when I open it, I try to hide my embarrassment by looking angry, but Pam storms into the room along with my sister, Suzie.

Pam screams, You cheating bastard! Now I know for sure! It's over! I'm through with you!

Just as she turns to leave the room, Huck walks in and Suzie tells him she's taking him home. He starts to cry and I tell him it's OK, that it's better for him to go with Suzie.

I sit on the edge of the bed and bury my goddamn head in my hands. In one big surge, all the pain and hurt I saw on Pam's face come together with all her previous pleas to save our marriage, and I am at once sorry and frightened to tears.

Go after her, you idiot! You've been a goddamn fool! She's everything you've ever wanted, and you know you can't lose her. I repeat those words to myself all the way home. *I can't lose her. I just can't lose her.* And I pray to God that I haven't.

The next several weeks are like a bad dream to me, full of lonely shadows and inexplicable thoughts. Half the time I walk around grieving and in a daze, the other half in a fit of rage. *If I could only talk with Pam alone, I know she'd come back. She loves you man. She's crazy about you.* But her goddamn parents have her under siege. They've taken the brand-new Triumph sports car I bought her and hidden it so she can't leave the house.

One Sunday morning I pull into her parents' driveway and honk the horn. Pam's mother opens the front door and shouts, If you don't leave right now, I'm calling the police.

Call them, goddammit! I'm not leaving until I talk to Pam.

Pam steps around her mother. Pat, please leave now. Dad's got a gun on you and he's not fooling around.

I've gotta talk to you, Pam.

The first shot rings out and a clump of dirt springs out of the ground about ten feet in front of me. Mr. Dotson is standing at the corner of the house aiming the pistol at me. He says, Get the hell off my property!

I'm not going any goddamn where!

He fires again. This time the bullet lands only a few feet in front of me, spraying my bare feet with dirt and dew.

You-son-of-a-bitch! I yell, retreating to my car and speeding off in a rage. *Doesn't he know there's more than one gun in the goddamn world? And doesn't he know I'm a little bit crazier than him?* The next time I come back, I decide, I'll bring my own gun along.

Why is it that whenever I get what I want, I don't want it anymore? And now that I've lost what I had, all I can think about is getting it back.

I start to neglect the business, relying on Tom to handle just about everything except for the payroll. As a diversion to the desperation and sickening loneliness I feel every waking minute, I start hanging out at the club Sal wants to buy. He gives the owner a deposit on the place while he waits to see if he can get the liquor license transferred to his name. As a result, we both have the run of the place, like we own it already.

Sometimes at night I work behind the bar long enough to meet a girl and take off with her. One night, I take this tall blond named Nykki to the Bayou in Georgetown. We dance until the place closes and then I take her home with me. After that, she shows up at the club every night looking for me. She tells me she's in love with me and she'll do anything in the world for me.

Nykki and I are in bed one night when Sal shows up with the bank teller Eddie Lawson from the Peoples National Bank on St. Barnabas Road. He's a cocky young punk who once tried to flirt with Pam when she came in to clean the bank without me. He fancies himself a professional gambler and he and Sal have a high-stakes card game going on; they're playing Tonk for a hundred dollars a hand. Nykki and I sit and watch them play until Sal's up two grand.

The next morning Sal hands me a wad of money.

I say, What's this for?

He says, That's a down payment for part of your business.

My cleaning business?

Yeah.

It ain't for sale, Sal. Forget about it.

Well, keep it anyway, he says. And there's plenty more where that came from.

What the hell do you mean?

He says, There's something big brewing, man, and we're both going to have a nice chunk of change.

In addition to being a compulsive gambler, Sal says Eddie Lawson is a goddamn embezzler. After Sal wiped him out, Eddie spilled his guts and cried like a little girl. The kid's been gambling with his bank's money for six months now and he's down almost eight grand. Sal says the little bastard has a friend who works at the main branch and tells him when the auditors are coming each week. To make his drawer even, he takes money out of the night deposit bags and puts it in his drawer. After the audit he returns the money to the bags. Sal says the kid doesn't know how much longer he can go on like this, but he has a great offer to make Sal.

Here's the deal: He'll give Sal the combinations to all five of the tellers' safes as well as the night deposit safe. Sal can go in the bank late one night and clean out all the safes. This way the kid's embezzlement will go undiscovered and Sal will become very rich. *The cameras don't come on unless they're activated by the alarm system, and the alarm system will be turned off. No one will see the burglar enter or exit the bank, and there'll be no fingerprints because the burglar will wear gloves. A gravy job. A piece of pineapple upside-down cake.*

That night, the three of us go inside the bank at two in the morning and Lawson shows Sal how to deactivate the alarm system. It takes Sal about ten seconds to open each safe and twice as long to catch his breath each time he opens one and sees all that money.

I'm driven by my compulsion to experience excitement at its highest, but I feign disinterest because I don't want the kid to associate me with what he is setting up for Sal. After Sal opens the last safe, he tells Lawson to have an alibi for next Sunday night and he better keep his mouth shut if he knows what's good for him.

A little after midnight on Sunday night, I drop off Sal behind the St. Barnabas Road building. Twenty minutes later, Sal comes out the back door of the building dragging a pillowcase. The stocking cap he wore into the place is now bunched up on top of his head and he reminds me of a character in *Alice in Wonderland. The queen of hearts makes some tarts. The knave of hearts steals them.*

The heist yields a little over sixty-two grand, which is more than enough to pay cash for the nightclub Sal wants to buy.

A couple of days later, two Prince George's County detectives come into my office to talk to me.

Did you know that one of your banks got robbed?

Yes.

How many sets of keys do you have to the place?

One.

Where is it?

The old couple who cleans the place for me has it. Here's their name and address.

Do you know Salvatore Ignatius Totaro?

Yes.

Do you know where we can find him?

No.

Do you know Eddie Lawson?

Yes, I met him.

How do you know him?

He and Sal play cards sometimes.

Did you enter the bank two weeks ago at two o'clock on a Saturday morning with Sal Totaro and Eddie Lawson?

No.

Would you be willing to come down and take a polygraph exam?

No way.

Why? Do you have something to hide?

Hell, no. I took one of them when I was a kid and it wasn't right.

Well, you don't have to take the polygraph, but you have to come with us now.

Am I under arrest?

Not yet, you're not. Would you mind coming with us?

On the way to the sheriff's office, the cop in the passenger's seat says matter of factly that Lawson cracked like an egg. They know all about his gambling addiction and how much money he stole from the bank himself and how he gave Sal and me the combinations to the safes. Then he reads me my rights and tells me if I cooperate, they'll look out for me. It's Sal they want and they want the money back.

I say, I don't know any goddamn thing about this.

Sal sends a lawyer to the county jail to see me. The lawyer says they got nothing on Sal or me, and the only reason they're holding me is because I had the keys to the building. He says Lawson's saying anything he can to get out of the trouble he's in and they're working on getting me out on bail.

I sit in the county jail another week before the bail bondsman comes and gets me out. I go to my office and my secretary tells me I've lost all the Peoples National Bank accounts. Sal made out the payroll and paid some bills while I was away, and he cashed a check for four thousand dollars.

When Sal walks in, I say, What the hell are you doing cashing a four thousand dollar check?

He says, I needed to pay off some bills of my own and I've been working for you for six months and haven't been paid a dime. I loaned two thousand of it to a guy for a month at 50 percent interest every two weeks.

You did what! Not with my goddamn money, you didn't! Where's all the goddamn bank money, Sal? Don't tell me you lost it gambling!

Relax, man. That money's put up. Don't worry. You got your half coming. This guy owns a used-car lot and he needed the money just for a couple of weeks. We'll go collect it at the end of next week.

But the guy doesn't have the money and Sal takes up for him. He tells me to stop worrying about it,that everything's under control. I tell him he'd better drive up to Buffalo and get my goddamn money and we end up getting into a fistfight right in my office. The secretary Janet comes in and she's hysterical. She says, If you two don't stop right now, I'm walking out of here.

Later that night, Nykki and I are watching television when Sal pulls into my driveway. He's drunk. He stands in the front yard, yelling for me to come outside. I raise the window and tell him to get away from my house and leave me the fuck alone. But he wants to have it out. He pulls his .45 out and starts waving it in the air and says to open the door or he'll kick it in.

Kick your mother in, you guinea bastard! I yell.

No sooner do I talk about his mother than he kicks the front door open and steps into the foyer. I stop his forward momentum by shooting him five times with the .32 he gave me. The first shot grazes the side of his stomach, but the second one hits him in the meat of his thigh and brings him to his knees; the third shot goes through his leather jacket and into his forearm; the fourth one grazes the top of his head; and the fifth bullet passes right through his lips and into his mouth. It shatters his dentures and stops.

When the police arrive, Sal's lying on the front lawn. He tells them a burglar shot him. Nykki tells them she was in the bedroom and only heard the shots ring out. When they ask me what happened, I tell them I was in the back bedroom with Nykki and didn't see who shot Sal.

Even though they don't have the weapon—I had gotten rid of Sal's and my gun by the time they arrived—and Sal himself said it was a burglar who'd shot him, they still arrest me for assault with intent to murder.

Two days after the shooting, Sal's out of the hospital and down at the county jail to see me.

You crazy motherfucker, he says, smiling. You could have killed me.

I'm sorry as hell, Sal. I thought you were gonna shoot me. I'm glad you're all right.

At the preliminary hearing, Sal takes the stand and testifies that a burglar broke into the house and shot him. The judge has no choice but to drop the charges. I'm free to go home.

Something happened during my stay in the county jail. Though I'm free once again from physical confinement, I can't escape the feelings of overwhelming loneliness and sheer disgust.

Every night in jail this time, thousands of lonely thoughts and images crawl across my mind like armies of red ants. I'm tormented by guilt, self-loathing, and shame. I hate myself. I hate the business, I hate my new house and all my material possessions, and I hate life itself for boring down such pain and torment on me.

Most of all, I hate myself for what I've done to Pam and our marriage. I long for her and grieve for her day and night. Missing her is not merely a matter of nostalgia, but a deep suffering. No woman could ever measure up to Pam in my eyes. Once again I start prowling the nights away, sleeping with women whom I want nothing to do with the next morning.

Something else happens shortly after I get out of jail that serves as a catalyst to my eventual demise. Sal has hooked up with a fellow just out of the Maryland House of Corrections and in desperate want of money. He's a twenty-four-year-old dope fiend named John Cooley Hanson. He's a smooth-talking fellow who tells me over and over how he's this big stickup artist.

One afternoon, I walk into my basement and find him sticking a needle in his arm. I watch as the drug casts its spell on him. First, his breathing increases suddenly. Then his facial expression changes; his eyes brighten and shine like marbles.

I ask, What is that shit?

It's speed, man. Bams. You wanna shot?

What's it do to you?

Man, you gotta try it. It makes you feel like heaven, man. There ain't nothing you can't do. Let me get you where I'm at.

I don't like needles, man. I hope you know what the fuck you're doing.

Don't worry, brother. You won't feel any pain at all.

I watch as he cleans out the syringe with cold water and then draws up the liquid that's left in the spoon. When he's ready to stick me with the needle, I look away and squint. Suddenly I feel a quick coolness spreading across my body causing my skin to shrink and the hair on the back of my neck and arms to rise like little chaffs of wheat. Then a tide of euphoria rushes in and sweeps across my mind, instantly drowning the voices, the noises and confusion, and all my self-loathing and contempt. What a sensational and fascinating transformation it is!

After I spend several minutes raving about the way I feel, Sal gets so excited that he wants to try it. Now we're both hooked on the feeling.

I'm so instantly hooked on this wonder drug that I drive John Hanson into the ghettos of Southeast Washington to find the dope man. On the way he tells me that Bams is the street name for Preludent, a strong amphetamine pill that's prescribed for people who are overweight. The pills sell for five dollars a piece on the street. I give him a hundred dollars and tell him to spend it all.

For the next several weeks, I get good and wired and drive around day and night looking for Eddie Lawson, the punk who implicated me in the bank burglary. After a day or two, I sleep for two days and then start the whole cycle over again.

Even preparing the drug for injection becomes a ritual. I get a thrill out of watching the needle pierce my skin and into my vein, then watching the blood shoot back into the syringe and then back into my vein again along with the liquid potion.

By now, I'm neglecting the business altogether. If it weren't for Tom's loyalty, I'd be without a single account.

He runs the business without any assistance and he's doing a fine job.

I also completely neglect my family and relatives to the extent that when my grandfather dies in the spring of '75, I'm told to stay away from the funeral. I failed to spend a single day visiting him while he was in the hospital dying from cancer. Even though my actions don't show it, I loved my grandfather dearly and I'm ashamed and guilt ridden by my behavior and the dark course my life has taken. As a result, I sink deeper into drugs.

The speed makes me feel invulnerable. Sal drives me to the used-car lot to meet the fellow he loaned *my* money to and who is now two weeks late with the payment. The guy's real nonchalant about the whole thing, which makes me want to rip his head off. I grab a tire iron from his garage floor and start smashing car windows on his lot. *You'd better pay me my goddamn money!*

A week later I return and the guy only has a couple of hundred. This time I grab him around the throat and threaten to kill him if he doesn't have all the money he owes me by the end of the week.

A couple of days later, I lose the contract to the Citizens National Bank in Landover. Before I turn the keys in, I make a duplicate set and sell them to John Cooley Hanson for ten grand. I already have a story to tell the cops when they come to talk to me, and I know they will. I've had three different workers clean this bank over the past year, and any one of them could have made a copy of the keys.

John Cooley Hanson doesn't waste any time getting his money. He unlocks the front door of the bank at quarter to eight in the evening and walks inside with a vacuum cleaner and a feather duster in his hands. It's the close of business and the two tellers who've been working the drive-up windows are just pulling the shades down. After he handcuffs them to a soda machine in the back room, he empties their safes and walks out with the vacuum in one hand and a black trash bag filled with twenty-seven grand in the other.

Within two weeks, Hanson spends his share of the take and gets arrested by the FBI. After cutting a deal, he implicates Sal and me. We're both charged with the bank robbery and extortion. The extortion charge is the result of Sal loaning the used-car dealer my money and me threatening to kill him. The last time we were at his garage, he wore a wire.

Bail is set so high that neither of us can pay it. As a result, we sit in the federal section of the Baltimore city jail all of March, April, and May until our jury trials are over and we're found guilty. I never bother to contact my mother or any of my family during these months, as I am thoroughly disgusted with life and myself. Though I know I have no one to blame but myself, I blame the bank teller, Eddie Lawson, who brought the law down on me initially, and the sewer-rat-dope-fiend John Cooley Hanson.

Eddie Lawson, the bank teller, gets ten years probation for embezzlement, John Cooley Hanson gets the federal youth act in exchange for testifying against Sal and me, Sal and I get twenty-five years for the bank robbery and extortion convictions.

After sentencing, they send Sal to the U.S. Penitentiary in Atlanta and me to the notoriously violent U.S. Penitentiary in Lewisburg, Pennsylvania.

Chapter 23

The U.S. Marshals' Greyhound bus rolls through the rear entrance to the U.S. Penitentiary in Lewisburg. The massive stone walls close around me like a tomb. As we drive around the inside perimeter of the prison, all I can think is that I've never been more alone in my life than I am now.

The bus stops at the side of the administration building. We spill out, thirty-five in all, and we're met by a line of club-wielding guards dressed in blue suits and ties.

I fight back the tears as I walk through the gauntlet and into the prison. This time it isn't Johnny Fear that overwhelms me; it's the stark realization that I've ruined my life and have no one to blame but me. Here I am, twenty-three years old with a twenty-five-year sentence to serve in a prison that's over three hundred miles from home. As miserable and disgusted as I am with myself, I can't afford to dwell on it long, for I know I will need all of the artful dodger within me to survive this place.

For two weeks, they keep me on the orientation block. On the third day I run into a fellow I met in the county jail after I shot Sal. His name's Bobby Hamilton and he's a two-time bank robber. Early in the morning, he comes to my cell with a bundle of clothes under his arms. He's the only man in the joint I know and I'm glad to see him. He lays a pair of Bermudas, a couple of colored t-shirts, and a green army jacket at the foot of my bed.

How's it going, Pat? He says. I had a feeling I'd be seeing you. How much time did they give you?

Twenty-five big ones, Bobby, I say. They knocked me right out of the goddamn box.

Damn. That's eight years and four months before you see the parole board. I'll be doing most of that with you. They gave me twenty.

Give me the rundown on this place, Bobby. What's it like?

A fucking madhouse, man. There's been at least one killing a month since I've been here. Just stay to yourself and mind your own business. That's all you gotta do. I've gotta go to work now. I'll tell you more later.

Before he leaves the cell, he tells me to look inside the lining of the army jacket. I pick up the jacket and an eight-inch knife with a four-inch handle covered with black electrical tape falls out of the lining.

What the hell's this for, Bobby? I ask.

In case you need it. This place is crazy. Everybody has one.

I'm not in general population a week before I see my first stabbing. I'm standing in the breakfast line when a black prisoner walks from the back of the line all the way to the front just so he can be with his friends. *Whack!* The Cuban prisoner he butts in front of stabs him in the side of the neck. Down he goes, the shiv, rusty and bent, still stuck in his neck. The scene unnerves me and I shiver like a frightened dog. I watch the reaction of those around me and to a man everyone seems indifferent and callous. I immediately force myself to change my countenance.

The cat on the floor ain't nobody anyway. He got what he deserved. Who in the fuck was he to cut in front of somebody anyway? Mind your business and everything is gonna be all right.

Two weeks later I'm lying in bed on a Saturday morning, listening to the radio and thinking about my family. All of a sudden I hear an explosion that's so loud and powerful it shakes the bed frame. I jump out of bed and look outside my door. A prisoner's screaming, *Oh, God! Motherfuck! God! Somebody help me, please!*

The door to the cell two cells down from mine is buckled. Debris is all over the hall. The screaming prisoner stumbles from the cell and falls to his knees in the middle of the hall. His back is ripped open and the blood flowing from his wounds has already dyed his white boxer shorts crimson-red. Other prisoners appear from their cells. I wait to see if anyone's going to help this cat who's now sprawled out on the floor. No one goes near him.

The prisoner loses consciousness as other prisoners parade by his cell. Glass from his cell window is all over the floor, as are fragments of what was once a big black radio. As I stand there watching the prisoner bleed to death, I hear one prisoner tell another, That was one hell of a pipe bomb!

What in the fuck did this guy do to catch this? I wonder. *Did he bump some asshole and forget to say excuse me, or did he just look at a cat the wrong way? Maybe he did something more sinister? Maybe he crossed the dope man. Maybe he took some ass and got what he had coming. Or maybe he was a thief or a snitch or a lousy goddamn shakedown artist.*

Hundreds of possibilities flash across my mind. I watch the two guards and nurse move with the urgency of a mortician as they place the fellow on a canvas gurney and carry him away.

In the morning, I find refuge standing over a trough peeling potatoes and carrots. It's one thing to be afraid, and another thing to show it. To show it in here is tantamount to wearing a sign around your neck that says, I'm waiting to be somebody's bitch. Any seasoned prisoner can read the fear in another's eyes. The trick is to camouflage it. I learn to walk with my eyes focused on some object far ahead of me, all the while looking cold and hard and as mean as any man around me.

In the vegetable prep room, I work alongside several Puerto Rican fellows. It's the first time in my life I've been around Spanish-speaking people and I'm both fascinated and amused by their quick-tongued language and strange intonations. *Los Americanos. Los gringos. Espanol. No ingles. Pocho.* It's sweet poetry to my ears.

With the exception of the Russian spy and a couple of very old prisoners, just about everyone walks with someone; everyone belongs to a clique. There are racial cliques; neighborhood cliques; religious affiliation cliques; dope fiend cliques. The tension between some of these cliques is so charged you can feel it the closer you get to them. The Nation of Islam Muslims segregate themselves from the other Muslim sects. Puerto Ricans and Cubans constantly stare one another down. A Puerto Rican prisoner can be seen walking with a white or black prisoner, but never with a Cuban.

Even in sports there's no truce. When a Puerto Rican comes up against a Cuban in a handball tournament, the competition is fierce and sometimes violent, as is the trash-talking in the stands.

One day I ask a Puerto Rican brother named Puma why there's so much animosity between the Puerto Ricans and Cubans. He waves his hand in the air in disgust, and the muscles tighten in his face, revealing his wide, bright-white teeth. He says, *Ah! Macho. Macho. E's a macho thing, amigo, tha's all.*

He offers no more, and I ask no more.

There are many other rivalries. The brothers from Baltimore hate the brothers from D.C. The brothers from Pittsburgh get along with everyone except for the brothers from Philly. The brothers from Philly have it in for everyone; their worst enemies are themselves. Brothers from West Philly are constantly at it with the brothers from North Philly or South Philly. I learn that these brothers have all grown up gang-warring over nothing more than pride—the pride that comes simply from growing up in one part of the city as opposed to another.

I settle into a disciplined routine and get along well at first. I get hooked on playing handball, a game I've never even heard of before coming to the joint, and I get good at it. I play every day with the New York Italians and Puerto

Ricans. In the afternoons I start lifting weights with Phillie DeGasaro, a young Italian fellow from New York City who's also serving time for bank robbery. We like each other from the start. It isn't long before we start telling one another about our families and lives. We both went to Catholic school and were altar boys; we like the same kind of music, too.

What impresses me the most about Phillie is that he's far more mature than his twenty-four years. He doesn't engage in horseplaying or joke telling, and he takes the situation we're in very seriously, which only reinforces my tendency to do the same. I'm also impressed by the fact that he's a college graduate and was never in trouble in his life until he robbed a bank to pay off his gambling debts. He has a girlfriend who comes to see him every two weeks, and all he wants to do is stay in shape and get the hell out of this place so he and his girl can get married.

On Sunday afternoons, Phillie invites me down to his cellblock for a spaghetti dinner. He lives on J Block, one of the two honor blocks in the prison, where most of the Italians live. The heroes of the mob—Vinnie Aloi, Johnny Dio, Big Paul Castellano, and Rick Ferri all live next to each other on the first floor of J Block.

When I walk on the block, the spicy aromas that waft from the hall remind me of my mother's kitchen. The place is immaculately clean and there's lots of laughter and camaraderie. A few old men are standing around a large pot of spaghetti that's simmering on a portable burner in the hall, and they're ribbing each other in Italian. One of them says, Who're you here to see, kid?

Phillie DeGasaro, sir.

Two doors down on the right.

Thank you.

As I pass the first door I know immediately why J Block is called the honor block. There aren't any bars or locks on the doors. The doors are made of solid wood with a small rectangular glass window. I knock on Phillie's door and when it swings open, a short bull of a man who's as bald as an egg gestures me to come in.

Hey, Richie, let my friend Patty through the door, would you?

Phillie introduces me to Richie the Bull and then to the other four fellows who are sitting around a table playing cards and telling stories. After some small talk, Phillie tells me to follow him down the hall.

He knocks on a door and this tall, handsome man opens it.

Vinnie, this is my friend Patty.

Vinnie tells us to come in and close the door. After the introductions are over, Mr. Vinnie Aloi, the second most influential prisoner in Lewisburg and a captain in one of the Mafia families in New York City, asks me all kinds of questions. How much time I'm doing. What I'm in for. Where I'm from.

Just when I think he's finished, he says, You don't use drugs, do you, Patty?

No, sir, I lie.

Well, that's good. Because if you do, you wouldn't be welcome on this block.

I understand that, sir.

Hey, come on with the sir crap, kid. Do I look that old to you?

No, sir. I mean, no, not at all.

All right. You going to stay and have something to eat with us?

Sounds good to me, Vinnie.

With that, Phillie and I return to his room and he tells me all about the intricate workings of prison politics. The Italians rarely allow outsiders into their clique, he says; they associate with a few blacks and Puerto Ricans out of necessity.

He says, We have at least one mulunyan from Philly, one from Baltimore and D.C., and two or three from New York on our payroll.

Mulunyan is a slur similar to nigger, I learn, and they keep the toughest blacks in the joint in their pocket as political pawns.

I also learn that even though there are no guards, counselors, or unit managers stationed inside J Block, you still have to get permission to enter the block and that permission has to be gained by one of the top mob guys.

Few of the Italians work in the kitchen, so they rely on other prisoners to provide them with cooking utensils, fresh bread, meat, vegetables, and fruit. Even these outsiders are screened before they're ever approached. If you're a suspected snitch or homosexual or dope fiend, you can't mule for them.

It isn't long after I meet the dapper and courtly Vinnie Aloi that I begin to work as one of his mules, delivering grocery bags filled with fresh vegetables, raw steaks and hamburger meat, and all sorts of spices to J Block on a weekly basis. In return, I'm given carte blanche to come on the block anytime I want. Eventually, I come to know all the New York Italians by their first names and J Block becomes a sanctuary to me. I hang out there every night and become a part of the Italian clique.

Three weeks after I start muling for the mob, I'm stopped in front of the dining halls by a guard who wants to search my grocery bags. There are two dozen steaks in the bag and several pounds of hamburger meat. The guard escorts me to the captain's office where I'm handcuffed and taken to the hole.

For thirty days I feel like a heel as Phillie and the mob guys smuggle cigarettes, coffee, and snacks to me every week. Every day, Phillie stops by the cellblock across from the hole and yells out the window to me. And every day he asks the same two questions: Are you all right? Do you need anything?

When my thirty days are up, Phillie and the mob guys are waiting to greet me when I come on their block. The next day I go back to working in the kitchen and muling for the mob.

It's almost a year before my real troubles in Lewisburg begin. I'm on my way to K-Dorm to visit Mr. Frank Bruno, an old man who was a magistrate in Pittsburgh. I start down the steps when I meet a prisoner who's stumbling upstairs, clutching the handle of a single shear from a disassembled pair of tailor's scissors. The long blade is buried in the center of his chest.

He tries to shout for help through a throat gurgling with blood. *Po-leece! Po-leece! Oh, Je-sus!*

The man takes three steps in front of me, collapses on the floor, and convulses several times. Then he dies, the purple blood oozing from his mouth and chest cavity like an artesian well.

I'm standing three feet from his sprawled-out body and I can see death's door in his eyes. The scene sends my mind into the twilight zone. *Jesus fucking Christ! He croaked, man! The fucking guy croaked right in front of you, goddammit! You gotta go! You gotta get away from this shit! That judge never said anything about having to go through this bullshit! This ain't right and you know it! You gotta get the fuck out of here!*

I'm petrified to no end after seeing this fellow die. Up until now, I've managed to stay ahead of my fears and worries by numbing my brain with marijuana every morning when I wake up. Smoking reefer barricades Johnny Fear every time. But images of this last scene—the man's bloody hands wrapped around the end of the shear, his bulging eyes reeking with shock and desperation, the blood spurting from his mouth like a pump—seize me and won't let go.

To harness my fears, I turn to a potent high-performance drug called crystal methamphetamine, better known as crank, monster, or go-fast. Up until now, I've avoided the hard-core drug scene because it's a dangerous game. Any drug you want is available here, and often only a knife or a piece of pipe separates the haves from the have-nots.

Until now, I've reasoned that getting involved in the drug scene could only compound my problems and put my life in needless jeopardy. But now, fear is running up and down my back like so many tire tracks. Now I need a fix that will put me far out in front of my fears. The crystal meth does just that. They call it crank because it cranks you up; they call it go-fast because it makes you go fast; and some call it monster because you can turn into one if somebody fucks with you.

Every day since I've been here, I've watched drug transactions go down in the cellblocks, in the hallways, and out on the yard. By the time I get involved, I know all the dealers in the joint. My lawyer was in possession of over ten grand of mine and I have five grand in my prison account. I can afford to get high as often as I want.

Initially, I hook up with my friend Bobby Hamilton and a dope fiend from New York named Mikie the Blond. These guys are thorough hustlers whom I trust as much as I trust anyone here. Even though they don't have money on their books, they manage to get high almost every day by dealing drugs for other prisoners and riding on the coattails of other dope fiends. A couple of times Bobby turns me on to heroin, his drug of choice, but I don't like the high. Heroin puts you in a nod, a euphoria of total resignation; speed, by contrast, creates a euphoria of excitement and hope.

On a Friday afternoon in the winter of my first year, another kind of hope arrives in the form of a letter from my old girlfriend Nykki. She tells me she's been trying to find out what happened to me and now that she knows, she wants to come and see me. How I long to smell and feel a woman again. For two weeks, she's all I think about.

When she walks in the visiting room and I see her, it's the first time in over a year that I truly feel alive. I hold her for a long time before I turn her loose and step back to look closely at her. She's gorgeous. She's cut her long blond hair and now it falls to the top of her shoulders, accenting her delicate white throat. Her large wistful blue eyes are filled with tears that drop one by one on her beautiful red dress.

We take our seats in the back corner of the visiting room and Nykki doesn't waste any time bringing me up to date on her life. She's never stopped loving me or thinking about me, she says. She wants to move near the prison where she can be near me and visit every day she's allowed.

How can I refuse her offer? Visitors are allowed to come six days a week for up to six hours a day. The way I figure it, I can be in a woman's arms for a quarter of every day. What's more, though there are rules that limit how much a prisoner is permitted to kiss his visitor, these restrictions aren't enforced. There are blind spots all over the large visiting room, and Phillie has already schooled me on the ways couples have quick sex whenever the place is good and crowded.

Though I'm not in love with Nykki, she's quite beautiful and I know she loves me and will do just about anything I ask her to do.

But then she drops a bomb on me when she tells me she's become a devout Jehovah's Witness. For the past year she's been witnessing for Christ with other JWs down in Ocean City, Maryland, where she's been living.

At first I tease her until she breaks down and cries. Here's a girl who's gone from being a nymphomaniac to toting a Bible and a packet of Jesus Saves tracts and telling me how much Jesus loves me. *She can't possibly think she has a prayer of converting this fellow.*

I don't bother to tell her that I tried Jesus once and failed. I decide to test her and see just how far gone she is. Before our first visit is over, I tell her to be prepared to make love the next time she comes to see me.

She says, I'll be back next Saturday.

Within a month, Nykki finds an apartment five minutes from the prison and starts visiting me almost every day. She needs money to pay her bills and buy food, but she's not the kind of girl to take a regular job. I tell her she can make all the money she wants smuggling drugs into the prison. All she has to do is make one trip a week to Philadelphia or Baltimore or New York to pick up a package.

Heroin, crystal meth, pills, acid, and reefer—whatever drug my connections want smuggled in, Nykki goes after. She charges a couple hundred dollars for making the trip, and I usually get a piece of the package right off the top for myself. Depending on how the packages are wrapped when she gets them, Nykki opens them and skims and undetectable amount off the top. She wraps the skim separately and brings it to me to sell for her. She's as cunning as a weasel.

My daily routine changes completely now that Nykki is on the scene. Gradually, I stop lifting weights with Phillie and acquire a whole new set of friends. Phillie and I remain friends, but I stop hanging out on J Block after quitting my job in the kitchen and muling for the mob guys. In the evenings, I hang out on the yard selling drugs to a select clientele, while my business partners, Bobby and Mikie the Blond, negotiate deals with the low-life slicksters who would grease their own mothers if given the chance.

When Nykki and I are together, we create our own world. We dream and scheme and fantasize about our future together. Sometimes, we imagine we're invisible to everyone around us and take turns role-playing. One of us pretends to by shy while the other plays the role of seducer. These are the most intimate moments we have together. Almost every day we kiss and caress each other into a frenzy of passion and orgasms. Here is my only opportunity to feel loved and express love, and the absence of privacy is a small thing.

Nykki's in love to the hilt. One day I say to her, half jesting, half earnest, I have this idea that's pretty crazy. I know you're gonna laugh like hell when I tell you about it.

She says, No, I won't, silly. I promise I won't laugh. Tell me.

OK. What if? What if I could be with you right now? What if we could go off together right now? Only it wouldn't be legal.

What do you mean?

I mean, what if I walked right out of this joint without making parole? Would you go on the lam with me?

I'd do anything to be with you, Pat, you know that.

Well, anyway, I was just joking. I couldn't get out of this joint even if I tried.

The truth is I've been studying the prison as intensely as the men who built it must have studied it. My fantasy of escaping is purely instinctual. Every prisoner dreams of escaping at one time or another, but only a few ever act on that dream.

In the spring of 1976, though, almost a year after I arrived at Lewisburg, something happens that causes my instinctual curiosity to dissolve into do-or-die urgency. I let my guard down for two seconds and get stabbed three times by a prisoner named Rabbit.

I'm about to make a drug transaction on the third floor of D Block where no guards are posted. As I pull back the curtain that's hanging at the entrance to a fellow's cell, I step inside and right into an ambush. A notorious booty bandit named Rabbit rushes through the curtain behind me and sucker-punches me. The blow grazes the side of my head and knocks me off balance.

I say, Man, what the fuck did you do that for?

He says, Shut up and get on the bed.

Are you crazy?

He throws a second punch, but I drop down and charge right at him. The momentum carries us both through the doorway and into the hall. I'm trying to hold on to him with one hand and get my knife out from under my shirt with my other hand. Before I can get it out, he stabs me in my right thigh two times and once in my buttock.

I finally get my knife in my hands, and I'm trying to stab him, but he moves like a bat out of hell. I keep stabbing the air and holding him at the same time and the one time I feel the knife penetrate his side, we free ourselves at the same time. I run down the steps and walk quickly back to G Block where I live, the blood running down my leg and my heart pounding like a son of a bitch.

Inside my cell, I pull my pants off and discover that my wounds are only superficial. I sit on the edge of the bed, squeezing the knife tightly in one hand and wiping the blood off my leg and ass cheek with my other hand. When the bell rings for evening lockup, my heart's still pounding and I'm crying like a goddamn baby because I never thought something like this would ever happen to me.

Right then and there I decide with every grain of determination I possess to break out of this place. I've got to do it before I end up dead or killing that scumbag Rabbit. I have to escape before this prison destroys me completely.

In the morning, I shove my knife down the side of my pants and watch for Rabbit everywhere I go. I'm determined to stick my knife straight through his neck if it comes down to that.

I walk around the exercise track alone, taking mental notes on the three guard towers in the yard. I estimate how much of the yard each guard can see from his post, how often the guards stand and peer around, and the exact time when they receive their meals. I picture myself scaling the wall at the corner of the tower and catching the guard asleep or with his back turned, and overpowering him. Just because no one else had ever made it over the wall, I reason, doesn't mean it can't happen

The folklore of escapes and attempted escapes interests me from the first time I hear a couple of old heads passing these stories along on the yard one evening. The most recent escape occurred only a few months after I arrived. Two bold young white cats had made their way to freedom inside the prison trash truck. They'd managed to somehow jam the compressor once they got inside, and they lived to tell about it. Another successful escape occurred in the early seventies when the notorious McCoy brothers hijacked the trash truck and rammed it through both rear gates. They were later killed in Virginia Beach in a shootout with the FBI.

There are stories about failed attempts too. Several men tried going over the wall and either were shot in the process or gave up. Then there was the fellow who worked on the docks loading the freight from the prison industries into railroad cars that come right through the prison. He had planned to ride the rails to freedom, but when the late-afternoon count came up one man short, they locked the joint down. They found the poor fellow stowed away in a sealed cardboard box.

To increase my chances of succeeding, I confide in an Alabama bank robber and escape artist named Tommy Brooks. Tommy's serving a hundred years for robbing a slew of banks. He's already escaped from two county jails and an Alabama road gang, so there's no questioning his heart. He makes it clear to me that he isn't about to try anything stupid. It has to be a high-percentage shot, he says.

We set out scrutinizing every part of the prison landscape. We come up with a plan that absorbs us day and night. The guard tower in the front right corner of the prison is only a hundred feet from our cellblock. It just so happens that this tower's not manned from ten at night to six in the morning. We'll go over the wall at the corner of the tower early one morning when the fog rolls in.

With my knowledge of geometry, I calculate that we'll need to secure six bed boards to get to the top of the wall. A bed board, which is nothing more than a heavy sheet of plywood with a frame around it, is issued to prisoners who have problems sleeping on the worn-out bedsprings. We can easily convert the bed boards into a portable ladder by cutting slots into the underside of each board and then connecting each board with pieces of two-by-fours.

Routine is so contagious in prison that even the most idiosyncratic and unpredictable guards are consistently predictable. On alternate nights, Tommy and I take turns timing the guards' rounds. After only a week, we have their routine down pat. One guard comes like a thief in the night. Hoping to stumble upon some nefarious activity, he silences his keys by holding them tightly in the palm of his hand. He's still predictable, though; he arrives at precisely five minutes to every hour. His relief arrives at just about the same time every night too, his keys dangling and jangling.

But almost as quickly as our hopes and enthusiasm for the plan have been raised, they're put to rest. The plan, we decide one night after picking it apart, is just too risky. We would need hacksaw blades to get us out the window of our cells and, to secure the blades, we'd have to pay a prisoner who works in mechanical services to steal them. That would mean putting another person on notice about our plan. We would also need at least two other prisoners to stash a bed board or two in their cells until the night we'd make our move. Then there's the matter of the trip wire that runs along the top of the wall. It's possible to get over the wall without touching the wire and setting off the alarm, but highly unlikely. There are just too many variables outside of our control, we decide.

Disappointed? Yes. Discouraged? No. Over and over I tell myself, *There's a way out, man. You just gotta find it.*

On every visit, Nykki reinforces my train of thought. After I tell her I'm searching for a way out, she joins right in with, *Have you thought about this? Have you thought about that?* Her excitement further inspires me.

I say, Nykki, we're gonna need money when I get out. Are you willing to rob a bank or two with me?

She smiles. I'll be the getaway driver, she says. We'll be like Bonnie and Clyde.

The one emotion that drives me like a man possessed stems from my encounter with Rabbit. One evening we stand face to face in the phone line. He knows I'm strapped and I know he's strapped. He says, Hey, man. You all right? You cool?

I know damn well he doesn't give a rat's ass how I'm doing, but I play the game because I'm just as afraid of dying as he is.

No matter how much self-confidence you have, you don't do to another person what Rabbit did to me and not be paranoid about the other man retaliating. And just because weeks have gone by and we've passed each other in the halls and on the courtyard and I haven't retaliated doesn't mean I'm not going to. The bottom line is that he doesn't know if

I'm a plain coward or just biding my time and waiting for an opportunity that's on my own terms.

I look him square in the eyes and answer in a calm, cold tone, Yeah. Why wouldn't I be all right?

I'm hoping he knows what it's like to squirm in fear.

Between my daily visits with Nykki and my evening vigilances wherein I go about like a prisoner of war, clandestinely gathering and exchanging information with Tommy, my goddamn father comes to see me one afternoon with his wife and their two kids—my half-brother, Jimmy, who's ten, and half-sister, Anne, who's eleven.

I'm thankful my father's brought his family along, because he and I don't know what the hell to say to each other. Talking with the kids is much easier. They go on and on about how wonderful my brother Michael is. They just met him a few weeks back when he came to Columbus for a visit. He brought them each a gift and took them for a ride in his new Corvette. *Yes, yes, yes! Mike's a real classy guy and that's why everyone in the world loves him!* I say.

When the visit's over, I breathe a big sigh of relief. I did well. I showed his ass a little class of my own, what with the fine way I smiled the whole goddamn afternoon, pretending that the son-of-a-bitch had been in my life all along. Hell, I deserve an Academy Award for the way I smoothed him and his family right into my life like spreading peanut butter over a piece of whole-wheat bread. Not once did I ask him one of those troubling questions that had weighed me down so in my youth. *Where in the hell did you go, Pop? Why didn't you give me a call, man? Why didn't you stop by? And where in Christ's name did you run off to after you came to visit me in the hospital?*

No sirree, I had too much class for all that. Even after they all passionately swore to return for a visit next month, I had enough goddamn class to refrain from telling them that I just might not be home when they get here.

I'm just as cordial and hospitable when they return the following month. We have more to talk about this time, as we've written letters in the interim and there are lots of questions to answer and ideas and emotions to clarify. Like the first visit, I spend most of my time talking with the kids and getting to know my father's wife, Rae. At one point, Rae and I take a walk to the vending machines. She says, Pat, your father tried many times to see you when you were little, but your grandfather and aunts told him to stay away. It tore him up, Pat, it really did. There was nothing he could do, though, you know?

Once again I show my class. What she shares with me unlocks a room full of memories. Images and accompanying emotions stir in my mind like bats in an attic. *Slam the door shut! You don't need to deal with this shit now!*

Yeah, Rae, I say. I'm sure it did hurt.

But I wonder why she's telling me this. Why doesn't my father tell me? Why doesn't he just say, *Pat, man, I tried. I really tried to see you kids, but they wouldn't let me.*

It doesn't really matter anymore. And, besides, I've never been one to hold a grudge for long.

At the end of the visit, Rae pledges to write and visit every other month. Daddy asks me to call once in a while, too. I kiss the kids and Rae good-bye, and Daddy and I shake hands like two strangers. I'm sick and glad when they're gone.

Not two weeks later, the three people I love most in the world come to visit me. My two brothers Michael and Huck and my mother walk through the visiting room door and I almost break down and cry when I see them. I hug each one of them like I never want to let go. Moma cries and cries.

Please don't cry, Moma. I'm doing fine, I say.

Are you sure?

Yes, ma'am. Hell, this place isn't bad at all.

Huck, who's almost six feet tall and as handsome as all outdoors, wants to know what prison's like. I wouldn't dare tell him, so I glaze over it.

No one mentions my criminal case or asks when I'm getting out. They only want to know if I'm safe and getting along well. Goddamn, how I want to tell them how terrified and alone I am inside this place, and how desperately I need to escape before I lose my mind or my life. I want to tell them about the stabbings and beatings I've seen, about the fellow with the shear buried in his chest who died right in front of me, and about the knife fight I was in. But I don't. I fake all sorts of pleasantries: The food's good. I lift weights and play handball every day. Yes, I attend Mass every Sunday. No, I'm not in any danger whatsoever. Yes, I have other visitors, my girlfriend, my father and his family.

There are so many secrets burning inside of me that I must keep from them. I merely sit there knowing I'm about to do something that's either going to get me killed or placed on the FBI's most-wanted list, and I can't say a word about it. When the visit ends, I go back and take a long shower just so I can cry in peace under the cascading water.

In September, fifteen months into my sentence, I find my way to freedom. I'm sitting in the baseball dugout in the middle of a windy and cold rainstorm, feeling miserable and dejected, when a vehicle I've never seen before enters the rear gate of the institution. It's a large green dump truck with high plywood sidings and it's being used to collect the prison's daily trash. The driver stops at each building and gets out and empties the trash barrels. Then he drives to the trash shed behind the kitchen and backs up to the shed door.

To gain a better vantage point, I walk onto the exercise track and watch with amazement as two prisoners who work the trash detail begin dumping fifty-five-gallon barrels from the shed into the back of the truck. The whole time, the guard remains seated in the cab alongside the driver, a Chinese prisoner who lives out on the farm. *Oh, sweet Jesus! This is it! I just know it!*

The rain has let up by the time the truck pulls away and rolls to a stop at the rear gate. The gate guard crouches down and looks under the belly of the truck and then motions the driver to proceed on.

What happened to the big new trash truck with the hydraulic compactor? Did it break down? Will it be back on line tomorrow? And what about the two fellows who work in the trash shed? I know the one fellow, Johnny Mongello. But can he be trusted? What about his partner? Would they go along with my plan?

I walk the rest of the afternoon off and make a mental list of the people I need to talk to after supper. As I'm walking along, I look up in the sky and see a magnificent cloud formation, a rainbow arching across the sky, and a wavering curtain of sparrows flying over. The air hums and flutters as the birds rise and fall and rise again like a curtain.

After supper I make a trip down to K Dorm to see Frank Bruno.

I say, Frank, I know you know Johnny Mongello from the streets. I need to know if I can trust him.

Son, I've known that boy and his family all his life. He's a stand-up kid. He's no rat.

So I can trust him then, Frank?

Well, if you're worried about him telling on you for something, you don't need to. He'd go to hell first. That's the code he grew up with.

Thanks, Frank.

Ten minutes later, I find Johnny Mongello standing in the pill line getting his evening Valium. We walk back to his cell and I tell him my plan. Not only does he agree it will work, but he says he'll help me pull it off. The move will have to be made within the next couple of days, he says, because the hydraulic trash truck will be out of the shop and back in service soon.

Jesus Christ, man, thanks! I say. I really appreciate this. I'm going to have my girl check out some things tomorrow so I know where the hell I'm going once I get off the federal reservation. I'm going to leave two days from now.

You'd better not wait any longer than that, dude, he says, because that other truck will be back any day now.

By the way, I say. There's another fellow coming with me.

That's not a problem, as long as you trust him.

Nykki's ecstatic when I call her and tell her the news. She'll leave her apartment as soon as we finish talking and hike around the perimeter of the federal reservation the prison sits on until she finds the trash dump. Then she'll draw a route for me to follow right to her.

The next morning she's all business as we take our seats in the visiting room. The trash dump is a mile from the prison, she whispers. There's an eight-foot chain-link fence surrounding the dump. Once you get over the fence, you'll have to cross an open field until you come to a set of railroad tracks. When you—

Wait a minute, Nykki! Slow the hell down. How far is it from the open field to the railroad tracks?

About a hundred yards. When you reach the tracks, all you have to do is follow them to the highway. There's a restaurant right there. I'll be sitting in the parking lot waiting for you.

How far is it from the railroad tracks to the highway?

I'm not sure, baby. Close to a mile, I'd say.

She goes over the route one more time.

OK, I want you to leave now, Nykki. I've got a lot of things to do, and so do you. Be in that parking lot by no later than twelve thirty tomorrow afternoon. Don't leave that fucking place, girl! I'll be there!

I hold her tightly for a while before I let go and walk away.

Tommy Brooks, the blue-eyed bank robber with the Alabama accent and a hundred years to serve, sways like a weed in the wind when I tell him I've found a way out and we're leaving tomorrow. Even after I go over every detail with him twice, he turns and says, But something might not be right, man. We need more time to look this thing over. What about the other guy who works the trash detail? How do you know he's all right?

Look, Tommy, I'm going whether you come or not. I've checked these guys out and they're down with it, man. This is a chance of a lifetime. These people have dropped their fucking guard, goddammit, and I'm going.

All right, he says. I'm in.

I sleep very little throughout the night, and I can't resist playing a final round of what-if: *What if the guard gets out of the truck and watches Johnny Mongello and his partner dump the trash barrels into the truck? After all, that is his fuckin' job! And what if the guard gets out of the truck at the dump and watches the trash fall out of the truck? Well, then, your goose will be cooked, won't it? Maybe not. Not if you get to him and put him to sleep with the piece of pipe you're taking with you.*

After I take out the photos of my family and look at them one last time, I say all five decades of the rosary before I fall asleep.

At ten o'clock in the morning, I take a long shower, dress, and then inject a heavy dose of crystal meth into my veins. The engines roar, the tires screech, and Johnny Fear is left eating dust. When I leave my cell for the last time, I'm wearing the green army jacket Bobby Hamilton gave me fifteen months ago. Stashed inside the lining are a photo of Moma and Huck, my little red address book, and a ten-inch lead pipe.

I walk outside and around the exercise track until it's time to meet up with Tommy and Johnny Mongello and his work partner. We meet on the docks of the prison industry building and the four of us stand there in complete silence, smoking cigarettes and waiting for the dump truck to come through the rear gate.

This is your last chance to change your minds, dudes, Johnny says.

Fuck that, I say. I'm ready like Freddy, man.

Another ten minutes and the truck rolls through the second gate. Johnny and his partner jump off the dock and head toward the truck. Johnny, says, You gotta be inside that shed before the truck backs up to the door.

We'll be there, motherfucker! Don't worry about it.

After they walk away Tommy turns to me and says, I ain't going, man. There's too many variables—

Jesus fucking Christ, Tommy! This is a chance of a lifetime. Whatever, man.

There's no time to argue or debate. We shake hands, he wishes me luck, and I head off toward the shed.

No sooner do I get inside and crouch down behind an empty fifty-five-gallon barrel than I hear the truck backing up to the door. Thirty seconds later the shed door opens and Johnny whispers, Come on, for Christ's sake!

I bolt out of the shed and to the front corner of the truck bed. Johnny and his partner begin dumping barrels of trash over and around me while they carry on a crazy-ass conversation about their favorite NFL teams. During their exchange, the guard, who sits undisturbed in the cab of the truck, yells not to take all morning.

Finally, the driver starts the engine and pulls away. When the truck comes to a halt at the rear gate, my heart beats like an African war drum as I hear the guard in the truck speaking with the rear-gate guard. Then there's the electric buzz of the first gate opening and the truck eases forward. Only when we're through the second gate and the truck speeds up do I begin to breathe normally again.

The truck reaches the dump and begins to back into the pit. I work my way around, through and over the mounds of garbage to the rear of the truck. The bed of the truck begins to rise, and I spit coffee grounds out of my mouth and prepare to jump. When I do, I land in a pile of rotted vegetables and yesterday's slop. Instantly, I'm showered with oatmeal and more coffee grounds.

As the truck begins to move away, I keep my head down until I can no longer hear the sound of the engine. I can't remember ever being as excited and thrilled as I am at that moment.

I stand and quickly brush away the food and garbage from my clothes, face, and hair, and then I do a fifty-yard dash to the chain-link fence that Nykki told me about. I'm up and over it in one continuous motion. I start running across an open field until I reach railroad tracks that cut right through a cornfield. I don't stop running until I see the highway and restaurant parking lot where Nykki sits waiting for me.

She sees me coming out of the cornfield through her rearview mirror and gets out of the car. Hurrying toward me, she pulls up a foot short of being in my arms.

Pew! Mother of God! You smell like coffee grounds and rotten eggs! I'm not hugging you! She gets back in the car and throws a blanket over the passenger seat.

I'll bet Clyde Barrow never smelled as horrible as you smell, she says.

I kiss her on the neck as she pulls out of the parking lot. Maybe not, I say. But Clyde Barrow never escaped from a federal penitentiary in a goddamn trash truck either. Did he, Bonnie Parker?

No, I guess not, she says. Now where to?

We drive along glancing at one another and smiling cautiously.

Keep driving, Nykki, I say. Drive until we run out of road.

Afterword

By Sister Helen Prejean

In my introduction to *Dead Man Walking*, I discussed two situations that make for interesting stories: when an extraordinary person is plunged into the commonplace and when an ordinary person gets involved in extraordinary events. After reading *Incorrigible*, I believe there's a third situation: when a not-so-ordinary person finds himself in a not-so-common place.

Patrick Middleton fits into this category because he had more opportunities in his young life than most of the death-row prisoners I've come to know over the past twenty-five years: he attended a fine Catholic school where he was showered with love and attention from the Sisters of the Immaculate Heart of Mary, and he had a plethora of loving relatives and understanding counselors, juvenile probation officers, and judges who tried to help him along the way. Sadly, he was unable to shake off the darkness and volatility that existed in his home environment.

Perhaps the most tragic irony of all was when he believed he had to escape from prison before he ended up dead or killing someone, and less than twenty-four hours after he climbed inside a trash truck and got away, he committed a murder during a senseless robbery.

While trying to hot-wire a car, Patrick was confronted by the owner, who screamed. In an effort to quiet her and take away her keys, Patrick struck her in the head with a piece of pipe. He took her keys and wallet and stole her car. Tragically, she died two days later from the blunt-force trauma to her head.

Patrick was on the lam for several days before he was apprehended by the FBI in Washington, D.C., and returned to Pennsylvania. He eventually pleaded guilty to the robbery and second-degree murder charges and received a life sentence. The judge ordered that he serve his sentence behind the walls of Western Penitentiary on the north side of the city of Pittsburgh. As far as society and his family were concerned, Patrick's life was over now.

But something extraordinary happened to him in his first year at Western. As he was passing through the stages of despair that most prisoners with a fresh life sentence endure, Patrick made a profound discovery:

> Alone in my cell at night, stuck in a mire of self-pity and despair, I cried like a baby as I relived my past and contemplated a hopeless future. That I had taken another person's life in a stupid, stupid act and felt overwhelming guilt and shame, that I had been ostracized by society and my very own family, these things were only part of what made me think about taking my own life. Every night there was a growing restlessness stirring inside me, the kind that stirs when you know something's terribly wrong, but you can't put your finger on what it is. At times, I thought I was losing my mind.
>
> Surely it would be better to be dead, I thought, than to spend the next fifteen years—for that was the average time a prisoner served on a life sentence—living under such hopeless circumstances. The idea of escaping again was completely out of the question, for it was clear to me that to do so would only make my life more miserable than it already was; that is to say, even if I were to succeed in escaping again, I was aware that I couldn't escape from myself. (From

I Shade My Laurels: The Memoir of a Prison Scholar
a work in progress and the sequel to *Incorrigible*.

One day while he was exploring his new environment, Patrick found himself climbing the stairs of the second floor of a converted warehouse, where the University of Pittsburgh had set up its prison-branch campus. He peered into classrooms, read the advertisements and notices on the bulletin boards, and watched a prisoner as he painted a giant mural of a cathedral of learning on the wall in the main corridor.

As Patrick mingled among the other prisoners, what amazed him the most was how the professors and graduate students from the main campus interacted so freely with the prisoners. He would soon learn that these professors and students had carte blanche to come and go morning, noon, and night.

Patrick didn't go unnoticed for very long that morning. When an administrator from the university asked him if he was there to register, he said he wasn't sure. But then he spent the next two hours filling out Pell grant and new-student application forms. This marked the beginning of a most extraordinary journey that lasted for the next twelve years.

Almost immediately, Patrick distinguished himself in his classes with his eagerness for learning and his ability to grasp new concepts. He finished his first year at the top of the freshmen class and was inducted into the national freshman honor society, Phi Eta Sigma. As remarkable as his academic achievements were—he earned straight As!—his personal growth and development were even more extraordinary:

> All my life it had been easy to be enthusiastic about some new experience, only to grow bored and lose interest completely after the novelty wore off. That never happened to me when it came to learning. Every night I studied and wrote for four to five hours.

What I read about in my psychology and literature courses, I wrote about in my journals as the concepts and topics pertained to my own interests and experiences. My hunger for understanding was ferocious.

In my own coursework, I would begin with a syllabus to follow, and in no time some secondary topic would beckon me to follow. It was in an introductory psychology course, for example, that I was first introduced to the term *existentialism*: the twentieth-century branch of philosophy that stresses that man is what he makes himself and is also responsible for what he makes of himself. "How can I live the remainder of my life so as not to consider myself a complete failure?" That was the question that guided my daily living.

I have had the privilege of reading excerpts from Patrick's journals describing these years, and what amazed me more than anything was how he beat the commonwealth out of the punishment it had meted out to him. Here he was supposed to be doing hard time among hardened men, but, instead, he had turned his prison into a college. He made friends with students on the main campus. His professors took a personal interest in not just his intellectual growth, but also in his personal and spiritual development.

He also started seeing a prison psychologist, who taught him about transactional analysis and the art of introspection. His entire family came back into his life, which led him back to the Church and into the confessional for the first time since childhood. When his father came to see him, Patrick was able to confront him about why he had abandoned the family, and from there they began to heal and become genuine friends.

Patrick earned his bachelor of arts Degree (summa cum laude) in English in 1983, graduating in the top two percent of a senior class of close to two thousand students.

He also earned an $1,800 chancellor's undergraduate scholarship award as a senior, and used that money to help pay his first year's tuition in graduate school.

While working on his master's in language communication, he taught high school English and literature, and the university placed him under contract to teach undergraduate English composition and reading courses. From his teaching stipend, he paid the Department of Corrections 17 percent for his room and board.

Around this time, one of his graduate advisers, the internationally renowned reading specialist and author Dr. Harry Sartain, invited Patrick to conduct research with him. Together, they created the first language arts curriculum for adult learners in a prison environment. Other professors soon got wind of Patrick's knack for conducting research and joined in with him. By the time he earned his master's, he had created an entire college-level learning skills component in reading and writing. He had also designed, administered, and evaluated a battery of placement tests for new students. Along the way, he won a prestigious teaching award in English and several small literary prizes.

In every stage of development as a graduate student, Patrick made a new contribution to the university's undergraduate program. As he completed his statistical work in the School of Education's doctoral program, he began to design and then teach statistics courses to undergraduate psychology majors. His course was so highly praised by faculty members in the psychology department that they began to incorporate his exercises into their program.

By the time he completed his experimental methods courses for his doctorate, he had attracted the attention of the chair of the psychology department, Dr. Donald McBurney, who invited Patrick to collaborate on the second edition of Dr. McBurney's *Experimental Psychology* textbook. Patrick ended up writing the exercises for each chapter, and he was the senior author of the instructor's manual that accompanied the textbook.

In 1990, Patrick Middleton became the first prisoner in the United States to earn his doctorate degree in a classroom setting (as opposed through correspondence courses). He went on to assist in the third edition of Dr. McBurney's textbook, and he was again the senior author of the new instructor's manual and test battery for the third edition.

It has been seventeen years since Patrick graduated from the University of Pittsburgh and left the world of college academia. Over the years he has continued to grasp all he can from life. In the early '90s, he sang with a popular oldies group called the House of Relics that appeared on commercial radio stations and on PBS, and he once performed with the famous rhythm and blues group, the Marcels.

In 2004, his highly acclaimed self-help book, *Healing Our Imprisoned Minds: A People's Guide to Hope and Freedom*, was published by Infinity Publishing. The book is being used in writing and alcohol and drug programs in several states. It has been so well received that it is about to go into a second edition. Presently, Patrick is working on the sequel to *Incorrigible*. This second memoir is called *I Shade My Laurels: The Memoir of a Prison Scholar*.

In his journals, Patrick wrote that literature was his greatest passion and gift because it was through reading and vicarious experiences that he had learned to recognize a truth and internalize it.

Perhaps the one truth that saved his life and made a decent man out of him came from the great Russian writer Fyodor Dostoyevsky, as recorded in Patrick's journal: "Life is life everywhere. Life is in ourselves, not in the world that surrounds us."

About the Author

In 1979, Patrick Middleton began his search for self-understanding and inner freedom while serving a life sentence for second-degree robbery-homicide. Along the way, he became the first prisoner in America to earn his Bachelor of Arts degree (summa cum laude), Master's degree, and Ph.D., in a classroom setting behind the walls of a maximum security prison. During his tenure as a graduate student, Patrick taught and lectured undergraduate students enrolled in the University of Pittsburgh's writing and psychology programs; paid room and board to the Department of Corrections; and won several fellowships, teaching awards, and literary prizes. He also co-authored a teacher's manual for a textbook in experimental psychology.

Today, 33 years into his incarceration, Patrick continues working in the field of academia, and is finishing the final chapters of his next memoir, *I Shade My Laurel: The Memoir of a Prison Scholar.*

To contact the author, write to:

Patrick Middleton, AK-3703
c/o SageWriters
Box 215
Swarthmore, PA 19081
PMiddleton@comcast.net
SageWriters@comcast.net
610-328-6101